Gendered Labour and Clitoridean Revolt
Leopoldina Fortunati
and Carla Lonzi

Gendered Labour and Clitoridean Revolt
Leopoldina Fortunati
and Carla Lonzi

Edited by
Arlen Austin, Sara Colantuono,
and Jaleh Mansoor

Fillip, Vancouver
Folio Series: G

Contents

Jaleh Mansoor

Value's Negative, and the Negative's Capacity

An Introduction to Leopoldina Fortunati and Carla Lonzi through the Lens of Claire Fontaine's Model for a Dereified Life for Women (and Everyone Else)

We identify marriage as the institution that has subordinated women to the male destiny. We are against marriage. We identify in unpaid domestic labor the service that allows private and state capitalism to survive.
—Carla Lonzi, Carla Accardi, and Elvira Banotti, *Manifesto Rivolta Femminile*, Rome, 1970[1]

Italian Marxist feminist theorist Leopoldina Fortunati's (b. 1949) *L'arcano della riproduzione: Casalinghe, prostitute, operai e capitale* (*The Arcane of Reproduction: Housewives, Prostitutes, Workers and Capital*, 1981), finally published in English by Autonomedia in 1995 and retranslated by Arlen Austin and Sara Colantuono for Verso in 2024, circumscribes women's specific historical position within capitalism—within social relations organized by and for capital, and that which political economist and philosopher Mario Tronti has called the "social factory."[2] And yet for all his acumen, Tronti and the Italian left missed the real matrix of class: women.

Since the turn of the millennium—and most immediately the anticapitalist movements precipitated in Italy following the murder of a G8 summit protester Carlo Giuliani (by riot police)[3] and subsequent waves of protest such as Occupy and #MeToo—attention has increased on Fortunati's writings on the origin and circulation of value across the whole of society through its interstices. Here, woman, and above all the figure of the housewife, is revealed to be the invisible pivot of capitalist social totality, insofar as she both reproduces the daily life of all classes and is a vehicle for the replication of labour power itself. As such, women, particularly women who are not part of the formal economy and who do not receive wages, constitute a sub-proletariat that consumes its own labour capacity in the replication of others. Moreover, this invisible universal class drives much of the metabolism of capital valorization, since it is positioned as a consumer class. Fortunati's theories on gender and class have particular relevance to feminism and labour studies but also to Italian studies, due for renewed attention. Her propositions are at once practical, intuitive, and epiphanic in their elegance. They have reverberated across spaces of protest, within classrooms, and in cultural production.

Taking an approach distinct to the existential line favoured by thinkers such as Simone de Beauvoir, Fortunati contends that the subject position of "women" is forged by a historically entrenched relationship to value production. This relationship is indirect and negatively negotiated through family and property relations, rather than formed through direct access to wages. While value derives from labour time, Fortunati locates the conditions needed for value production to occur in the first place in the work of women; this is a group whose labour is not measured by the wage but rather whose historical *exclusion* from waged labour allows capitalist value production to proceed. In other words, while the capitalist system often excludes women from wages, and always excludes them from equal wages, it does not exclude them from value production, however much that may seem to be the case.

Instead, women are included as a *negative* function. Here, the hierarchy between figure and ground in visual culture lends a way to understand these social relations and the circuitry of value that undergirds them. Women (the ground) are occluded within a system that depends on them for the replication and circulation of value, creating the structure upon which both labour and profit (the figure) can exist.

Surplus value—the endgame of the capitalist mode of production situated within a social totality—rests on this occluded, invisible, and negatively accumulated work of women for the production of labour power as well as its daily maintenance. This work takes the form of reproduction, domestic labour, elder care, affective and sexual labour, and family maintenance in the so-called private sphere. But this contradiction—indispensable yet invisible; necessary and occluded—is foundational. Women's work supports the totality of the "social factory," even as its infrastructure overwrites their contribution. It is unpaid, unvalued, and unseen—and necessarily so, for this unseen sector is, indeed, the very matrix of capitalism. Fortunati calls this unseen matrix "the arcane of reproduction." Secret and inscrutable, this layer of work and discipline obfuscates any coherent materialist analysis of everyday life. Still, women are rarely thought of as "workers."

Fortunati offers a metaphor of optical reversal to articulate the at once dialectical and co-constitutive relationship of visible value and its invisible support, mapped along the axis of gender: women's work "presents itself as a photograph printed back to front, as mirror image of the process of commodity production."[4] This "back to front" relation of invisible (women's) work to formal (men's) work is doubly hidden. Karl Marx called the space of value production, such as the factory floor, "the hidden abode." Yet the hidden abode, as the crucible of surplus value, hides its own doubly hidden matrix of domestic replication, which in turn is the hidden abode's enabling condition. By using the analogy of a film negative to a photographic image to describe those captured in a wage relation without receiving formal remuneration, Fortunati acknowledges how this political-economic dynamic comes to determine perception, or the social visual field.

To put it another way: Women don't simply generate the condition for value in the straightforward way the photographic negative generates the picture yet is also contained within it. Rather, women's expenditures across time are structurally overwritten and denied. Passive dependency becomes violent denial. The very existence of the negative is erased.

Nevertheless, the analogy to a photographic negative affords Fortunati a way to consolidate a coherent understanding of "class" less vague than other activists and political economists of the Italian ultra-left. Among them are, for example, political philosopher Antonio Negri, who uses "multitude" to describe an expanded post-class inclusive of women, immigrants, and a sub-proletariat, but without decentring the wage. By locating the double function of the wage—that is, its capacity to operate negatively and indirectly as well as directly through paid wages—Fortunati introduces the crucial insight that its operations are both economic and political. The wage, then, is a matter not of remuneration in an isolated transaction, or even the rational distribution of resources, but rather the disciplinary structuring of the social totality in order to exact total exploitation—not only among family and intimate relations but insofar as these cast their shadows into the organization of the public sphere, invisibly.[5]

As such, *The Arcane of Reproduction* pushes past the blind spot of much of Italian ultra-left workerist and post-workerist theory by noting the need for unwaged, yet still measured, labour. Because all of society—not only official workers but also the daily lived experience of women and children—is disciplined by clock time and the temporality of work. Simply put, the commodity of labour power, as well as its production and maintenance, depends on invisibly and negatively mediated women's time. Even simpler: Without unwaged labour, capitalism would not function. In parallel to this structure of value production, in which women are required to occupy the negative component, Fortunati locates the seat of revolutionary struggle in a similarly *negative* relation to power and capital. This linked and double position posits all deskilled work as "feminine," which enables Fortunati to find a subject of struggle that does not conform to the historical understanding of the working class. A traditional understanding of class, for Fortunati, is a category to be discarded because it has been shaped by the masculinist parameters of the wage, the medium of value.

If Fortunati addresses the occluded structural conditions that *objectively* determine the impoverishment and dispossession of women's lives through the logic of value, then Carla Lonzi (1931–82), alongside her Rivolta Femminile (Women's Revolt) group, emphasizes the ineffable *subjective* dimension of everyday life for women. Here, consciousness raising and forms of separatism became key strategies. Lonzi encouraged feminists to distance themselves from leftist movements, as they are built on the concerns of men. As such, Rivolta Femminile's project became enabling women to reach subjectivity, against the objective determinations that confine them to supporting roles in the production and circulation of value. This project requires "women's reciprocal subjectification [to be] created where nothing existed; they invent the freedom that they represent for each other, the words to tell it and to keep making it happen in their lives."[6] This elaboration of a separatist autonomy for women, in which individual women are encouraged to find "authenticity" in relation to other women, requires a shift away from the piazza—the space of protest, riot, and strike—and toward spaces formerly unseen, if not deemed utterly nonexistent, in the political social lives of men: the myriad corners of the private and intimate realm.[7] However, despite Lonzi's call to disengage from leftist movements, much of her autonomist feminist language takes an ultra-leftist and even insurrectionary register. It summons the barricade, the strike, the revolt.

While Fortunati hopes to illuminate the negative space, the compulsory hell of social reproduction, as an unseen and therefore materially impoverished support matrix for value-productive labour, the extraction of women's labour through unpaid time turned over doubly to the boss as the condition for the possibility of the wage that is everyday life for most women, Lonzi wants to light the path to its exit. In "Sputiamo su Hegel" ("Let's Spit on Hegel," sometimes translated as "We Spit on Hegel," 1970),[8] her best-known text and a de facto manifesto for the Rivolta Femminile group, Lonzi encourages forms of consciousness raising.[9] She is suspicious of the organized left, structured by the dominance of men's analysis, which is founded on women's exploitation. And so, the barricade is reimagined as that which each woman must forge for herself in order to then build it collectively.

Elaborating on the inquiries begun by these two philosophers in the late twentieth century into the present day, the contemporary artist collective Claire Fontaine build their prognosis of the present and its potential for the future around a logic and tone of polarization. They take Fortunati's analysis and set it into generativity dialectical, if not antagonistic, relation to Lonzi's voice, spirit, and tone. For instance, the very title of Claire Fontaine's essay "Raising the Uprising" takes social reproduction and the task of producing future generations almost as an inevitability, while glossing the text with Lonzi's acerbic lucidity as it takes the form of a manifesto or rallying cry. The assumption that future generations will express themselves through uprisings commonly would be considered the care work of a rather paradoxical and counterintuitive subject position; rather, mothers are usually presumed to expect stability for their children, so that those children can produce the next generation. Claire Fontaine, citing Lonzi throughout, harness the philosopher's tone of acidic rebellion and "the total negation of all things existing" (as Marx described communism) insofar as all things existing—and above reproductive social relations—act as external constraints that limit women's freedom and creativity. If Marx (and Marxists, including Fortunati) strove to overcome class and the value form, then Lonzi could be said to want to find freedom and creativity for all women. By forcing the two into synthesis, Claire Fontaine tries to arrive at a feminist position that sacrifices neither analytical rigour nor militant passion.

At the core of their project and its debt to the contradictions within Italian feminism and its twin poles of Fortunati and Lonzi is the concrete potential of "the negative." This negative is located, historically and materially, in the invisible social dimensions of value extraction and, culturally, in women's foreclosed imaginaries. Where Fortunati's lucid analysis speaks to the *logic* of gender and an equally precise identification of a place from which to dismantle it from a materialist-feminist vantage, Lonzi's voice expresses its passionate affect, in excess to a purely rational inquiry. We could say that Fortunati's precision and Lonzi's attitude constitute the respectively Apollonian and Dionysian sides of an art project that will not accept the division between public and private, political and ethical, and, above all, will not accept the gendered libidinal economy of state capital. The gambit of taking these polarizing voices as a matrix for an art practice is finding a model to finally overcome the divide between theory and practice.

The aspiration is—for Fortunati and Lonzi, as much as for Claire Fontaine—women's autonomy to practice creative freedom, even within the most private spheres of life: that is, sexuality and reproduction. Women's creative freedom of course exceeds those spheres. But given the total colonization of women's lives at the most molecular level, the revolutionary proposition here is to start with that everywhere and nowhere (because invisibilized) logic of gender—with the private sphere, with the domestic. So, the "blockade," or riot or strike, can take place in any number of spaces and in any number of situations, from practice to discourse to consciousness to intimate life, in the kitchen as much as on the street, in the bedroom as much as along supply chains. Claire Fontaine begin with historically domesticated and privatized social relations only to demonstrate not only the artificiality of the divide but the extractive economies inherent in these naturalized forms of intimacy and association, thereby performing the way in which the artwork—like work, despite the differences between those forms of labour—starts with the diffuse and omnipresent "every yet nowhere" of gender difference. It is precisely this mapping of the unlocatable that allows critique to go in any direction, a kind of dérive of otherwise invisible social terrain.

In deference to Lonzi's entire oeuvre, Claire Fontaine write: *Running the blockade will be something that we do within ourselves; it will be the human strike by which we break our complicity with what imprisons us in spite of ourselves and we will create the social and collective relations in which this illegible revolt will become inspiriting and contagious. Running the blockade means confronting oneself and pushing oneself to read Lonzi as a friend that we have created in our reading mind in order to bring into existence that we who is capable of freedom.*[10]

Claire Fontaine live this blockade. The texts by Claire Fontaine collected in this book—drawn through the artists' practice across the sphere of gendered labour and across the equally primary divide between intellectual and manual labour (artists write as much as they make artwork; they raise children as much as they work the art circuit, etc.)—offer us a glimpse of what a dereified life might look like. And the warp and weft of that practice are Fortunati's analysis and Lonzi's affect.

This volume offers an introduction to two critical voices who articulate the spectrum of Italian feminism's analysis and its contribution to the present. Italian studies scholar and translator Sara Colantuono and media studies scholar Arlen Austin present readers with a translation of one of Carla Lonzi's most discussed but previously untranslated texts, "La donna clitoridea e la donna vaginale" ("The Clitoridean Woman and the Vaginal Woman"), striking for the way it situates the author's exploration of social reproduction in relation to models of consciousness, alongside other previously untranslated pieces, such as Lonzi's classic reflection of her experience of the feminist movement in "Itinerario di riflessioni" ("An Itinerary of Reflections") from 1977. We are also elated to present selections from Leopoldina Fortunati's *The Arcane of Reproduction*, newly translated and annotated by Colantuono and Austin in collaboration with Fortunati herself.

Accompanying the primary texts are contextual essays

by myself, Colantuono, and Austin, alongside reprints and updates of secondary literature. To demonstrate the significance of Fortunati's and Lonzi's discourse to our present, Maya Gonzalez, a Marxist feminist political economist who rediscovered much of Fortunati's contribution to both feminism and Marxist value-form theory, has generously allowed us to reprint her early essay "The Gendered Circuit: Reading *The Arcane of Reproduction*." "The Hidden Abode Beneath/Behind/Beyond the Factory Floor, Gendered Labor, and the Human Strike: Claire Fontaine's Italian Marxist Feminism" situates this discourse historically and traces its reverberations through contemporary art. Reprints of the collective's own writing most immediately indebted to Lonzi and Fortunati also appear in this dossier, including "The Refusal to Work as a Life Form" and "On the Illegible." The Folio closes with a conversation among Lonzi scholar Giovanna Zapperi, myself, and Fulvia Carnevale of Claire Fontaine.

1. Trans. Sara Colantuono.

2. Mario Tronti, "Factory and Society" (1962), in *Labor and Capital*, trans. David Broder (1966; repr. London: Verso, 2019), 12–35. "On the one hand, value, dead labor, which dominates living labor, is personified in the capitalist; on the other, instead, the worker appears as labor power purely objectively, as commodity."

3. The 27th G8 summit was held in Genoa in July 2001.

4. Leopoldina Fortunati, quoted in Maya Gonzalez, "The Gendered Circuit: (Re)reading *The Arcane of Reproduction*," p. 235 in this volume.

5. The trope of "invisibility" resonates across the Italian ultra left of the *operaisti* and Autonomia, most obviously by writer Nanni Balestrini in *The Unseen* (London: Verso, 2011), originally published as *Gli Invisibili* in 1986. See also Evan Calder Williams, "Invisible Organization: Reading Romano Alquati," *Viewpoint Magazine*, September 2013. https://fillip.ca/bl59.

6. Claire Fontaine, "Carla Lonzi or the Art of Running the Blockade," in *Human Strike and the Art of Creating Freedom* (South Pasadena, CA: Semiotext(e)), 237.

7. Maud Anne Bracke, "Feminism of Difference," in *Women and Reinvention of the Political: Feminism in Italy, 1968–1983* (New York: Routledge,

2014), 70. Bracke makes the case that Lonzi purposefully emphasized a turn away from political movements in contrast to "neo-Marxist" feminist groups like Lotta Femminista (Feminist Struggle), whose mission is best signalled by the volume Mariarosa Dalla Costa and Selma James, *The Power of Women and the Subversion of the Community* (Bristol, UK: Falling Water, 1972). See also the critical anthology on Carla Lonzi's *Autoritratto* (*Self-portrait*): Francesco Ventrella and Giovanna Zapperi, eds. *Feminism and Art in Postwar Italy: The Legacy of Carla Lonzi* (London: Bloomsbury, 2021). Finally, see Anna Curcio, "Marxist Feminism of Rupture," *Viewpoint Magazine*, January 2020, https://fillip.ca/cg61.

8. Here and throughout we use Lonzi's own preferred English translations in addition to the formal references to the published Italian text. These translations are drawn from archival documents held in the Lonzi archive at the Galleria Nazionale in Rome.

9. For an introduction to Lonzi's activist writing, including the 1970 English-language anthology *Let's Spit on Hegel*, see Paola Bono and Sandra Kemp, eds., *Italian Feminist Thought: A Reader* (Oxford: Basil Blackwell, 1991). See also Carla Lonzi, *Self-portrait*, trans. Allison Grimaldi Donahue (Brussels: Divided, 2021), originally published as *Autoritratto* in 1969.

10. Claire Fontaine, "Carla Lonzi or the Art of Running the Blockade," 248.

Claire Fontaine
The Refusal to Work
as a Life Form

In a text from 1980, sociologist Lucio Castellano describes the progressive disconnect between the world of production and the world of human and social life that took place in Italy during the 1970s. This shifting of the solid structures in relation to which subjectivities had formed themselves up until that moment created a profound lack of love for the existing reality and new loves for the possible; a total distrust of the perspectives that had hitherto constituted the proletarian horizon, as much on a political as on a personal level; and a trust in ways of being that seemed previously unthinkable. The revolution of 1977, in which this process culminated without exhausting itself, was so unexpected that it was illegible, in the sense in which feminist activist Carla Lonzi uses this category.[1] Those born under the sign of the rejection of an unreformable world terrified the power to the point that their rebellion was punished in a disproportionate and ruthless way. (The rest is the history of counterinsurgency.)[2]

In that revolt, despite its fragility and its youthful inconsistency, there was the promise of a political, monetary, and libidinal economy based on renewable energies such as the hope-force, the love-force, the revolt-force, and a new sensibility to the emotional fabric of life. This sustainable development, created by the proximity of free souls, showed even housework as exploitation; also, the work of love and the conditions of heterosexual pleasure appeared in need of a radical transformation. Castellano writes: *The factory no longer commands through the labour market, the set of social behaviours and social cooperation appears wider and richer than that which animates the productive work of capital… while the working time of everyone is not only sub-jectively experienced as expropriation of life, as condemnation and misery, but objectively it empties itself of knowledge and creative force; instead, free time increasingly ceases to be the subordinate time for the reproduction of the workforce and it becomes a time rich in exchanges and social relationships, that carries communication, elaboration, coordination, filled with huge resources and knowledge.*[3]

Whether the space for these rich subjectivities who affirmed a new possible world had been generated by the strength of their political refusal, or whether it was the result of the loss of symbolic relevance of a gasping Communist Party and a patriarchy already suffering from a violent crisis of delegitimization, is not known to us. Certainly, the cadences and the extraction of living energies from the bodies became unbearable and created a wave of shared hostility that swept from the factories into the streets and the houses. Suddenly, new creatures began to populate the urban space and that of desire; they belonged to a world in which everyone's life was an experiment. Historian and philosopher Umberto Eco was already observing this strange phenomenon with a posthumous gaze and expressed the justified fear that its complexity might remain misunderstood. He explained, in a (much criticized) review of *Alice è il Diavolo—sulla strada di Majakovskij: testi per una pratica di comunicazione sovversiva* (Alice is the devil—On the road to Mayakovsky: Texts for a practice of subversive communication) by the collective A/Traverso in *Corriere della Sera*, an Italian daily newspaper: *Whoever picks up the book I'm talking about without knowing what is happening in Italy, or anyone who reads it in the library in thirty years' time, will have a strange impression. One would not see seasonal, unemployed, long-haired people in train station waiting rooms, naked bodies looking for new contacts. If anything, one would be under the impression that a new "cultural" group is talking about these things and that in order to do so they invented new channels and new expressive styles.*[4]

The life forms that grew in the interstices of capitalism in fact look enigmatic to us when seen from our present, where the very interstitial spaces between beings are the object of the most violent colonization. Totally ignorant of collective life, we exist today in a network of psychologically vulnerable loneliness connected by social media and electronic communication. We no longer know anything about the materialist sensibility that arises in the daily experience of proximity, nor do we know anything about a politics of rejection, which sees responsibility for what we are not responsible for as the first thing to rebel against; today we feel accomplices of the disaster, and we know well the depression that comes from this specific guilty loneliness. The infrastructure already revealed itself as the place where power was settling, monitoring, regulating, terrorizing, and extracting value. The historical refusal to work was the displacement of the struggle on an existential level, precisely on the ground that power colonized during the 1980s through the world of soulless commodities and endless work. The space of this new frontier of control was that of the *infrathin*: the warmth of a chair from which someone has just gotten up, the tobacco smoke that comes out of the mouth and joins with that coming out of the nose, the slightest difference between two objects, which makes one a potential readymade and the other just a thing to use trivially—these are some definitions that artist Marcel Duchamp gives of the infrathin. It is difficult to imagine that this type of perception was born in an exploited or productive body. Duchamp prided himself on doing nothing, on being inactive, and in this desertion toward the world of usefulness his rebellious sensitivity toward the poetry hidden in banal things grew, and so did his relentless rejection of the use value and decoration of the retinal. Duchamp's first readymade, *The Bicycle Wheel*, dates back to 1913 and speaks of idleness. Watching the wheel turn, the artist said, relaxed and comforted him; it was an opening toward something different from everyday life: "I liked the idea of having a bicycle wheel in my studio. I enjoyed looking at it, just as I enjoyed looking at the flames dancing in a fireplace."[5] In 1975, two World Wars later, the figure of the artist had become a worker on the assembly line of existence: Carla Lonzi breaks up with sculptor Pietro Consagra because they do nothing but live in function of his work, in the absence of social relations. "He who dictates the law is the work," writes Lonzi in *Vai pure (Go Then)*: *Then the work needs a certain atmosphere to be produced.... At this point the relationship becomes a burden, a farce for who sees in the relationship the ultimate meaning of her life. When I feel that you…are ready to betray me, to betray the reasons for the relationship to give space to the reasons for the work, that is, you prefer to bring the work and yourself as the author to life rather than yourself as a participant in the relationship, I have hit rock bottom.*[6] That living together with someone who lives only to be a worker would be unbearable seems today an incredible luxury.

This is why the refusal to work in the 1970s seen today, in the dim light of our antisocial and busy present, is dazzling. Refusing work back then meant not only affirming a vital positivity outside of wage exploitation but also rejecting the latter as the only battleground, as the sole origin of contractual identity and of life form. It also meant rejecting equality and equivalence as facts and objects of desire, and rejecting the language of rights, with its reverent hypocrisy toward those who have always used the law to better oppress. The revolutionary aspect of this political perspective lies in the adoption of a new self-produced system of values, one that saw precariousness and marginality in relation to work, and the partial or total exclusion of the political grids of the party and the unions as a resource. Being a woman, a marginalized person, a youth, an immigrant were experiences whose existential and political richness was at that point valued and whose subversive force threw into crisis families, collectives, and everything that was organized according to the transpolitical values of patriarchy. Social class appeared a limiting category compared to the infinity of desires experienced by the singularities. Precisely because productivity and functionality already haunted the subjects up to their revolutionary engagement, overturning this situation through ironic slogans (1977 was a goldmine for those), fancy dressing, and the defunctionalization of language created a new sense of reality, a revolt within the revolt. Feminist scholar Lea Melandri evoked an intelligent barbarism, an ironic sensuality, a wise naivety that seemed possible at the time. "For this little hope," she writes, "it is worth fighting the sad, the boring, the needy, the miserable: the red ascetics."[7]

The emergence of the sensitivity that at the time was called the "richness of social needs" shows us a winding path leading out of the confusion of our present. The life forms that converged into Autonomia,[8] mutually reproduced and reinforced in neighbourhoods and groups, gave rise to an unexpected evolution of the subjects who formed the movement, but they were also the result of the new sensitivity formed in reaction to technological and political transformations in the world at that time. Urbanism and the world of work, with their demeaning ugliness, clearly outlined the sinister contours of the productive subjectivities they needed: the revolt consisted in seeing something else, in making oneself sensitive to a representation of life that was more faithful to the intuition of a collective possibility of salvation than to the awareness of the oppressive and separating control. At the same time, the continuity of the factory, within the social factory of the couple and the family, began to be politicized—*Numéro Deux* (1975) by Jean-Luc Godard and Anne-Marie Miéville remains a cornerstone of this process. The atmosphere of the social housing in Grenoble (and in the rest of the West), the anguish of the sexuality of a productive couple, go straight to the heart of the viewer, through sounds that are as dry and raw as proletarian life. The voices and noises, not smoothed by the remixing, immerse us in the precise emotional tonality of the working class of lower Grenoble. Sandrine, the protagonist, blurts out: "When you no longer get along with a man, you can always leave him, but what do you do when it is an entire social system that rapes you?" At the origin of feminist sensitivity, which is the disturbing hidden mother of the refusal to work, there is an experience of the physiological reality of desire that is contagious and is not only of a sexual nature—even if sex was a great protagonist of this awakening. A pact with the living, different from that imposed by extractive capitalism, could emerge then, because use value and exchange value were, and always will be, governed by a rationality that does not explain illness, frigidity, anxiety, depression, the climate disaster; we have called the sensitivity that gave birth to this liberating complicity with life "magic materialism."

The strike that took place at that time in the name of these values is the only one possible for us today: a strike disconnected from the identity of a worker or a class, which erodes the intimate complicity with everything that oppresses and takes away dignity from physiological and social life. The human strike owes the movement of '77 its emotional intelligence and the ability to stand on the side of life against government, control, and poverty. Even if we want to put aside the feminist matrix of this movement, its context is however that of the social factory, the transition from the social worker to the mass worker, that clearly appears in the analyses of postwar theorists Mario Tronti, Antonio Negri, and Romano Alquati.[9] Because, on the one hand, the disappearance of the traditional worker undermined the Marxist dialectical scheme of antagonism and the seizure of power, of the reappropriation of the means of production, of which today we know the profoundly problematic nature (not only are harmful and polluting things the majority of what is produced, but the very philosophy of today's production process is toxic). On the other hand, the emphasis placed on the social, on the creation of what the Situationists in the 1960s described as "situations," established a new relationship with immanence and therefore with the reproduction of oneself and others, a suspicion toward procrastination that animates both the logic of waged labor and that of militancy.

Politicizing the present in its imperfect wholeness allowed everyone to see the political potentiality of the personal dimension enlightened by consciousness raising. Upon this existential horizon, what we call "magic materialism" was born. Any knowledge that privileges an energeticist approach over a mechanistic one, an activist vision rather than an accumulative one, based on a dynamic idea of production processes—seen as creative processes—and not on a hypostatization or systematization of procedures and structures, is a form of magic materialism. Whether it is agriculture, medicine, relationships within society, or the actions and rituals put in place to stabilize an emotional or physiological situation (world making), magic materialism is based on a feminist epistemology that attributes equal value to production and reproduction—thus placing itself in bitter conflict with Marxism—to the care required for production, and to the regeneration of the producers themselves. Care lies at the heart of the concept of magic materialism as a practice that mobilizes a series of highly specialized and singular (nonmechanically transmissible) skills that involve the emotional investment and singular affective intertwining of objects and subjects, both animate and inanimate, which is typical of practices historically defined as magic.

The idea of "magic," as formulated by anthropologist Ernesto De Martino, has no connection with a romantic position of idealization of precapitalist knowledge and practices. It is instead linked to the concern that the positivist attitude of the researcher could lead to a refusal to understand phenomena that are not scientifically explainable, disqualifying them as the effects of a suggestion or fakes. "The problem of magic powers," writes De Martino, "involves not only the subject of judgment but also the judging category itself, the category of reality."[10] Magic, in this context, defines an action based on cause-and-effect relationships that Western science does not contemplate. What philosopher Michel Foucault describes as the revolt of subjected knowledge connects the two references of De Martino and Silvia Federici, which can be used to create an epistemic paradigm allowing for a transvaluation of humanity—currently impossible within the dominant production processes of commodities and thought. Federici starts from the feminist standpoint in her intention to re-enchant the world.[11] Free from any romanticism, her method reveals the "magic" operations carried out by capitalist accumulation processes, among which she cites the witch hunt as a foundational moment that, along with the enclosure of the commons, generated the Industrial Revolution as the mass production of docile bodies.[12]

In 1977, there was talk of "*untorelli*" to describe those who propagated a libertarian epidemic as well as "metropolitan Indians," figures born for fun as incarnations of existential foreigners, colonized by capitalism, who embodied an epistemic exteriority to the logic of capital, another notion of physical and mental health, of hygiene, of pleasure. Lonzi writing about clitoral orgasm seemed inappropriate and offensive, and it was not immediately clear why this concept would bring Hegelian (and Marxist) dialectics to its knees along with the rest of Western philosophy. It was fundamental to create the short circuit that made it clear what ignorance the patriarchal emancipation project was nourished by; thus, this operation had to pass through channels that were not simply discursive and traditionally political, and in this sense we might speak of decolonization. Using the words of the enemy to rationally explain the forms of one's exclusion was thus not enough (as it is not sufficient today for American people of colour). Disobedience passes through the incarnation of oneself outside the power relations that constitute us as subjects, first of all sexuality and production. There is an infrathin connection between things and bodies that must be rediscovered and that emerges only in the refusal to work, in the reappropriation of the processes of subjectivation. Magic materialism is the child of idleness as a form of struggle, of human strike as self-defence, and its emergence provides the strength that allows us to refuse to collaborate with destructive forces. In the struggles to come, we will fight to live by honouring a rationality that respects our own physiological reality, rejecting the normalization of power relations that produce bare life, whether it is through the extermination of migrants or police brutality. A life in which the greatest masterpiece is the use of one's time, a program whose depth has not yet been measured. Only through the human strike can we refuse work in the factories of subjectivities, refuse the persuasions of targeted advertising and algorithms, refuse a life that is toxic for the planet and degrading to us. Feminism showed us the path because it broke the deepest and most indispensable complicity of Western culture—that between men and women—revealing to the oppressors that they were more miserable than the oppressed, that there was a possible shared pleasure beyond the loneliness experienced by both sexes.

This text is an invitation to consider the fear of losing one's privilege as the most politically dangerous thing within the present historical moment. The only part of humankind that can still rise up are those who have not yet been deprived of everything by war or who have not yet fallen foul of the climate disasters that have occurred so far. They can refuse to correspond to the image they receive of themselves by perceiving the murmur of worlds silenced in the name of profit, the only worlds that can save our sick planet. Magic materialism is the bearer of an existence that does not place reproduction at the service of production and that reappropriates the means of production of a present that comes accompanied by its future.

This text was originally commissioned by OGR Torino on the occasion of the 2021 exhibition *Vogliamo Tutto*, curated by Samuele Piazza and Nicola Ricciardi, and published in Samuele Piazza and Nicola Ricciardi, eds., *Vogliamo Tutto: Cultural Practices and Labor* (Milan: Lenz, 2021).

1. Carla Lonzi, *Taci, anzi parla. Diario di una femminista* [Speak not, no, speak: Diary of a feminist] (1978; repr., Milan: Scritti di Rivolta Femminile, 2010), 1, 172–73. In Italy, the revolt of the '77 movement was also described as "diffuse irrationalism."

2. See, for example, New York Committee Against Repression in Italy, "April 7: Repression in Italy – CARI," Libcom.org, October 26, 2019, https://fillip.ca/178v.

3. Lucio Castellano, "Il rifiuto del lavoro," in *Gli autonomi*, vol. 2, ed. Sergio Bianchi and Lanfranco Caminiti (Rome: Derive Approdi, 2007), 16.

4. Umberto Eco, *L'anno nove* in *Sette anni di desiderio* (Milan: Bompiani, 2004), 60.

5. "Marcel Duchamp, *Bicycle Wheel*," MoMA, accessed May 3, 2024, https://fillip.ca/hip1.

6. Carla Lonzi, *Vai pure. Dialogo con Pietro Consagra* [*Go then: A Dialogue between the Author and Pietro Consagra*] (1980; repr., Milan: Scritti di Rivolta Femminile, 2011), 10.

7. Lea Melandri, "Una barbarie intelligente," in Bianchi and Caminiti, *Gli autonomi*, vol. 1, 245.

8. "Autonomia" denotes the emergence in Italy, particularly post-1973, of an ultra-left that examined possibilities for subsisting autonomously from processes of capitalist accumulation and disarticulated itself from official governmental organs, such as the party, the union, and the state apparatus itself. These entities had come under scrutiny for the betrayal of the proletariat in favour of the state and the reproduction of capital in the aftermath of World War II and Cold War international relations—not least the way in which American dollars informed the Italian economic miracle at the expense of the Italian worker. The CIA-backed coup in Chile in 1973 had led the Italian Communist Party under Enrico Berlinguer to form an alliance with the more "moderate" Christian Democrats in the "Historic Compromise" (*Compromesso storico*), increasingly foreclosing the possibility of a radically anti-capitalist movement within the country's official political system. In their organic formation of a postparliamentarian, postrepresentational (nonelectoral) politics, various Autonomia groups turned to an analysis of a social totality within capital, a "social factory" (Mario Tronti, Antonio Negri) that opened the path to acknowledging the struggles of those previously deemed to hold apolitical and/or non-capital-producing subject positions (including women, among others): a social heterogeneity that political philosopher Antonio Negri would eventually call "multitude." However, the specificity of various aspects of this larger multitude are lost within Negri's term, an aporia whereby the Italian feminist positions examined in this volume offer greater precision in regard to the gender-specific production of capital.

9. Tronti, Negri, and Alquati were theorists in the core group behind *Quaderni Rossi*, the original journal of *operaismo* from 1961 onward. They sought to theorize, through a reinterpretation of Marxist concepts, an autonomous working-class militancy that could effectively resolve historically and geographically specific social issues left unattended by the reforms proposed by the Italian Communist Party. The term *operaismo* is widely accepted and used in anglophone academia as synonym for Italian workerism, but in some instances it is used to indicate a more specific group: Potere Operaio (1969–73). As a synonym of workerism, *operaismo* is understood as a multifaceted political and intellectual movement that begun in the early 1960s and that actively changed the course of history throughout that decade, until the Hot Autumn of 1969.

10. Ernesto De Martino, *Il mondo magico. Prolegomeni a una storia del magismo* (1948; repr. Turin: Einaudi, 2022), 54.

11. Silvia Federici, *Re-enchanting the World: Feminism and the Politics of the Commons* (Oakland, CA: PM Press, 2019).

12. Silvia Federici, *Caliban and the Witch: Women, the Body and Primitive Accumulation* (New York: Autonomedia, 2009).

Sara Colantuono and Arlen Austin

Lonzi and Fortunati

Difference and Feminist Rupture

Why pair the writings of Carla Lonzi and Leopoldina Fortunati? While they share obvious correspondences of temporality, geography, and entwinement in the inescapable political upheavals of Italy throughout "the long '68"—which extended through the 1970s—their differences at times make them incommensurable. Of course, both might be included in the unorthodox processes that artist duo Claire Fontaine has defined as "human strike": an ongoing "revolt within a revolt" indicating immediate transformations in the libidinal economies of political-textual movements that defied traditional forms of organization and mediation. However, Lonzi's and Fortunati's modes and means of engagement were profoundly different, even often at odds, in the context of 1970s feminist factionalism and the antagonisms of the Italian parliamentary and extraparliamentary left in the Cold War era. They are united, though, in understanding feminism itself as an ongoing revolutionary rupture and in their different, but equally nonnegotiable, criticism of hegemonic Marxist ideologies: in the culture of 1970s Italy, a true "revolt within a revolt."

Although both engaged in radically heterodox writing projects and organizational forms, Lonzi is perhaps more widely acknowledged for such activities, given the relevance of her work for art historians and her insistence on the prescriptive erasure of any (patriarchal) cultural forms—or, as she calls them, "moments of creativity"—including any form of art making, from women's lives.[1] Confronting the paradoxes of her own work as both a decrier of cultural forms and a former art critic, Lonzi understands the very possibility of her subjective persistence as contingent on feminism as an ongoing historical rupture. As Lonzi reveals in her journals: "Before feminism, the possibility that someone could believe in me, in my existence and in the contribution of this existence, did not exist culturally."[2] After founding the separatist group Rivolta Femminile (Women's Revolt) in the summer of 1970 with Carla Accardi and Elvira Banotti, Lonzi worked relentlessly against the grain to continually undo and re-create her feminist practice, risking, at every turn, a collapse back into hierarchical relational forms and self-defeating politics. Such a slippage could be avoided only through the collective practice of *autocoscienza* (consciousness raising), a practice requiring that feminism be consistently written and spoken in renewed, living form.

In a 1977 text, Lonzi describes Rivolta Femminile in 1970 as an alternative to the feminist tendency to "come to terms with Marxism," a tendency she harshly condemns: "the Marxist tendency within feminism represented a form of emancipation: some women had assumed the demagogic behaviors that characterized the parties of the left and were an example of a well-done male operation."[3] It was in response to the first attempts to organize a feminist movement by women who considered "theorizing that women constitute a class" to be "a conquest" that Lonzi wrote "Sputiamo su Hegel" ("Let's Spit on Hegel").[4] In "Itinerario di riflessioni" ("An Itinerary of Reflections," translated here for the first time to English), Lonzi writes: "When I first started to do feminism I wrote 'Sputiamo su Hegel' for many reasons, but also to cleanse a space where I felt that we all should have grown."[5] That space was other than that of feminist Marxism, and other than what Lonzi calls "the way of emancipation."[6]

Within such a system, existing feminisms are not spared—neither preceding forms of Marxist feminism nor emerging forms of "radical feminism" or "difference feminism," as they have come to be known in the Anglo-American context. The approach to a feminism of difference, like those of philosopher and psychoanalyst Julia Kristeva or scholar and journalist Lea Melandri, in which the feminine persistently questions or undermines a masculinist logic and logos, is, for Lonzi, a Sisyphean task. "Bringing vases to Samos," as she terms it, fails to add anything new to a cultural patrimony that dooms women to reinforce a fundamentally masculinist culture.[7] If subjection to the role of "eternal irony of the community" is a fate to be avoided at all costs, then Lonzi constantly worries that her own thought may be structured around persistent dichotomies in the patrilineage of Hegelian Marxism. In her diaries, she writes: "After so much effort in attempting to unhook myself from Marxism, I have preserved it fully: the idea of identifying value with a category of the oppressed is Marxist."[8]

At the same time, Lonzi is mercilessly scornful of a Marxist politics that would shield men, based on their class position or commitment to class struggle, from the critique of feminism. No man should be spared the righteous hatred of women, whose subjectivities constituted the blind spot in male "Politics," with its capital P. Lonzi asks pointedly: "Is it that in other contexts one is accustomed to treat those who should realize they are abusing others kindly?" Why should a feminist politics be suspended "until they can be placed between two quotes of Marx" approaching them "as if they were children to whom one has to present truth in the language of their ABCs?"[9] Every woman (alone and in common) must, for Lonzi, perform a necessary passage into embodied speech while simultaneously refusing the criterion of submission to patriarchal culture as arbiter of recognition. If such a refusal necessitates a certain illegibility and invisibility, then so be it—it is also a vital necessity.

Fortunati's appropriation of the Marxisms of *operaismo* may appear rather tame and deeply compromised in relation to Lonzi's standards.[10] Unlike Lonzi, Fortunati does not shy away from employing Marxist categories, however heterodox her use of them, engaging them with a rigour akin to musical exercises as she plays through variations on the category of labour power in its relation to the sphere of reproduction. While Lonzi's milieu was the small *autocoscienza* groups of Rivolta Femminile, Fortunati's was the circle of feminists in the Mestre area, including Mariarosa Dalla Costa, who, in 1971, co-founded Lotta Femminista (Feminist Struggle). The group's members, though often seeking refuge from the intense misogyny of male groups of the extraparliamentary left, remained in close contact and debate with them. By 1972, Lotta Femminista fractured further by joining the international Wages for Housework movement.[11] Although seldom remarked upon in current scholarship, an unmistakable class difference existed between the two groups and their membership, which reflects their divergent focuses and interests. While Rivolta Femminile members were artists, art critics, and educated upper-class women who met in Rome and Milan, Lotta Femminista was born in the suburban factories of one of the most industrialized petrochemical manufacturing regions of Northeastern Italy.

However divergent the discourses and political practices of Rivolta Femminile and Lotta Femminista may appear today, the urgency of developing a feminist project without existing institutions and practices led to the groups' writings appearing side by side in key publications as well as in the reading lists of nascent feminist groups in the early 1970s. They coexisted among a host of appropriated texts endowed with local meanings from emerging feminist movements globally. As historian Maud Anne Bracke has noted, "non-Italian texts and encounters were used strategically and eclectically" (particularly those from French and American traditions) and the same was sometimes true for texts from divergent traditions within Italy itself.[12] As Lotta Femminista groups expanded beyond the Mestre region, however, Rivolta Femminile made sure to clarify, in a 1972 *volantone*,[13] that its members did not share a project with Lotta Femminista and that the two groups' projects and politics should not be conflated. Dalla Costa recalls that branches of Rivolta Femminile generally refused to distribute Lotta Femminista's literature in their spaces. Judging from Dalla Costa's own archive, which scrupulously documents Lotta Femminista's development in relation to local and global movements of the era, the lack of engagement was mutual.[14]

In retrospect, however, Dalla Costa writes that Lotta Femminista was one of the "two great souls of feminism" in the Italian context of that era, "the other being that of *autocoscienza* (consciousness raising)."[15] Though she specifies that the latter movement "had little sympathy for demonstrations and, even on large issues of the Feminist Movement such as abortion, it sometimes preferred not to participate" (which was part of rejecting what Rivolta Femminile characterized as "external commitments"), Dalla Costa nevertheless claims a profound commonality. Even if unrecognized at the time, this common ground for Dalla Costa was one of refusing what she refers to as the "vice of homologation"—that is, any capitulation to demands for equality or recognition within a capitalist division and distribution of life and labour. For Dalla Costa this refusal—at least in retrospect—seems to outweigh particular institutional commitments or discursive formations.

If there is one unquestionable similarity between the works of Fortunati and Lonzi, it is that both have been scarcely translated into English. Equally true is that it is impossible to present excerpts from either's written contributions to the 1970s feminist movement without doing injustice to the rigour and specificity of their original interventions. Both authors are "untranslatable," even given the standard apologia mandated by deconstructionism that all texts are such. In the case of Lonzi and Rivolta Femminile, translation must acknowledge that many of the writings ("*scritti*," as Lonzi calls them) were experimental written expressions, tools in the relational practice of *autocoscienza*, and not intended to be reified as "texts." That is to say, they are not easily decontextualized and reproducible but rather should be understood as context bound, ephemeral, and unique. As Lonzi declares in the introduction to the 1974 collection *Sputiamo su Hegel. La donna clitoridea e la donna vaginale e altri scritti* (*Let's Spit on Hegel: The Clitoridean Woman and the Vaginal Woman and Other Writings*), much of which is translated in this volume for the first time: *The risk of these writings is that they can be taken as theoretical sureties, whereas they only reflect an initial way for me to come out into the open, one in which scorn prevailed, born of my realization that masculine culture, in all its aspects, had been theorizing women's inferiority.*[16] As unpublished letters and manuscripts reveal, Lonzi was a meticulous writer who feared and reacted angrily to most attempts to translate her texts, accusing translators across the world of not being faithful enough to her painstakingly edited essays. The writings we present here, translated with the utmost care, are from the Scritti di Rivolta Femminile series and were collected and self-published by the group's publishing company in Milan. Up until now, they have remained largely inaccessible to non-Italian-primary readers.

In Fortunati's case, a certain "untranslatability" results from the appearance of familiar categories in the inverted world of reproduction, where they become imbued with new significance through the great feminist refusal of housework, the work-discipline of the family, and compulsory heterosexuality. The traditional Marxist-Hegelian interplay between appearance and reality is doubled in the displacement of the subject of productive waged labour by the feminist subject of reproduction and her refusal. Of course, such conceptual difficulties are compounded by the state repression of the Italian left in the late 1970s and 1980s, particularly the intellectual circles of *operaismo* in the northeast, which Fortunati was affiliated with and which resulted in a bleeding of revolutionary lives from the country, the belated release and translation of texts, and the stagnation or erasure of some of the movement's most vital debates.

Lonzi's relative obscurity was, to a greater degree, self-willed, given that Rivolta Femminile had already articulated a deep awareness of the compromised nature of any public engagement—not to mention any publicized individuality as inevitably a commerce with patriarchal power—in its first manifesto. However, 1980s feminist groups would come to adapt and appropriate the practice of *autocoscienza*, with the addition of psychoanalytic language. These women, associated with the Libreria delle Donne di Milano (Milan Women's Library) and the women's philosophy group Diotima, are now relatively well-known in English translation and include, among others, prominent figures like Luisa Muraro and Adriana Cavarero.

While this Italian feminism of difference is often considered to be historically derived from Lonzi and Rivolta Femminile, Lonzi herself—in the 1978 text "Mito della proposta culturale" ("The Myth of Cultural Proposal")—distanced herself from a feminist movement she saw as "led astray by the ambition of demonstrating its weight on the old political terrain."[17] Here Lonzi responded to what she believed to be a reactionary return to traditional psychoanalytic categories visible in the "hijacking of relations, within feminist groups, toward the analysis of the depth, or the practice of the unconscious ('*pratica dell'inconscio*')."[18] If the essay's declared target is the work of Lea Melandri, its goal is to discuss how dismissing the practice of *autocoscienza* in favour of practices derived from psychoanalysis was ultimately destroying feminism: "Feminism as a topic has already created a phenomenon of massification: in almost ten years of life feminism has come increasingly to conform only to those aspects of feminism men understand."[19]

Sexuality and the Master-Slave Dialectic in Lonzi and Fortunati

The collection *Sputiamo su Hegel*, published in 1974, includes the primary statements of Rivolta Femminile and the foundational texts Lonzi composed in the previous five years of her engagement with the movement.[20] We translate much of the collection in this Folio, with the exception of the group's founding text, "Manifesto di Rivolta Femminile," and "Sputiamo su Hegel," as they are readily available in English.[21]

While the practice of *autocoscienza* came to be focused as a mode of writing and speaking that was intimate and active at the level of the subject, as opposed to directly and programmatically political, the discourse of these early texts does not lack a comprehensive theory of sexuality and sexual oppression. Even though Lonzi always refused to use the term "theory" ("feminism is not an idea, it is a practice"),[22] her rigorous thinking is above all a theory of withdrawal and reinvestment: a process of *deculturizzazione* (deculturation) or *fare tabula rasa* (wiping a clean slate) that attends to women's potential to subsequently reach (and redefine) subjectivity as such. "Sputiamo su Hegel," published in 1970, had mocked the heroic dramaturgy of Hegelian Marxism and called for a mass feminist withdrawal from institutions at large, from culture, and, above all, from the Hegelian march of History. The group claimed that feminism could, in fact, do more than remain in thrall to the logics of an equality achieved through revolutionary progress and instead imagine a new subject: "Not being trapped within the master-slave dialectic, we become conscious of ourselves; we are the Unexpected Subject."[23] For Lonzi, equality is merely a juridical category, the admittance into a world already made by others, a world always already foreclosing the possibility of feminist subjectivity.

Two of the 1971 texts included in this volume, "Assenza della donna dai momenti celebrativi della manifestazione creativa maschile" ("The Absence of Woman from Occasions Celebrating the Manifestation of Male Creativity") and "La donna clitoridea e la donna vaginale" ("The Clitoridean Woman and the Vaginal Woman"), define the continuity that Lonzi articulates between women as celebrants and spectators of masculine culture and their seemingly passive role in vaginal sex. Once revealed, the correspondence between the spectator and the vaginal woman, on the one hand, and, on the other, the refusal of vaginal sex and absence from the art world, is evident throughout Lonzi's corpus. In this specific phase of Lonzi's feminist practice, participation in moments of male creativity and acceptance of reproductive sex in fact prevent any possibility of developing autonomous subjectivity. The third 1971 text we translate, "Sessualità femminile e aborto" ("Female Sexuality and Abortion"), written that summer with the women of Rivolta Femminile, takes a stand on the ongoing public debate on abortion and brings to an extreme the thesis outlined in "The Clitoridean Woman and the Vaginal Woman." Lonzi links the problem of abortion to vaginal sex, a model of sexuality defined as having the goal of men's pleasure and which has always been sold to women as natural. For Lonzi and the rest of Rivolta Femminile, abortion was not a solution but a dangerous, misleading freedom that could strengthen social structures and behaviours that the group understood to be manifestations of structural subjugation and exploitation. Lonzi contended what instead needed change was the conception of sexuality itself, achievable only through "the disruption of the vagina-penis sexual model."[24] The fourth text, "Significato dell'autocoscienza nei gruppi femministi" ("The Meaning of *Autocoscienza* in Feminist Groups"), from 1972, marks the practice of *autocoscienza* as the primary means of deculturation, revealing woman as the "unexpected subject"; that is, one that emerges from outside of History in a sense, or, more precisely, from what Lonzi refers to as women's "millennial absence from history."[25]

Lonzi's theorization of sexual politics directly invokes this removal of women's bodies from history, wherein the choice of sexual practices (between vaginal and clitoral sex) serves the cause of feminism. Even if Lonzi appears to recuperate some of Sigmund Freud's fundamental theories of sexuality in "The Clitoridean Woman and the Vaginal Woman"—particularly the homology between clitoris and penis invoked in the essay's opening lines—she in fact opposes Freud as much as she does Karl Marx or Georg Wilhelm Friedrich Hegel in her vast critique of patriarchal culture. She identifies Freud and his successor Wilhelm

Reich, a prominent proponent of the "sexual liberation" championed within the New Left, as engaging in a "cultural mutilation" of the clitoris, and thus performing a violence commensurate with or worse than that of patriarchal pre-capitalist cultures. While such a reading inevitably appears as strongly essentialist and ahistorical to a contemporary audience, one can also note that Lonzi makes consistent use of figures of anticolonialism to describe women's emancipation—traditions popular in forms of Maoism, Fanonism, and other Third Worldist discourses that permeated the Italian extraparliamentary left at the time.[26]

If various factions of the extraparliamentary left could quote great anticolonial passages from Mao Zedong and Frantz Fanon, it was unlikely that they could confront the misogyny that structured their own homes and workplaces. Though never attentive, in a Fanonian sense, to the co-construction of race and gender, Lonzi's texts are highly provocative and problematic in their insistence on the possibility of a feminist subjectivity that transcends a history and culture forged and received in the violence of patriarchy. At their best, they may be read as marking a radical critique of the sexuality of modernity, confronting the dualism of its epistemic structures and refusing to reproduce them—at least not without a struggle.

On its surface, "The Clitoridean Woman and the Vaginal Woman" seems to mark a strongly dichotomous and essentialist distinction between the vaginal woman as "passively" assimilated into patriarchal culture and the clitoridean[27] woman as "liberated," at least on the plane of sexuality, possessed of what Lonzi refers to as an "authenticity" that might achieve autonomy on both a bodily and a cultural plane. Lonzi deploys both anticolonial and insurrectionary figures to mark this distinction (running the blockade, the barricade, the deculturation of the colonized subject, and so on). The great irony turns out to be that there is nothing essentialist or necessarily liberatory about the clitoridean woman: *The clitoridean woman is not the liberated woman, nor the woman who has escaped from suffering the male myth—these women do not exist in the civilization in which we find ourselves—but the one who faced this myth moment by moment and was not captured by it. Her operation was not ideological, but lived.... The clitoridean woman has nothing essential to offer man and expects nothing essential from him.*[28]

However, the final text we've translated—"Itinerario di riflessioni" (An Itinerary of Reflections), from 1977—shows something of Lonzi's capacity to divest from presupposed dichotomies and begin to reinvent them. Radically different in style, composition, language, and structure than the 1974 *Sputiamo su Hegel* texts, "An Itinerary of Reflections" displays all the specificities of Lonzi's second feminism. After the first period of exhausting daily group meetings (1970–72) and the years spent in "a strong state of concentration" while writing her diary (1972–77), Lonzi began to operate in a different register, with the practices of autobiographical writing and *autocoscienza* becoming the bedrocks of her feminism. The first text made public, five years after her last publication in 1972, was this essay, "Itinerario di riflessioni," contained in the collection *È già politica* (It is already politics, 1977). This book, still published under the name Rivolta Femminile, established an entirely new set of references as well as historical and cultural coordinates. If, in her first feminist period, the declared target was the culture of men, in this second period the focus was all on the relationship among women, both in the past and in the present. The volume's opening page contains a photograph of Saint Thérèse of Lisieux (Plate 5), an image Lonzi defines as "the exact image of my self-portrait, the presence of two forces, both active and overlapping in my life, to which I was seeking a solution."[29] Alongside other saints and nuns, as well as sixteenth- and seventeenth-century authors and poets, Saint Thérèse is presented as the leader of a cluster of "comrade(s) of liberation"—women whose writings and lives came to constitute a model for a different mode of relation.[30]

Fortunati with and against Lonzi

There are ways in which Fortunati's feminist subject, as much as Lonzi's, emerges from outside or beyond "history" though a radical break. However, coming from a feminist discourse so engaged with Marxism, Fortunati's approach might not be admitted within the Lonzian paradigm. Fortunati composed her definitive early work, *L'arcano della riproduzione: Casalinghe, prostitute, operai e capitale* (*The Arcane of Reproduction: Housewives, Prostitutes, Workers and Capital*), throughout the 1970s. Finally published in Italian in 1981, it only belatedly found release in English, in abridged from, by Autonomedia in 1995.[31] Composed in dialogue with the *operaismo* and Autonomia movements, the work circumscribes women's specific historical position under capitalism within what the *operaisti* had defined as the "social factory,"[32] originally defined by Mario Tronti, Antonio Negri, and other philosophers. For this tradition, a certain transition was key: the one between the "formal" and the "real" subsumption of labour, as such a distinction was understood in relation to global advancements in capitalist organization—particularly in the Italian context. Here, "advanced" industrial production sought to incorporate and organize an extended terrain and community devoted to its own reproduction and advancement in processes of global accumulation.

In such a context, Fortunati defines that which constitutes the subject position of women as a function of a historically entrenched and indirect form of labour, mediated through negation in its relationship to value production. While, in traditional Marxian accounts, value derives from waged labour time in production, Fortunati locates the condition for the possibility of value production first and foremost in the work of women and the equating of such work with an extended "Kingdom of Nature" where it "naturally" occurs. In fact, value is based on the *exclusion* of reproductive work from the traditional calculation of labour time upon which the wage and money form depends. In other words, value production does not simply "exclude" women any more than it excludes "nature" as a category that it constantly defines and redefines in its own interest. Both "nature" and "women's work" may be glorified—made hypervisible—even as they are exploited and uncompensated. Thus neither can be said to be "erased" in any simple sense, all while they are subsumed as naturalized functions that constitute what Fortunati refers to throughout *L'arcano della riproduzione* as a *"forza naturale del lavoro sociale,"* or a "naturally occurring labour power of the social."

One might take the title of Fortunati's work as emblematic of the complexities of such a simultaneous occlusion-inclusion of feminized labour—what she refers to not as an erasure but as a more complex "ideological orchestration" (*orchestrazione ideologica*) that occurs in the realm of reproduction.[33] The title of *L'arcano della riproduzione* was translated for the first English edition as *The Arcane of Reproduction*, but this rendering limits the original title's evocative power. The adjectival form "arcane," meaning simply "mysterious or obscure" in common contemporary English usage, obscures the Italian title's primary associations. On the one hand, Fortunati's title is a somewhat humorous reference to the Major Arcana of the tarot, the twenty-two cards that act as the "trump" cards in the seventeenth-century deck, capable of causing dramatic reversal in the occult meanings of the other cards as well as each other's significance. Making this reference inescapable, the original Italian edition's cover reproduced two of these Major Arcana cards: Strength (*forza*), numbered XI, and the World, (*il mondo*), numbered XXII. The former is generally represented as a woman taming a lion, and the later depicts a naked woman astride four symbols of the cosmos (Plate 9).

Referencing these figures of the tarot might be affiliated with classic "second-wave" invocations of premodern forms of women's power against a contemporary patriarchal capitalist system, fitting among the era's various feminist invocations of traditions of witchcraft, goddess worship, and—particularly prominent in Italy and France—historical and mythical figures such as Diotima and Hypatia, representing the basis of philosophical and scientific traditions. Here, however, arises a particular Marxist-feminist twist. The Strength card, when paired with women's power represented in graphic form in relation to the World, could certainly suggest a feminist détournement of a Marxist analysis of labour power and its relation to the totality of a capitalist accumulation process.

Such an interpretation finds reinforcement in the title's use of the term *l'arcano*, which might be obscure to those unfamiliar with Italian translations of Marx. The most popular Italian translations used in the 1970s render the first section of the classic last chapter of *Capital*'s first volume, "The Secret of Primitive Accumulation,"[34] as "*l'arcano dell' accumulazione originaria*." Marx's original "*Das Geheimnis der ursprünglichen Akkumulation*" becomes, literally, "the secret of originary accumulation"; in *Capital*'s final section, this phrase appears in reference to the dispossession of the future worker from other means of sustenance necessary for the capitalist accumulation process to be set in motion.[35] Thus Fortunati's "*l'arcano*" also refers to a form of so-called originary ("*sogenannte ursprüngliche*") accumulation lodged at the heart of daily processes of gendered labour and exploitation as well as a form of accumulation lodged at the heart of the commodity form itself. The Italian translations of Marx also deploy the term "*l'arcano*" in the early chapters of *Capital* to translate "*Geheimnis der Plusmacherei*" ("the mystery of surplus value," in most English language editions), becoming: "*il carattere di feticcio della merce e il suo arcano*" ("the fetish character of commodities and their mystery").

In the original Italian title and cover design of her book, therefore, Fortunati invokes forms of exploitation lodged in both a "timeless" deep history of precapitalist patriarchy and the "innovations" of a new stage of capitalist development. It is of course quite impossible to represent such continuity and transformation in any straightforward way, and as such Fortunati chooses a metaphor of optical reversal to articulate the dialectical and co-constitutive relationship of the visible in terms of its constitution of value and its invisible support mapped along the axis of gender. She writes: "This sphere is not simply the opposite of the productive sphere, but rather it conceptually 'presents itself as a photograph printed back-to-front, as mirror image of the process of commodity production.'"[36] Attentive to the relationship between verso and recto, this "back to front" of a "hidden abode" and its doubly hidden enabling condition structures the "face" of appearances. By evoking a photographic negative's relationship to a printed picture to analogize those captured in a wage relation without being recipients of the wage or engaged in value-productive work, Fortunati acknowledges that this political-economic dynamic comes to determine perception—the social visual field in general. Of course, women don't simply generate the condition for value the way the analogue negative generates the photograph while remaining contained within it. Women's expenditures across time are structurally overwritten and denied. Passive dependency becomes violent denial.

The work of Leopoldina Fortunati and Carla Lonzi testifies once and for all to the multifaceted richness of feminist thought as it developed against all odds in the post-Fascist reconstruction of one of the most Catholic and most conservative countries of the Western world, torn between the interests of American capitalism and Soviet state socialism in the Cold War era. Direct knowledge of these authors is essential to avoid the exoticism and reductive characterization that too often accompany presentations of Italian feminism for an English readership. To an attentive reader, then, Fortunati and Lonzi—especially in the first part of "The Clitoridean Woman and the Vaginal Woman"—display an array of striking similarities that draw a faithful picture of the cultural reality of what political theorist Ida Dominijanni has long defined as "the Italian laboratory."[37] The surgical analysis they each perform on the condition of women stems from the same understanding of the world as structured by interlocking planes of oppression, "a patriarchal utopia where the woman is *de facto* programmed as the last human being repressed and subjugated to sustain the grandiose effort of the male world as he breaks for himself the chains of repression and slavery."[38] In such passages, it is hard to distinguish one author from the other. For Lonzi and Fortunati both, the "patriarchal utopia" needs to be neutralized with highly specific tactics so that women's liberation can take place. The two thinkers often present the same tactics in their texts, and they employ one above all others across their very different forms of analysis and action: the tactic of refusal. For Fortunati and her Lotta Femminista allies, it was refusal of housework; for Lonzi, it was refusal to celebrate manifestations of male creativity and refusal of vaginal sex as a social practice. To recognize this matrix means to begin an exploration of Italian feminist thought with a critical, but historically accurate, eye.

1. See in particular Rivolta Femminile's 1971 statement "Assenza della donna dai momenti celebrativi della creatività maschile," translated in this volume as "The Absence of Woman from Occasions Celebrating the Manifestation of Male Creativity," beginning on p. 59. This essay was one of the few to be adapted shortly after its publication, published in the first issue of *Heresies* by the New York–based feminist art collective of the same name. See Rivolta Femminile, "On Woman's Refusal to Celebrate Male Creativity," *Heresies* 1, no. 1 (1977), 100.

2. Carla Lonzi, *Taci, anzi parla. Diario di una femminista* [Speak not, no, speak: Diary of a feminist] (Milano: Scritti di Rivolta Femminile, 1978), 142–43. All translations are the authors', unless otherwise noted.

3. See Maria Grazia Chinese, Carla Lonzi, Marta Lonzi, and Anna Jaquinta, *È già politica* [It is already politics] (Milan: Scritti di Rivolta Femminile, 1977), 110.

4. Carla Lonzi, Marta Lonzi, and Anna Jaquinta, *La presenza dell'uomo nel femminismo* [Male presence in feminism], Scritti di Rivolta Femminile 9 (Milan: Scritti di Rivolta Femminile, 1978), 146.

5. Lonzi, *Taci, anzi parla*, 29.

6. Lonzi et al., *È già politica*, 110.

7. Lonzi's expression "bringing vases to Samos" refers to the Greek island of Samos in antiquity, famed for its production of the most advanced pottery of the era. Thus "bringing vases to Samos" would entail a redundant contribution to an already defined culture. See the translation beginning on p. 109 of Lonzi's "Itinerario di riflessioni" ("An Itinerary of Reflections").

8. Lonzi, *Taci, anzi parla*, 548.

9. Carla Lonzi, "Mito della proposta culturale" [The Myth of Cultural Proposal], in Lonzi et al., *La presenza dell'uomo nel femminismo*, 141.

10. For those unfamiliar with *operaismo*, or "workerism," the term generally refers to an analysis privileging working-class revolt as the active force driving capitalist "development," as opposed to narratives of capitalist planning and control. In the Italian context the movement is most associated with the journals *Quaderni Rossi* (Red Notebooks), founded in 1961 by Raniero Panzieri, Antonio Negri, and Mario Tronti, among others,

and *Classe Operaie* (Working Class), founded in 1964. For an overview of the major actors and theories of *operaismo*, see Steve Wright, *Storming Heaven: Class Composition and Struggle in Autonomist Marxism* (London: Pluto, 2022).

11. See Louis Toupin, *Wages for Housework: The History of an International Feminist Movement, 1972–1977* (London: Pluto; Vancouver: UBC Press, 2018), 83–121, 220–240.

12. Maud Anne Bracke, *Women and the Reinvention of the Political: Feminism in Italy, 1968–1983* (London: Routledge, 2014), 18.

13. This two-page *volantone*, or cyclostile broadsheet, was titled simply "Per l'identificazione di Rivolta Femminile." It is available in the Archivio di Lotta Femminista per il salario al lavoro domestico. Biblioteca civica di Padova, Sezione 6 – Serie 1–36.

14. Dalla Costa's archive, housed in the Biblioteca civica di Padova, includes over 100,000 documents scrupulously chronicling trends in global feminist, anticolonial, ecological, and broadly anticapitalist movements from the 1960s onward. The collection focuses most intensely on Italian feminist movements of the 1970s yet includes only two of the short *volantone* produced by Rivolta Femminile (the one mentioned above and the statement on the importance of *autoconscienza* practice reproduced elsewhere in this book). It includes none of Lonzi's individual works, save those essays that were collected early and published in important Italian feminist readers such as *Donna è Bello* (Woman is beautiful) from 1972, which coupled texts from *Notes from the Second Year* and other early feminist publications from the French Mouvement de libération des femmes (Women's Liberation Movement) and journals such as *Sottosopra* (Upside down), founded in Milan by members of Libreria della Donna (Woman's Bookshop).

15. Mariarosa Dalla Costa, "Introduction to the Archive of Feminist Struggle for Wages for Housework," *Viewpoint Magazine*, October 31, 2015 https://fillip.ca/tgkh.

16. Carla Lonzi, *Sputiamo su Hegel. La donna clitoridea e la donna vaginale* [Let's Spit on Hegel: The Clitoridean Woman and the Vaginal Woman and Other Writings] (Milan: Rivolta Femminile, 1974), 7.

17. Lonzi, "Mito della proposta culturale," 145.

18. Lonzi, "Mito della proposta culturale," 152, 145.

19. Lonzi, "Mito della proposta culturale," 154.

20. Carla Lonzi, *Scritti di Rivolta Femminile 1, 2, 3, Sputiamo su Hegel. La donna clitoridea e la donna vaginale* (Milan: Rivolta Femminile, 1974).

21. See Carla Lonzi, "Let's Spit on Hegel," in *Italian Feminist Thought: A Reader*, ed. Paola Bono and Sandra Kemp (Oxford: Basil Blackwell, 1991), 40–59. The volume also includes translations of Rivolta Femminile's 1970 manifesto as well as "Sessualità femminile e aborto" ("Female Sexuality and Abortion") from 1971.

22. Lonzi, "Itinerario di riflessioni," 33.

23. Lonzi, "Let's Spit on Hegel," 59.

24. Lonzi, *Sputiamo su Hegel*, 140.

25. Lonzi, "Let's Spit on Hegel," 41.

26. For an informative discussion of Lonzi's concept of *deculturizzazione* and the *tabula rasa* required of

feminism in relation to anticolonial movements of the era, see Liliana Ellena, "Turbulence Zone: Diasporic Resonances across Carla Lonzi's Archive," in *Feminism and Art in Post-war Italy: The Legacy of Carla Lonzi*, ed. Francesco Ventrella and Giovanna Zapperi (London: Bloomsbury, 2020), 111–36.

27. Members of Rivolta Femminile used the plural term "donne clitoridee" or the singular "donna clitoridea" to refer to one another and as mutual recognition of a shared sexual politics. English-language translations vary between "clitoral" and "clitoridean." The latter has the benefit of the suffix "-ean," generally referring to broader forms of geographical, categorical, or other belonging, while the former as an English adjective has a somewhat more limiting reference to the clitoris as a sexual organ. We therefore generally prefer to translate the term as "clitoridean" when its broader associations seem more in line with the original text.

28. See the new translation of Lonzi's *An Itinerary of Reflections* in this volume, on p. 109. Originally published as "Itinerario di riflessioni," in Lonzi et al., *È già politica*, 23.

29. Lonzi, *Taci, anzi parla*, 34.

30. Lonzi, *Taci, anzi parla*, 223.

31. Leopoldina Fortunati, *L'arcano della riproduzione: Casalinghe, prostitute, operai e capitale* (Venice: Marsilio, 1981). Published in English as Leopoldina Fortunati, *The Arcane of Reproduction: Housework, Prostitution, Labor and Capital*, trans. Hillary Creek (Brooklyn: Autonomedia, 1995).

32. Mario Tronti, "Factory and Society" (1962), trans. David Broder (1966), in *Workers and Capital* (London: Verso, 2019). "On the one hand, value, dead labor, which dominates living labor, is personified in the capitalist; on the other, instead, the worker appears as labor power purely objectively, as commodity."

33. Fortunati, *L'arcano della riproduzione*, 23.

34. Chapter 24 or 26, depending on the edition.

35. Karl Marx, *Il Capitale: Critica dell'economia politica. Libro Primo*, trans. Delio Cantimori (Rome: Editori Riuniti), 777.

36. See, in this volume, Maya Gonzalez's "The Gendered Circuit: (Re)reading *The Arcane of Reproduction*," p. 235. Originally published as "The Gendered Circuit: Reading *The Arcane of Reproduction*," in "The Workers' Inquiry," special issue, *Viewpoint Magazine*, September 28, 2013, https://fillip.ca/r03k.

37. See Ida Dominijanni, "Heiresses at Twilight: The End of Politics and the Politics of Difference," *Commoner*, no. 11 (Spring 2006), 89.

38. Lonzi, *La donna clitoridea*, 90.

Carla Lonzi and Rivolta Femminile
Selected Texts (1971–77)

Contents

Translated by Arlen Austin
and Sara Colantuono

The following includes a number of shorter texts published by Rivolta Femminile (Women's Revolt) in the early 1970s accompanied by an extensive passage from Carla Lonzi's classic text "The Clitoridean Woman and the Vaginal Woman." The former were generally released as two- to three-page cyclostyle "press release" statements articulating the collective's position on a particular issue or event.

They are translated here from the 1974 collection *Sputiamo su Hegel. La donna clitoridea e la donna vaginale e altri scritti* (*Let's Spit on Hegel: The Clitoridean Woman and the*

Vaginal Woman and Other Writings), edited by Lonzi and published by Scritti di Rivolta Femminile, a publisher that the group founded in 1970.

Following the "Premessa" (Premise) to this collection, authored by Lonzi in 1973 to introduce the book's contents, we present the selection of texts in chronological order. These texts belong to Lonzi's first feminist phase, which began in the spring of 1970 and ended approximately in the spring of 1973, when she distanced herself from Carla Accardi, her long-time friend and co-founder of Rivolta Femminile, as well as the original Rivolta Femminile group and moved to Rome with her partner, Pietro Consagra.

Finally we include a translation of an important later text from 1977, "Itinerario di riflessioni" ("An Itinerary of Reflections"), contained in the collection *È già politica* (It is already politics, 1977). This book, which continues to be published under the name of Rivolta Femminile, established an entirely new set of references, sketching out historical and cultural coordinates that operate as the baseline for a feminist practice that is radically different from that of Lonzi's first period. If, in her early engagement, the declared target was the culture of men, the focus later became the relationship with women, in both the past and the present.

—Arlen Austin
and Sara Colantuono

Carla Lonzi
Premise

These writings, both those signed by me and those written collectively,[1] mark my growing awareness (*presa di coscienza*)[2] from the spring of '70 until early '72, stimulated by the discovery of the existence of feminism in the world, and by the relationship with the women of Rivolta Femminile.

The risk of these writings is that they can be taken as theoretical sureties (*punti fermi teorici*), whereas they only reflect an initial way for me to come out into the open, one in which scorn prevailed, born of my realization that masculine culture, in all its aspects, had been theorizing women's inferiority.

Women themselves accept a secondary status if whoever convinces them of such seems to deserve the esteem of mankind: Marx, Lenin, Freud, and all the others. I felt stimulated to refute some of the principles of patriarchy, not only those of the past and of the present but also those advanced by revolutionary ideologies.

Our Manifesto contains some of the most significant sentences that the general idea of feminism brought to consciousness during the first relationships among us. The feminist key operated like a revelation. We welcomed our need to express ourselves as a synonym of liberation itself.

I wrote "Let's Spit on Hegel" because I had been very disturbed to notice that nearly all Italian feminists gave more credit to class struggle than to their own oppression.

When neither revolution, nor philosophy, nor art, nor religion enjoyed our unconditional trust any longer, we faced the central issue of our inferiorization, the sexual one. During a campaign for the abolition of laws against abortion, I asked myself: Is it more slavish to submit to clandestine abortion, or to become pregnant if pleasure was not experienced, that is to say, only to satisfy a man? Who has obliged us to satisfy him at our expense? No one. There, we are unconscious but voluntary victims ("Female Sexuality and Abortion").

Why does the woman not have her resolution in orgasm ensured as does the man? What is its physiosexual functioning? And the psychosexual? What is, finally, its sex? Clitoridean women and vaginal women exist: Who are they? Who are we? ("The Clitoridean Woman and the Vaginal Woman").

By becoming conscious of cultural conditioning—that which we do not know of, that which we do not even imagine having—we could discover something essential, something that changes everything, the sense of ourselves, of relationships, of life. As we went, little by little, into the heart of oppression, the meaning of liberation became more and more interior. Because of this, consciousness raising is the only way; otherwise we risk fighting for a liberation that then would reveal itself as only exterior and superficial, for an illusory path ("The Meaning of *Autocoscienza* in Feminist Groups").

For example, we risk fighting for a tomorrow, a tomorrow without conditioning for woman, a tomorrow so far off that we will not even be there. Man has always postponed each solution to an ideal future for mankind, but it does not exist; we can, however, reveal current humankind, which is to say, ourselves.

No one is conditioned *a priori* to the point that one cannot free herself; no one cannot be so free of conditioning *a priori* to be free. We women are not conditioned in an irremediable way, but an experience of liberation has not been expressed by us in centuries.

These writings have been nothing more than a step toward that experience, a premise of it, and a prophecy of it.

November 1973

Translated from Carla Lonzi, "Premessa," in *Sputiamo su Hegel. La donna clitoridea e la donna vaginale e altri scritti* [*Let's Spit on Hegel: The Clitoridean Woman and the Vaginal Woman and Other Writings*] (Milan: Scritti di Rivolta Femminile, 1974), 7–9.

1. [Original note:] Initially, some points of consciousness were spontaneously appropriated by specific Rivolta Femminile groups; therefore the piece of writing that enunciated them was signed collectively. Signed under my name are the elaboration of those themes in more extended writings. Now that phase is over: true *autocoscienza* brought to a strictly personal expression.

2. In the original, this process is described as "*presa di coscienza*," suggesting an increasing grasp of consciousness. For readability, we have translated the line as "growing awareness," though unfortunately this translation does not retain the reference to *autocoscienza* as the distinctive form of consciousness raising practiced by Rivolta Femminile. See also the notes on the translation of "*prendere coscienza*" on p. 61.

The Absence of Woman from Occasions Celebrating the Manifestation of Male Creativity[1]

We of Rivolta Femminile refuse to participate in celebratory moments of male creativity because we have become aware (*prendere coscienza*)[2] that, in the patriarchal world—which is to say in the world made by men for men—creativity too, which is a liberating practice, is implemented by and for men. Woman, as a subsidiary human being, is denied any intervention that would imply recognition of her as a subject: for her, no liberation is envisioned.

Male creativity assumes as its interlocutor another instance of male creativity, but as client and spectator of this operation such creativity maintains woman, whose role excludes competition. Woman is conditioned in a category that *a priori* guarantees the protagonist of creativity the appreciation of his values. While creativity is recognized as having a liberating function, art is institutionalized, and with it a neutral counterpart who witnesses the gestures of others. The action of a man, even in the domain of art, is always articulated as a competitive action that is performed together with another man, his partner. This action is also always performed in relation to a woman, whom the man demands behold him.

This is the character of patriarchal creativity, stimulated by both aggressive confrontation with one's rival and by the disarmed acceptance of women. The man, the artist himself, feels abandoned by woman the moment she forgoes the role and archetype of spectator: the solidarity between them rested on the conviction that, as a gratified spectator of creativity, the woman had reached the ultimate goal of the reincarnations granted to her species.

Instead, the woman discovers that the patriarchal world has an absolute need for her as a supporting element on which even the liberating efforts of man rest, and that female liberation can be achieved only independently of patriarchal speculations and the male dynamics of liberation. The artist expects from woman the mythologization of his gesture and she, until her liberation process begins, responds exactly to this need of male civilization. The work of art does not want to lose the security of a myth that leans on our exclusively receptive role.

By becoming aware (*prendere coscienza*) of her condition in relation to male creativity, woman finds herself with two options: one, used until now, to reach equality on the creative level as it is historically defined by the male, alienating for her and recognized by man with indulgence; the other—the one that the feminist movement seeks—is that of the autonomous liberation of the woman who recovers a creativity that is hers, fed by the repression imposed by the models of the dominant sex.

Participating in the celebration of man's creativity means giving in to the historical enticement of our colonization during its culminating episode, according to the strategy of the patriarchal world. Without women, the cult of male supremacy becomes a character clash between men.

By absenting ourselves from the celebratory moments of male creative manifestation we do not pronounce an ideological judgment on creativity itself, condemn or contest it; but, in refusing to embrace it, we undermine the concept that the benefits of art are an administrable grace. Not believing in a reflexive process of liberation causes an exodus of creativity from patriarchal relationships. With her absence, woman makes a gesture of awareness, liberating and therefore creative.

Milan, March 1971

Translated from Carla Lonzi, "Assenza della donna dai momenti celebrativi della manifestazione creativa maschile," in *Sputiamo su Hegel. La donna clitoridea e la donna vaginale e altri scritti* [*Let's Spit on Hegel: The Clitoridean Woman and the Vaginal Woman and Other Writings*] (Milan: Scritti di Rivolta Femminile, 1974), 63–66.

1. The title of this work is uniquely difficult to translate without causing a great deal of confusion for an English reader. The essay was one of only a few to be adapted by an American feminist group, published in the first issue of *Heresies* by the New York–based feminist art collective of the same name, where it was translated simply as "On Woman's Refusal to Celebrate Male Creativity." See Rivolta Femminile, "On Woman's Refusal to Celebrate Male Creativity," *Heresies* 1, no. 1 (1977): 100. The most literal translation of the title would be something like: "The Absence of the Woman from Celebrative Moments of Male Creative Manifestation."

2. The original text uses the term "*prendere coscienza*" as in "*autocoscienza*." We chose to translate *prendere coscienza* as "becoming aware" for readability, although this choice forcefully removes from the text a key reference to the process of *autocoscienza*. We trust the importance of *autocoscienza* in the process is evident throughout.

Female Sexuality
and Abortion

We of Rivolta Femminile hold that the one to three million clandestine abortions calculated in Italy every year are a sufficient number to consider the antiabortion law expired as a matter of fact. The female community has risked its life, the civil and religious ostracism of a patriarchal state, by clandestinely carrying out abortion practice, which still today is entrusted as the last word to remove oneself from an unwanted gestation process. We refuse today to endure the affront that a few thousand signatures, both male and female, would serve as a footing to request from men in power, from legislators, what in reality has been the argument expressed by billions of women's lives thrown to the butcher of clandestine abortion. We will access freedom of abortion, and not new legislation on it, alongside those billions of women who constitute the history of female revolt, because only in this way will we make this fundamental chapter of our oppression into the first chapter of our consciousness raising from which to undermine the structure of male domination.

Compulsory and repetitive procreation has submitted the female species to the hands of man, for whom she constituted the first basis of power. But today what liberating content can procreation "by free choice" have in a world where culture exclusively embodies a male point of view on existence, conditioning *a priori* every woman's "free choice"? Do free sexuality and free maternity—in other words, the premises of a woman as a person—still go, after millennia, through the affirmation of free abortion? Free maternity and free sexuality must find their meaning within our consciousness raising; only in this way will we be sure that the freedom they are talking about is ours, and that it is not that of the male, who realizes himself through us, through an even more occult oppression of ourselves.

Women have abortions because they become pregnant. But why do they become pregnant? Is it because they answer to a specific sexual need that they have intercourse with partners in a way that defies the primacy of conception? Patriarchal culture does not ask itself this question because it does not admit doubts on "natural" laws. It avoids asking if in this field what is natural for men is also natural for women: it takes it for granted and defends through every means possible patriarchal man's sexuality as a "natural" sexuality for both, man and woman.

But we do know that when a woman becomes pregnant, and she did not want to, this happened not because she expressed herself sexually but because she conformed herself to the act and to the sexual model surely favoured by the patriarchal male, even if that could mean she would become pregnant and thus have to resort to an interruption of pregnancy. In the patriarchal world—in the world where woman is immobilized in a subaltern and servile condition through a mythologization of men and a devaluation of herself that are systematically solicited by every instant of her social and private life—man has imposed his pleasure. Pleasure that man imposes on woman leads to procreation, and it is on the basis of procreation that male culture has marked the border between natural sexuality and unnatural sexuality, prohibited or accessory and preliminary. But when is the procreative end officially denied by the whole of society? In a world forced to adopt contraception and antiprocreation, we absolutely must intervene with the consciousness that nature has given us a sexual organ that is distinct from procreation, and it is on the basis of this that we will find our autonomy from man as our lord and dispenser of pleasure to the inferiorized species, and we will develop a sexuality that starts from our physiological centre of pleasure, the clitoris.

Man has left woman alone before a law that prevents her from having an abortion: alone, denigrated, unworthy of collectivity. Tomorrow he will end up leaving her alone before a law that would not prevent her from having an abortion: alone, gratified, worthy of collectivity. But woman asks herself: "For whose pleasure did I become pregnant? For whose pleasure am I having an abortion?" This question contains the germs of our liberation: by formulating it, woman abandons the identification with man and she finds the strength to break the silence that is the crowning of colonization.

Woman now reflects: if it was in the sexual model imposed by the other, by the man, that she challenged conception, then it was the man who challenged conception via her body. Conception therefore is the product of the violence of male sexual culture on woman, who then becomes responsible for a situation that she passively endured. By denying her the possibility of abortion, man transforms his abuse into woman's guilt. By allowing her such freedom, man lifts her from her condemnation, drawing her into a new solidarity that postpones to an unspecified time the moment in which she would ask if the fact that she becomes pregnant is because of culture, in other words man's dominion, or because of autonomy, in other words natural destiny.

Man has created the cultural conditions under which woman turns to abortion as a solution connected to her own reproductive nature. In reality, woman, if she does have this possibility that is inherent to the biological mechanisms of her species, also enjoys a sexuality that is external to her vagina, and as such can be affirmed without risking conception. Man knows that the woman welcomes his orgasm in the vagina while more or less emotionally or physiologically involved; he knows that it is his orgasm and not the woman's; he knows that as a consequence the woman can become pregnant against her will and therefore be forced to have an abortion. Just the same, man makes love as a virility ritual, and it falls on the woman to be fertilized in the exact moment that she is deprived of her specific sexual enjoyment, in the moment that the act that makes her sexually colonized is accomplished. Once pregnant, woman discovers the other side of male power, which makes conception a problem of the one who possesses the uterus and not of the one who owns the culture of the penis.

Under this light, the legalization of abortion asked of the male has a sinister aspect, because the legalization of abortion, even free abortion, will serve to codify the delight of passivity as an expression of the female sex and to reinforce what they imply: the myth of the genital act being concluded by the male's orgasm in the vagina. Woman will seal, through a downplayed exercise of her being used, sexual phallocratic culture.

Seeking to protect our lives through a demand for the legalization of abortion leads, under the pretext of philanthropic and humanistic considerations, to our suicide: in an indirect way, the prevalence of one sex over another is reconfirmed even as the other seems to meet its liberation.

As spokespeople of the endless number of women who have had and have clandestine abortions, we consider the antiabortion law expired as a matter of fact, but above all we consider expired that culture of the penis, within which the concession made to women to engage in maternity as a free choice is presented as a victory of feminism, while instead patriarchy consolidates and updates its management of the world.

Patriarchy reaffirms the prestige of a sexual culture that impregnates women by denying them the right to express themselves in sex and emphasizing instead their capacity to conform to and favour the pleasure of the other, of the patriarchal man. Through the spread of abortion practices and contraceptives he makes sure that this pleasure will not be troubled by the prediction of an insane overpopulation of the globe. Liberalization of abortion has become, through millennia, the condition by which the patriarchy intends to remedy its contradictions while keeping the terms of its dominion unaltered. What meaning does a male orgasm assume to our eyes in a vagina covered by spermicides and contraceptive rubber? Does our colonization truly lead us not to see any deceit in a sexual culture that finds its justification in the procreative structure and then, even when denying the procreative end, maintains a steady ban over the clitoris? On which scientific prerequisites is male culture still allowed to consider immature the clitoridean orgasm and to push woman to the tiring and unlikely attainment of vaginal pleasure—a process of acculturation if there ever was one in relationships of subjugation among groups, and that is sold as a spontaneous disinhibition and normalization of femininity? Is it perhaps an aspiration of the girl to become that opaque and subjugated adult woman, that physical and psychic appendix of man, to be his companion in the patriarchal world, proud only of redeeming her passivity in mythical, voluptuous agreements? Is this not the goal the girl rejects with all of her being? And when she finally reaches it, did she not carry out the final phase of her conditioning, instead of developing her own autonomy? She must know that the psychophysical relationship with man, toward which male culture presently drags her, reluctant and troubled, is the same as the one in which the Turkish slave or the favoured of the Indian harem have gathered the most intense pleasures. A moderately erogenous zone such as the vagina became, by virtue of male prestige, the sex of the woman. Horrified, we read about African tribes that practiced on young women the asportation of the clitoris, but what else did [Sigmund] Freud and [Wilhelm] Reich practice? And of what else did men avail themselves on women if not a substitutive sexuality that she developed on the cultural mutilation of her own sexuality?

This is the refusal of a history of millennia that, on the one hand, oppressed that whole part of female humankind that doubted the union with man under an effective state of slavery and mortified herself in frigidity, not being able to conform to this union in an effective state of slavery; and, on the other hand, when an agreement was made with the male during the explicit statement of his virility, what did the deep pleasures of the woman express if not an individual bred in complete passive adoration of the other? It was clearly a pleasure connected with a historical situation that no longer existed, because this kind of woman's eroticism was sustained by her feeling rewarded by a being superior to herself, and this is not verifiable in a condition that excludes precisely that mythologization of men.

Abortion admitted by society wants to prolong and artificially give new strength to a feminine eroticism that has paralyzed and destroyed women for four thousand years. We claim a part of our body that procures us pleasure without condemning us to procreation and that unhooks us from the emotional condition of she who gives herself as an inferior to a superior being. Because of this, vaginal pleasure has been emphasized by an entire male culture, Western and Eastern, and has found in the Freudian and Reichian theory the pillar to protract its glory for a millennium more. We feminists stop this conspiracy of male power and we save ourselves from complete ruin.

Let's think of a civilization in which free sexuality would not amount to the apotheosis of free abortion and contraceptives adopted by women: it will manifest itself as development of a sexuality not specifically procreative but polymorphous, in other words, untethered to vaginal finalization. It would no longer be about preparing for the encounter between the sex of a hegemonic subject and his instrument but between two human subjects, man and woman, and their sexes (with every predictable and unpredictable fluctuation of the heterosexual aspect of humankind). From a place of violence and pleasure the vagina becomes, at discretion, one of the places of sexual games. In such a civilization it would appear clear that contraceptives would be entitled to those who intend to enjoy a sexuality that is procreative, and that abortion is not a solution for the free woman but for the woman who is colonized by the patriarchal system.

Milan, July 1971

Translated from Carla Lonzi, "Sessualità femminile e aborto," in *Sputiamo su Hegel: La donna clitoridea e la donna vaginale e altri scritti* [*Let's Spit on Hegel: The Clitoridean Woman and the Vaginal Woman and Other Writings*] (Milan: Scritti di Rivolta Femminile, 1974), 67–76.

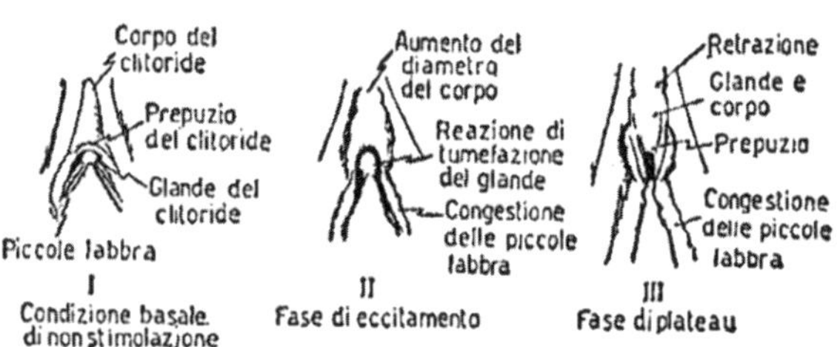

La clitoride nel ciclo di risposta sessuale femminile. La fase orgasmica è stata omessa per mancanza di dati.

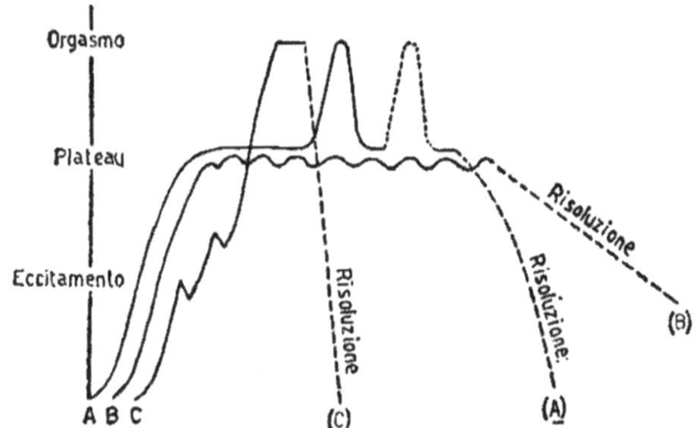

Il ciclo di risposta sessuale nella donna. (Diagrammi di tre tipi di comportamento indicativi dell'infinita varietà delle reazioni sessuali femminili).

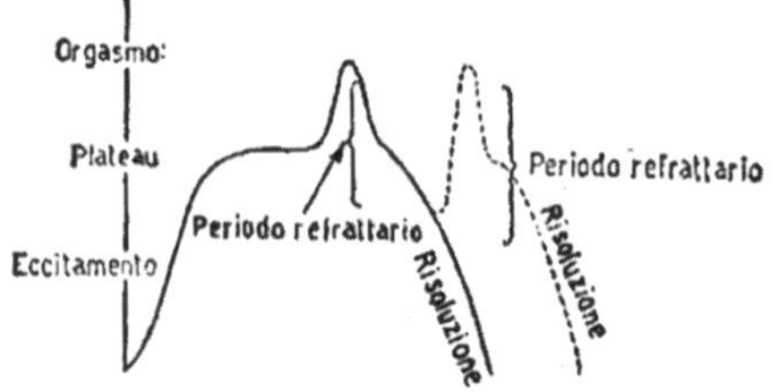

Il ciclo di risposta sessuale nell'uomo.

(I disegni sono stati tratti dal volume di W.H. Masters e V.E. Johnson « L'atto sessuale nell'uomo e nella donna », Ed. Feltrinelli).

Carla Lonzi

The Clitoridean Woman
and the Vaginal Woman

The female sex is the clitoris; the male sex is the penis.

The vagina is the cavity of the female body that welcomes the sperm of the man and forwards it into the uterus so that fertilization of the egg might occur. It is through this cavity that the body of the child exits from that of the mother.

The moment in which the penis of the man emits sperm is the moment of his orgasm. The vagina is thus the cavity of the female body where, in conjunction with the man's orgasm, the process of fertilization begins.

In men, the mechanism of pleasure is thus tightly bound to the mechanism of reproduction; in women, the mechanism of pleasure and the mechanism of reproduction are interconnected, but they do not coincide.

To impose on woman a coincidence that did not exist as a fact in her physiology was a gesture of cultural violence that does not compare with any other kind of colonization.

Once we were comrades,
but now I give you orders
because I am a man—you see—
I have the knife in my hand
and I operate on you.
Your clitoris, that you treasure so jealously,
I will rip it, I will throw it on the ground,
because I am a man, now.
My heart is made of stone:
otherwise I could not operate on you.
After they will care for your wound,
and I will know many things:

I will know those of you who take care of themselves,
and those who neglect themselves.

> —Initiatory chant of women elders
> who practice clitoral excision
> on Manja girls, in Ubanghi, Africa[1]

Do not speak this way, sisters.
My heart is scared.
I have great fear.
If I could mutate into a bird!
I would soon fly away!

> —Ritual chant of young Manja girls
> during the aforementioned operation

An apex of colonization was achieved when woman, deprived of the expression of her own autonomous sexuality, was also forbidden methods of abortion. An unwanted gestation is already in itself a consequence of an act of overpowering—one that responds to the sexual and psychological satisfaction of patriarchal man. The denial of the right to interrupt this process was a further act of overpowering, in light of which the values of the love relationship, through which male culture has obfuscated its imposition of a sexual model, are thrown into crisis.

Through man's imposed sexual model, woman, deprived of discovering and manifesting her own sexuality, acquires renunciation and submission as characteristics of her feminine being.

While enjoying pleasure in response to the pleasure of the man, the woman loses herself as an autonomous being, enhances her complementarity to the male, finds in him her motivation for existing.

Patriarchal sexual culture, being rigorously procreative, has created for woman a model of vaginal pleasure.

Contraceptives, abortion, sterilization reveal an inconsistency in the patriarchal world: they highlight that procreation and pleasure cannot no longer be equated. However, instead of questioning the procreative sexual model as a "natural" model, they reaffirm it by mobilizing a series of measures that render the procreative act nonprocreative.

Sexuality within a procreative model manifests itself for what it is: a culture, whose values and taboos reflect the concept of "nature" that has developed in relation to the purposes of the civilization that expressed it.

With birth control, women, who previously saw their sexuality devalued, also see motherhood devalued, in whose superabundance the world glimpses its next cataclysm.

The roles of wife and mother, in which woman should fulfill herself in the patriarchal world, thus risk being revealed as an alienated structure: sexual freedom in marriage and motherhood by free choice tend to restore social dignity to these roles, but they are surrogates for liberating content, true and real reforms.

While the patriarchal world and its culture, to remedy the demographic problem, are unable to implement any change in sexual culture that frees the level of pleasure from its condemnation to procreation, woman discovers the circumstance to perform that civilizational leap corresponding to her entry as subject into the erotic relationship.

Thus an organ of pleasure independent of procreation such as the clitoris loses that secondary and transitory role in the female sexuality that patriarchal man has decreed and becomes the organ upon which "nature" authorizes and solicits a type of nonprocreative sexuality.

The function of pleasure connected to procreation differs from the function of pleasure independent of procreation: in fact, the former guarantees the continuation of the species; the latter expresses a fundamental biological need of the individual.

Complementarity is a concept that concerns the woman and the man in the procreative moment, not in the erotic-sexual one.

Woman asks herself: On what basis is it postulated that clitoral pleasure expresses an infantile and immature female personality? Is it perhaps because it does not respond to the procreative sexual model? But isn't the procreative model the one in which the heterosexual relationship crystallized—even when the procreative goal was carefully avoided—according to the clear preference of the hegemonic penis? Therefore, clitoral pleasure is discredited, owing to the fact that it is not functional to the male genital model.

The erotic behaviour of the man relative to the woman, while on the one hand serving to excite her, on the other hand renders her a dependent succubus. This co-relationship opens up to the woman the possibility of psychically acceptable intercourse.

The woman does not need to appreciate herself through the attention that the man provides in courtship rites. If she were not so inferiorized and objectified, male adulation would no longer serve for compensation and redemption.

To fully enjoy the clitoral orgasm, woman must find psychic autonomy from man. This psychic autonomy is so inconceivable for male civilization as to be interpreted as a refusal of men and presupposed as an inclination toward women. In the patriarchal world, therefore, this woman is subject to all the ostracism traditionally reserved for a suspected openness toward homosexuality.

We do not make pronouncements on heterosexuality: we are not so blind as to not recognize it as a pillar of the patriarchy, nor are we so ideological as to reject it *a priori*. Each of us can study how much she likes or dislikes patriarchal man and how much the man.

From the patriarchal point of view, the vaginal woman[2] is considered the one who manifests a correct sexuality while the clitoridean represents the immature and masculinized and, for Freudian psychoanalysis, even the frigid woman. Feminism, on the other hand, affirms that the true evaluation of these responses to the relation with the oppressing sex is the following: the vaginal woman is the one who, in captivity, has been brought to a measure of consent for the enjoyment of the patriarch, while the clitoridean is she who has not acquiesced to the emotional coercion of integration with the other, that coercion that works on the passive woman, but rather expresses herself in a sexuality that does not coincide with coitus. Between these two poles of response to the conditioning and to male sexual culture are all those women whose sexual situation reflects a scarce possibility of identifying with the phenomenon, in an infinity of subjective and objective circumstances, which includes the absolute refusal of any form of sexuality.

Woman unconsciously senses the act of submission required of her to access heterosexual pleasure. The monogamous ideal imposed on her finds a point of connection to her authenticity: This ideal allows her to ennoble a "unique" relationship, a dedication to the other that, if extended to more men, would lose its ethical value: the value of a "specific" and "particularly" motivated choice. It would be revealed as a generalized conditioning of women in favour of men.

The monogamous woman spoken of by [Friedrich] Engels as the bearer of value in the couple is the woman colonized by the patriarchal system.

Male jealousy hardly subsides even when woman claims to have had pure sexual intercourse with no strings attached. But man knows that, in the current sexual culture, for woman there is no relationship without involvement: the man takes; the woman gives of herself.

All incitements to emancipation through activation of the female demeanour ("take the initiative") find an understandable resistance from woman. After all, what does it mean for you to urge a man to have sexual intercourse when what will take place will be sex conducted by the man?

The clitoridean woman represents everything that is authentic and inauthentic of the female world that has detached itself from visceral relations with men. The clitoridean woman has authentically claimed herself; the vaginal woman has simulated pleasure through estrangement, and sought the goals of man on the cultural and social level.

Asking man for the freedom to have an abortion to solve the problem of an unwanted gestation is as absurd as asking him for a sturdy penis, capable of lasting through various positions to bring woman to orgasm.

Vaginal orgasm, as a scientific problem, is now equivalent to the dispute over the sex of angels. There are women on whom the cultural conditioning for enjoyment during coitus is effective, and there are others—the majority—on whom it is ineffective. In the latter, either the woman finds a condition autonomous from the man and claims her orgasm in the clitoris or she hesitates to recognize herself in her own sex organ and stops at intermediate, painful, chaotic stages.

It is important for us to affirm our sex and not just to have it satisfied. What liberating meaning can the solution offered by the emancipated woman have? In presumed parity with the man who uses different techniques to vary sexual pleasure, she sees her clitoral orgasm satisfied, but she lacks awareness that she is expressing a sexuality of her own. She will therefore remain equally dominated by man and the male sexual model: she will double her skills to make the penis forget her betrayal and for the man to forget her unsuitability, by which she feels humiliated.

The clitoridean woman who becomes a vaginal aspirant is neutralized in her creativity and re-enacts, on the cultural level, that dependence on the male world that her sexual autonomy had questioned on the level of the erotic.

The vaginal woman, the one who reacted voluptuously in oppression, is doubly deceived. She has made available to man, for his particular mission, all the creativity of which a human being is the bearer, without ever finding the strength to want the entire arc of the creative experience for her own, which entails, before all else, a concentration on oneself. In fact, the vaginal woman feels anguish and guilt for every kind of pleasure of her own and associates herself with man in his contempt for the clitoral orgasm, because she is terrified of discovering herself as a human being outside the destiny of the couple, that is, outside the gratified union with a superior being.

The woman who, in the couple, declares herself lacking in resources and self-confidence, and in the meantime leads a dog's life in order to enhance the resources and self-confidence of her husband, must understand that she has been accustomed to performing a transference to which every woman is solicited by every man. She should try to withdraw the transference: all her energies will flow back to her.

For us, affirming our own sex does not mean impoverishing the encounter between man and woman, because we do not lose sight of the problem; on the contrary we wish to re-evaluate the human encounter with all its unexpected circumstances. Now, in an era in which the world of emotions drags us into mythic unions, into monogamous relationships of blackmail and opportunism, the so-called human relationship is very publicized, but in the meantime it is split from eroticism and has become a process that burns itself out in formality without a vivifying outlet.

The vaginal woman is reluctant to investigate sex because, having connected it with emotion, she is afraid of depriving it of the transcendence that surrounds it. Man, of course, remains behind the scenes and makes sure that his object is not deprived of the value created by an ignorance that makes it appear harmless. Man relies on woman's feelings for her to enjoy sex, and not on the knowledge of her sexuality.

We suggest meditating on how boring lengthy coitus is. Many amorous variations appear to be male fanaticisms, and as coarseness if, in addition, they neglect to guarantee a woman's orgasm.

Why does the vaginal woman hesitate to become aware of a problem as vast as that of woman in sex? How does she justify that female humanity is mostly disbanded and suffering from its sexuality? Identifying oneself with the condition of millions of women who lack a fixed point of reference in pleasure is very painful, but they can no longer be dismissed with patriarchal motivations by accusing them of being wrong or as still in slow transition from repression to normalcy. The millions of women who have expressed a profound universal discomfort in sex are a constant in the history of female humanity, a constant that denounces and reconfirms the need for a change in the world.

The category of repression, adopted by male culture to explain the dysfunctions that take place in the relationship between the sexes, is a new screen that hides the drama of women's oppression.

The study of infantile sexuality has a patriarchal character that enables the rationalization of women's oppression as a consequence of a childhood without repression. The fact that a repressed childhood yields "abnormal" results on a sexual level fails to consider the even more "abnormal" results that an unrepressed childhood yields for the purposes of a civilization in which women must be subjugated. In fact, if girl were to be kept in isolation from man, in the interdiction of autoeroticism and sexual games, in the mortification of her creative personality, she could grow mythomaniacal enough to submit to the male and to experience feelings of gratification with him. The young girl who begins to be raised partially free of those taboos cannot but pass through a series of conflicts and negative responses when later culture pretends that the result of her infant liberalization is a spontaneous adherence to subjection and the feminine role.

Whether they reach orgasm or not, many females draw satisfaction from the realization that the husband or sexual partner enjoyed the contact and from the realization that they made the pleasure of the male possible. We have biographies of people married for a large number of years, during which the wives never reached orgasm; nevertheless the marriages remained intact due to the high level of family harmony.

—Alfred Kinsey[3]

Feminism, for the woman, takes the place of psychoanalysis for the man. In the latter, man finds reasons that make his supremacy unassailable and scientific as an order definitively responding to the freedom of all; in feminism, woman finds the collective female conscience that elaborates the themes of her liberation. The category of repression in psychoanalysis is equivalent to the slave-master dialectic in Marxism: both are aimed at a patriarchal utopia where woman is de facto programmed as the last human being repressed and subjugated to sustain the grandiose effort of the male world as he breaks for himself the chains of repression and slavery.

Without the abolition of male sexual patterns and without an awareness of the vaginal woman, there is no feminism. And the patriarchy, as a historical epoch, is still sheltered from this end. In fact, it means that marriage will persist as a model of relationship, since it is contested only as an institution and not as a distribution of sexual roles and structuring of the couple. The erect penis is a sign of power, rank, and threat in the animal world that expresses the aggressive behaviour of the male; the female remains the alternative between submissive behaviour and escape.

The male copulatory organ is a subsidiary structure that developed at a later time and only in those animals whose behaviour during the sexual act was such as to adapt to its presence. The relationships of hierarchy and strength existing between the sexes played a role of primary importance in determining the position that the male and the female assume during mating. The stronger and more authoritative pursuer asserted his supremacy by mounting on his mate.... In mammals, including humans, it is not the case that copulation occurs this way because they have a penis; the opposite is true: they have a penis because the sexual behaviour of their ancestors who were without it paved the way for its development.

—Wolfgang Wickler[4]

The father is bad, the penis is bad: this is a reality of the patriarchal world. Why should the child be so blind that she considers them good and maintains a relationship of trust with them? Won't that trust be what betrays her, and when she wants to open her eyes, won't it always be too late?

Fortunately for us, many women have been children whose trust in the patriarch has collapsed in apocalyptic indignation or astonishment. Today, they bring to light moment by moment the unconscious contents of an operation whose audacity is still in full bloom.

When we claim to place our strength in the clitoridean woman, we do not intend to discriminate in value between women, only to indicate the temperamental reaction that contains the premises of *autocoscienza* (consciousness raising). In fact it is woman who, in all the intertwining casual and voluntary situations in her life, has tasted the intoxicating moments of herself constituted as an individual to find her natural outlet in feminism. And feminism acquires reality precisely from her previous experience; in fact, it exists as the affirmation of a point of truth that emerges, and not only as a lament. However exhausting the trials through which the woman not identified with her role is forced to pass, feminist awareness does not catch her without effort. Realizing the reason for each of her authentic gestures, she also realizes why they were not understood and why she did not feel completely frustrated and retained her courage. On the other hand, the vaginal woman can experience feminism as a trauma, primarily because she is not used to independent thinking and secondarily because it is precisely through independent thinking that she becomes aware of the deceptions of her own disposition to trust and union with man. For this woman, feminism is a turning point in life, not a continuation; therefore, autonomy from man can be accompanied by the painful aspect of a most complete disillusionment. But anger at a life lived in servitude is an indispensable remedy for feminism, as is equally so the rebellion of those who opposed servitude.

In anatomy and physiology it is no mystery that the part of the female body richest in nerve endings is the clitoris and that the vagina represents a reactive site only in the vestibule area, or external third, and that the rest is a real "anatomical impossibility" (Kinsey) as a site of orgasm. On the other hand, since the beginning of time, every erotic culture has raved about the need for particular techniques and erotic wisdom on the part of men to make women feel pleasure in coitus and to make them reach the liberating stages of sexual tension. In fact, during the act of coitus, an indirect rhythmic massage is produced on the clitoris—by stretching the genital membranes and also often through contact with the man's body—which, united with and multiplied by the psychic excitement transmitted to the clitoris and transformed by it, determines the orgasmic reaction: from the clitoris it radiates throughout the woman's sexual apparatus. The nefarious phallic analogy through which the clitoris was interpreted by [Sigmund] Freud has prevented us from identifying in the pleasure organ spontaneously found by the girl in autoeroticism the pleasure organ of the woman. But this is just the circumstance of a fatal mistake for generations of women and the pretext that allowed the patriarchal world to block the woman, at the dawn of her liberation, into the old state of dependence.

The fact that man wanted us vaginal against all physiological evidence should have made us doubt: because man has always wanted woman not in freedom, but in slavery. Woman has not expressed herself in any area of life, let alone in the reflection on her sexuality: she has not written her Kama Sutra, has not investigated her sex if not heeding assumptions already established by others. Was it possible that the fury with which men worried over her sexuality was not itself suspicious enough to show her the true way of femininity?

The affirmations that the stimulation of erotic fantasy in women is almost absent must take into account the fact that, by not expressing her sexuality on her own, she is eroticized by the psychic contents of the state of receptivity. She waits for man's suggestions and stimuli and adapts to them. This is not repression: it is the process of pleasure in women forced into sexual substitution.

The moment of union, when the complementary knows the end of its incompleteness by letting itself be deeply penetrated by man for his enjoyment, has become the psychic engine mobilizing desire in woman.

One wonders: Why is the vagina passive? Can't it be perceived as something that takes, that acts, instead of something that welcomes, conforms, and is subjugated? This is an interpretation offered by the man who suggests active emotions to a woman or rather varies his pleasure from possessing to being absorbed and possessed by the woman.

In patriarchal sexual culture it is not the man who seeks the woman, but his penis which seeks the vagina. What the woman experiences as the value of the union, the man experiences as an episode of sex, a passage to something else.

Every time she tastes the Purushayta, the woman must remember that, in the absence of a special effort on her part, her husband's pleasure will not be perfect at all and that therefore she will have to make an effort to be able to close and squeeze the Yoni (vagina) so that it moulds tightly onto the Lingarn (penis), stretching and compressing at will, similar, in a word, to the hand of the milkmaid Gopala when milking the cow. This can only be learned with long practice, and especially directing the will into the organ itself, as men do who exercise to sharpen the sense of hearing or touch. She who practices this is never lost. Then her husband will appreciate her above any other woman and would not mistake her for the most beautiful Flani (queen) of both worlds: so much is the Yoni precious to the man who locks himself up!

—*Kama Sutra: The Indian Art of Loving* (translated by K. Maliai)

Despite the courtly and loving literature that accompanies heterosexual intercourse in culture, the man does not become impotent even when knowing that the woman does not derive enjoyment. The penis thus manifests itself in all its truth as an authoritarian organ that values the place where its pleasure takes place for what it needs and not for reciprocity.

The woman has the fantasy of being raped during coitus: this is interpreted as the result of the repression performed by a civilization that has led her to accept pleasure only if lived masochistically and against her will. We believe instead that there is a truth in what faces the unconscious of the woman and, if she is pleased with it, it is because there is no other way than that of suffering to achieve vaginal pleasure.

The man has the fantasy of being abused by a woman during coitus: this is interpreted as the fruit of the repression operated by a civilization that has pushed him to eroticize himself in an irresponsible rapture of violence.[5] Also in this phenomenon we glimpse a different truth latent in the male unconscious: the woman really is used in the sexual act, and that she refuses and is finally taken serves to reflect back to the man an enlarged image of his virility, and therefore of power.

Why, then, does the man who is so proud of his availability in sex find his ideal state of equilibrium mirroring himself in a woman who lacks that disengagement and who gets involved with him every time? And why does he need to show his annoyance about the woman's attachment, and instead feels lost if he just assumes that he is facing a partner who has opened his eyes to her condition as an object, and she no longer adapts to it, no longer remains the object of those emotional delicacies—tremor, self-denial, admiration, etc.—which complement the pleasure of being consumed by the other? The man feels reassured by this, since the sex he performs so casually is not twisted against him, making him in turn an object.

The woman who, in the monogamous couple through a conscious and voluntary effort, passes from the clitoral to the vaginal stage observes that it was a matter of psychologically unlocking herself from the man in order to enjoy more absolute pleasures and total agreement. It is evident that accepting the role of wife and mother—and therefore of one who fulfills herself by doing the utmost for others—while claiming an independent sexuality in the relationship is a situation of unsustainable schizophrenia. By behaving like a bad copy of the vaginal woman—that is, as an unhappy vaginal woman, a slave continually dissociated from her reach toward autonomy and demystification of the man—she feels profoundly guilty. An available exit from this guilt is to reaffirm in sex her adaptation to these values she is addicted to by renouncing her real clitoral orgasm, promising and demanding like any outlet of autonomy, which truly recedes in her experience, since no part of her brain is willing to connect with him anymore. The other exit, the one that comes from feminist awareness, is to strengthen the urge to exist independently of the roles, in order to recompose a psychic unity based on self-affirmation and not on the pleasure of getting lost. This path does not have any legislation to guarantee it and cannot be gratified by the approval of patriarchal man: it leads to the unexpected for the imaginative gifts that the woman confidently assumes for herself.

Patriarchal society reproduces the privileges that mammalian communities have decreed belong to the aggressiveness of the male: it is true that the harem is a need of the horse as of many other animals, but the need of the mares is not to be dominated en masse by the stallion. So much so that to gather them and possess them, the latter relies on violence and they rebel desperately. Only when they have been bitten and bloodied in long fights and defeats do they acquiesce to the role.

By "masturbation," male sexual culture means not only autoeroticism but also any form of stimulation of the sexual organs other than coitus. This is an interpretation that merely expresses the supremacy of the virile activity of penetration and of those active sensations that have their privileged seat in the vagina; even if the term "coitus" is used for penetrations in other places, as in oral or anal coitus. Therefore, for this culture, female sexuality can be only implemented through masturbatory acts, even when these are performed by the partner. The conventional character of these distinctions is evident, since each achievement of orgasm is invariably produced by the rhythmic rubbing of the sexual organs. It is interesting to note instead that homosexual coitus in the female vagina, not being *a priori* coordinated with intercourse, is considered masturbation. It is evident that, corresponding with the idea of masturbation, there is a sense of pleasure experienced in solitude and separateness: how is it possible to use the same term to mean pleasures that are reciprocally procured in the solicitations of love making? In our opinion, the difference between masturbation and non-masturbation lies in sensing the presence of the other and in mutual eroticism and not in the execution of the model of coitus to the point of becoming accustomed to each other and ignoring each other or perceiving each other in a conditioned reflex. The latter is an imposition of the privileged act of the patriarch, who guards the virility and ideological values of procreative heterosexual penetration.

The preparation [sexual education] of human beings of the two sexes is very dissimilar, both in infancy and in puberty: while males are trained to exercise the act itself, females are nurtured to have an intense concentration to overcome the act itself in a catharsis of feeling in which the act seems destined to cancel itself out.

We are faced with two conditionings of the same phenomenon, which previously found resolution in marriage or the monogamous couple with the attendant oppression of women. But today, when young people are looking for an encounter, two strong differences make such conditioning fail to the point that there is no turning back and with dramatic consequences that no *a posteriori* settlement can heal.

Psychoanalysis is wrong when it affirms that the female human being's maturity consists in the disposition to give herself in abandonment to the other. This disposition is instead the one that, contrasted with the path discovered in the girl's autoeroticism, distances her from true eroticism and relegates her to the field of sentiment, where, pushed into this deception by man, she immerses herself in the pure carnal sensations, already autonomous and sufficient in themselves for achieving the highest states of pleasure.

We are wary of the optimism with which some emancipated women promote their sporting and drama-free arrangements with men as an example to emulate. Not only do we deny that any woman today can have satisfactory relationships in any area of the male world, but we observe that, by behaving according to woman's *noblesse oblige* associated with all male privileges and conveniences, she offers man an understanding that serves as a different type of servitude, while still integrating that of the traditional wife. Such has always been the case in the most fortunate historical periods and for those social categories of success and representation. The emancipated woman gives man the comfort of regulating her emotionality based on his, her need on his, her version of events on his, and thus kills her authenticity in the illusion of avoiding defeat.

Autonomy for woman does not mean isolation from man, as is the fear of vaginal women accustomed to finding wholeness in the couple, but it means reserving for oneself that power that for millennia has yielded to her lord.

The woman who has passed with greater or lesser difficulty from the clitoridean to the vaginal experience is the woman who most rejects autonomy from man as a value. She seems to have the solution to the problem ready to hand because she has a term of comparison on the level of pleasures between a minor and a greater psychic, and therefore physical, involvement with man. But the minor involvement she experiences as separation, and she essentially agrees with Freudian interpretations that consider mature the woman who is capable of abandoning herself to the other without reservation. In this case, lesser or greater involvement with man becomes synonymous with less or greater self-realization, and therefore with lesser or greater pleasure. The influence of these women—who constitute the true defence of patriarchal sexual culture and support imposing it on the great majority of women with the blackmail of claiming an objective and tested superiority of experience—is very great without their knowledge. The ingenuity in offering a convincing echo around the great voluptuousness of an orgasm achieved simultaneously with a man at the point chosen by him stems from having been predisposed to think that the height of eroticism is the achievement of this condition. The vaginal woman tends to remain estranged from any eroticism that is not a fusion with the other or the loss of consciousness linked to psychic emotions tied to the adolescent dream of falling in love. But eroticism is play and exalt in the possibility of dilation that they feel springing directly from the reciprocal responses of one another's bodies. Pure eroticism, coming from this state of consciousness, frees the human being to become an individual, while the woman, left to the sensation and ecstasy of union, has been subtracted from the carnal pole that, together with the ethical one, would have given her the sense of completion that leads to creative possibility.

Vaginal pleasure is not for woman the deepest and most complete pleasure, but it is the official pleasure of patriarchal sexual culture. Reaching it for woman means feeling fulfilled in the only rewarding model for her: the one that satisfies the expectations of man.

As is understandable, the maximum physiological intensity of the orgasmic response of the woman, felt subjectively or objectively recorded, was reached in the experimental sample by means of self-manipulation techniques or by mechanical means regulated by the same subject. Immediately after were the levels of erotic intensity reached with manipulation performed by the partner. The minimum level of intensity in the response of the target organs was recorded during coitus.

—William H. Masters, gynecologist,
and Virginia E. Johnson, sexologist

Man no longer recognizes the woman who emerges from her colonization and from the roles through which he was preparing an experience that has been premade and repeated over millennia: the mother, the virgin, the wife, the lover, the daughter, the sister, the sister-in-law, the friend, and the prostitute. The woman was a product pre-packaged in such a way that he had nothing to discover in her forms of human beingness.

Each role presented his guarantees; to escape those guarantees was to fall outside the consideration of man; it was the end. Every "different" woman today knows that every man in his heart wishes for her end because, failing to catalogue her, he feels irritated and helpless in the face of the fact that understanding between the sexes is no longer so clear. Aided by psychoanalysis, which reflects man's reluctance to admit that woman is his problem, they label any woman not identified with a role with a judgment on her psychosexual health.

"Among the hundreds of patients I observed and treated over the course of a few years," states [physician and psychoanalyst] Wilhelm Reich, referring to experiences circa 1920–25, "there was not a single woman who did not suffer from the complete absence of vaginal orgasm. In men, roughly 60 to 70 percent suffered from severe genital disorders." The others, the 30 or 40 percent who did not have obvious disorders, such as impotence or premature ejaculation, in describing their sensations and behaviour during the sexual act, convinced Reich that they too suffered from severe sexual disorders of some form. In the face of this, Reich still insists that it was impossible to find genitally healthy female patients. "The woman was considered genitally healthy when she was able to achieve a clitoral orgasm. The distinction between clitoral and vaginal arousal was unknown. In short, no one had the slightest idea of the natural functioning of orgasm." Reich began from the assumption of normal coitus with mutual self-abandonment, tenderness, and desire as a goal through which to bring together the neurotic personalities of the man, essentially a rapist, sadist, and exhibitionist, even when he is able to carry out the sexual act normally, and of the woman, who was incapable of vaginal orgasm and whose attitudes toward the partner reflect anguish, coldness, masculinity. To do so, Reich reinforces the Freudian ideology of the vaginal orgasm. We do not see how it can be argued that a woman capable of achieving clitoral orgasm and not vaginal orgasm is a woman incapable of orgasmic potency and how she compares, for example, to a man who declares himself lacking in pleasure during ejaculation. They would perhaps be comparable if the woman also claimed that she did not derive any sensory climax or discharge of sexual tension from her clitoral orgasm. But this occurs only when woman is made aware of the negative and transitory value that male sexual culture ascribes to clitoral orgasm, perhaps through the reaction of the partner, and of the "proof" that awaits her femininity in the transition to the definitively "superior" vaginal orgasm. Reich's conception of the optimal and uniquely "healthy" experience of simultaneous orgasm in a future culture in which the partners, having broken down the sex-phobic character-armoring derived from repression, give themselves to each other unreservedly is a hypothesis that perpetuates the sexual model responsible for female anxiety. The union between the sexes on the level of pleasure in a reality where the sexes are enemies due not to some tragic misunderstanding created by repression but to management of the world by man and exercise of male power, which has persisted for millennia, has always been a unity in which the woman was forced to fall. Today, woman wants orgasm not for reasons of the couple but for her physiological and mental health, because she finds the confinement, that for millennia has been proposed to her in arousal with her partner, frightening, but without knowing how to shake free of it or leaving to fate and her own deference to man the possibility of return. This is also why the alternative of refusing arousal is even more frightening, since it is not within woman's power to guarantee an exit for herself. On the other hand, the certainty of orgasm, of the knowledge and the right conduct required to achieve it, is what allows woman to react in sex and to actively participate in arousal. Woman's passivity is a remedy for those who would not collaborate in a process whose resolution she does not control; and this is the state of frustration that turns it into the other's tool. Woman is left with a realm of pleasure experienced on the verge of anguish. This attitude, held even by Reich, is a typically male worldview. Starting from terrifying facts of cruelty and suffering in sex, it arrives at the mirage of total-izing solutions in which patriarchy is secured. Such facts should rather convince male humanity to abandon its dic-tatorship: all the world's saviours are patriarchs, but the world will not be saved in this fashion. Within the patriar-chy, it is clear that she is not saved.

The woman is a silver cup in which man deposits his golden fruits.

—Johann Wolfgang von Goethe

Patriarchy makes all those who belong to the male sex reverberate with cultural prestige, and even those of relative mediocrity benefit from a surplus, which woman remains fascinated with in every relationship both of love and of work. This imposture has left woman at the mercy of man, stabilizing a condition of imbalance that none can recover from alone in her individual lifetime. Feminism prevents her from taking seriously the mania with which any man feels obliged to leave an indelible trace of himself on her, even if such a trace does not justify his efforts, even if, more serious a threat, such a trace does not justify the myth that woman has of the other's cultural operation, of which she cannot see the absolute superficiality.

The awareness of the real crisis between a colonizing sex and a colonized sex is lacking in Reich: if he deals with woman, it is because he cannot neglect she who is man's complement; but it remains man, the tragic protagonist in the years of fascism, Nazism, Stalinism, McCarthyism, that haunts Reich with a sense of the total perversion of instincts. It is for man that he prophesies a regenerating bath in the original energy of the cosmos. But female humanity must exorcize the power of the male through an evolution of the species and redeem it from the condemnation to which an imbalance of forces and functions destined it. The woman wonders if it is true that the female of other species of animals, up to the primates from which we presumably descend, is deprived of the vital surge of the orgasm, and she looks with skepticism at nature as men have called her to witness it. Witness what? Coitus was undoubtedly, for the human female, a result of an intelligence; the intelligence of a subjugated being that establishes with its superior a psychic bond unavailable to the female animal. But the intelligence that has allowed woman to emotionally acquiesce to the pleasure of hegemonic sex is the intelligence that since the beginning of time has kept her subjugated to the will of another. The only intelligence of woman that feminism recognizes is that which leads out of this captivity of man and manifests itself in the rejection of the theories that promote arousal and orgasm obtained during coitus as the expression of female sexuality. Aware of an orgasm obtained by suggestion of physical union of bodies, of which one belongs to the superior race, is an automatic condition of enjoyment; woman calls into consideration a sexuality of her own whose orgasmic resolution is not connected to any mental condition or acceptance of slavery. Woman begins to think for herself and does not listen to calls other than those of her liberation from the other sex, and she distrusts everything, of nature as well as of the cosmos. She does not want to hear emphasis on sex, union, pleasure. Finally in possession of her sexuality, she requires convincing from no one that her effort will be well rewarded and that the pleasure of a moment will be worth a lifetime as a slave.

Beyond the theories of the cosmic superposition and interpenetration of two orgonotic systems, woman, no longer subject to the sexual model myth of man, can easily ascertain that her clitoral orgasm and man's orgasm obtained in erotic reciprocity are the same phenomenon. As far as one insists on the biological-emotional values of the couple form and on abandonment to the other, we have understood it essential only to abandon oneself to this phenomenon.

To experience orgasm during coitus, the woman must have an idea of the man that transcends the idea she has of herself and convince herself that she is with a man who is worthy of the high idea that she has of that man.

There is a moment in the girl's life, which passes like a meteor. It is when she detaches herself from the parental home and, alone, confusedly perceives all the potentialities of her being. One may wonder why this period of autonomy is so short, why the approach of the boy entails such an immediate capitulation. The expectation of the encounter with man, which is the basis of her preparation for life, has created in her a disposition that is triggered before she can become aware of it: nothing of what was hers, not even the pleasure experienced in autoeroticism, maintains consistency in the face of the upheaval that contact with the male world causes. The ignorance, indifference, tolerance, or hostility of man toward her specific sexual enjoyment and toward ways of achieving it determine her reaction to pleasure. In the rush of youth, when the boy is absorbed by the exuberant exercise of his sexuality, the girl undergoes a sudden change of course that disorients and disappoints her. She loses the self-confidence that had burst into her psyche in a moment of loosened external pressure and she feels a collapse of personality that confirms her attachment to man. It is in this passage that a state of anxiety for her frailty establishes itself, and it is in this state of anxiety that man works. As an ancient Indian author says: "All maidens hear what men say to them, but sometimes they don't even answer a word."

Let's not forget that the moment in which woman touches the bottom of vital suffering in male culture is the one in which she unconsciously moves toward cultivating lack of pleasure as a habit that requires the imposition of a partner to satisfy needs connected to the mythologization of man and to his presence in her life, and not in eroticism.

Traditionally, women have sought self-affirmation in culture and, even more coveted, in male creativity. While losing ground in adolescence and youth, the girl, exalting herself or turning back on herself, sometimes spontaneously finds an outlet in expression and tries to embark on a creative destiny. Feminism today warns women about this process and invites them to reflect that the first operation from which female existence takes shape is that which starts where each woman leaves to free herself—recognizing in sexual colonization the basic condition of the weakening and subjugation of woman. If she gives precedence to expression in the male world she must know that she is carrying out an activity through which she cultivates and demonstrates a creative energy to ultimately measure herself with men in isolation and be admitted among them.

Feminism finds this kind of activity that precedes women's *autocoscienza* and respects it only if the woman obtains from it liberation from cultural subservience to man.

The vaginal woman is the woman who supports the myth of the big powerful penis and who guards the ideology of patriarchal virility. She is a projection of man's pride and she becomes the nightmare of his biological decline. But if it is true, as has been shown by [William H.] Masters and [Virginia E.] Johnson, that the orgasmic phenomenon occurs in women thanks to the work of the clitoris and it is the same, with the involvement of all the genital organs, through whatever stimulation is obtained—direct or indirect of the clitoris, somatic or psychic — and if it is true that in direct stimulation, whether personal or that of the partner, it is more intense and more quickly and surely achievable, why then do the same researchers who have discovered these data continue to speak of the vagina as the primary organ of female sexual expression compared to the clitoris, which is the "focal point of the female sexual reaction"?

What are the reasons for maintaining this dualism? And why does the fact remain uncommented on, though supported by extensive data, that, in the female sexual reaction, "a psychic component with consequent stimulus to the clitoris is invariably discovered"? And why are they surprised that the problem of orgasm was a "problem" of the woman, while for the man it is taken for granted and appears instead displaced onto the problem of erection? Obviously there is no answer available in a context that insists, despite all evidence, that "the function of the penis is to provide an organic means to the physiological and psychological phenomena of the increase and subsequent resolution of male and female sexual tensions." Because it is in this dogmatic passage that the counterfeiting knot is hidden, which has led and maintained the female sex to confirm the hypothetical nature of orgasm and the male sex the voluntary nature of an erection.

Man has subdued woman by making her the voluptuous instrument of his sexuality, but in this process he feels that he loses power as he loses virility: this is where the antagonistic relation with young people and the segregation and possession of women are triggered. Patriarchal phallic culture is a reflection of a male obsession once the identification—penis-power identification—is accomplished. The clitoridean woman, affirming a sexuality of her own whose functioning does not coincide with the stimulation of the penis, abandons the penis to itself. Everything concerning the penis no longer coincides with the expression of domination, from which man draws exhibitionistic stimuli and sadistic attitude, but with the pure and simple manifestation of pleasure. An erection is not required by woman, neither power, nor strength, nor anything. The penis is man's own sex and it is for him: it must rediscover itself in this new dimension of consciousness; the delusion of power that made him reflect it in female ecstasy, and made him obliged to do so, is a deception of his own domination. Woman has her own privileged and precious, perfect and infallible, point from which all the ecstasies that a human being can come to feel commence, and it is not directly connected with the penis. If the man draws grim forebodings from this feminist *autocoscienza* and feels threatened, it means that he sees no space for himself in the world except through the imposition of the myths of masculinity and the subjugation of women.

1971

Translated from Carla Lonzi, "La donna clitoridea e la donna vaginale," in *Sputiamo su Hegel. La donna clitoridea e la donna vaginale e altri scritti* [*Let's Spit on Hegel: The Clitoridean Woman and the Vaginal Woman and Other Writings*] (Milan: Scritti di Rivolta Femminile, 1974), 77–112. Pages 112 to 140 not included.

1. Ubanghi was a province in Zaire. This quotation's source is unknown and possibly not precise; the archive sheds no light on it.

2. [Original note:] It should be understood that the orgasmic phenomenon is unique to any woman and may occur with any stimulus. We refer here to the "vaginal woman" as one who obtains orgasm during coitus and the "clitoridean woman" as the one who obtains orgasm during caresses of the clitoris; the "vaginal orgasm" is the orgasm obtained during coitus and the clitoral orgasm that obtained while stimulating the clitoris.

3. Alfred Kinsey (1894–1956) was an American sexologist, biologist, and professor of entomology and zoology.

4. Lonzi's original text does not include complete citations. This is drawn from Wolfgang Wickler, a student of zoologist and ethologist Konrad Lorenz and a prominent sociobiologist. It seems likely that this is a quote from *Mimikry. Nachahmung und Täuschung in der Natur* [Mimickry: Imitation and deception in nature] (Munich: n.p., 1968).

5. The original text uses the Latin "*raptus*," referencing the term in Roman law meaning a crime of seizure of property, and so does not refer exclusively to rape as the act of sexual violence as generally understood in a contemporary context; however, this word is one basis for the etymology of the term in both legal and broader cultural connotations.

The Meaning of *Autocoscienza* in Feminist Groups

Woman belongs to the conquered species: conquered by the myth of man. Woman suffers from man's privilege over her, but suffers it in the deference and obedience that those who have imposed themselves as subjects inspire in her. The victorious species says to woman: "Make yourself worthy of me. Absorb, through the knowledge of the subject, the idea of who is completely human and universal. Under my guidance, you enter the subjective dimension."

In this way man not only justifies the control he exercises over woman's personality—at stake here is her well-being, and every little mistake can be fatal—but he also becomes the arbiter of her conscience, and finally the depositary for her inferiority: he promises to ransom her from her subservience; he lies. In fact, whoever obeys does not deserve to be recognized, because obedience is irreconcilable with autonomy, and it is autonomy that creates the stimulus for knowledge in the other. Thus, man does not know woman; he knows himself and her as much as he needs. Only through an unexpected act, one that is free, can the woman escape the role of object. But free means that she does not accept any mortgage on her salvation that is in someone else's hands.

After having induced in the conquered species the need for his approval, man has made a shadow of woman, who, disheartened in her ability to incarnate, projects onto him. The path that he indicates to her is, unbeknownst to woman, without exit: as long as she continually returns to him for evaluation of herself, man is ready to make every corner of his culture, his whole self, available to her. The honour is great, the opportunity unique. Woman does not see the deception because, as a creature defined on the basis of her vaginal path, of her functionality to man, she sees, in that destiny of complementarity and penetration, the symbol of a passage toward virtue, the virtue of the subject, granted to her as an outlet for her incompleteness.

But the virtues acquired are those of the vanquished, who make of them a useless treasure. When she enters into the thematic posed by man, woman becomes more and more enveloped in allegiance to the other and continually reaffirms the other's superiority over her. She is sure to trace her condition of dependence through a faithful apprenticeship to male culture, but each step forward is equidistant from a goal set to infinity: in the strategy of her subordination, the promise of subjectivity is a reward, not a real possibility. But woman has become accustomed to thinking that, beyond the struggle between the sexes, man is her saviour, as the one whom nature has predestined to have her salvation at heart.

The taste of deception can be attested to by those of us who, having enjoyed male culture, before feminism, experiencing some resonance at a level felt as our own, were abruptly brought back to consciousness of our subordinate condition with the advent of feminism. In fact, when those of us began to establish a feminist perspective within ourselves, we realized that, at best, man wanted to take control over this operation of ours as well: an indirect way of denying the legitimacy of the operation itself, emptying it of meaning.

This means that, in patriarchy, woman can reach the maximum degree of "subject supervised" by masculinity, that is, with the enticement of a resonance that emanates from herself but which is not of herself, because it is of others through herself. No longer an object, but a tool.

In the eyes of patriarchal man, woman, on her own ground, can magnify only those germs of her species' inferiority that he painstakingly tries to neutralize with a constant presumption of intellectual and emotional rectification that keeps her aligned with masculine culture, models, values. On her own land, woman is a plant of monstrous growth that gives man his worst dreams of humanity's decay.

Thus man, every man, offers to woman this deception as an instrument of cultural domination, domination that he did not intend but which at present he cannot but want: he relentlessly exonerates himself from any suspicion of guilt because he knows himself immune to any choice, although he defends his right to continue the status quo *ab antiquo*, for which he is not responsible. In fact, as a patriarchal subject, man needs not only his turn to be identified as subject, and thus by the men who hold subjectivity—at that level he is unreachable by woman—but to be mythologized precisely by those who are not subject, by women. This mythologization is a balm for his wounds as a man among men for whom prestige is hierarchical.

Retreating from woman's terrain is therefore, for man, an incalculable loss of the patriarchal dimension, and therefore of virility: his rank depends *ab antiquo* on the degree of subjection and veneration that he has managed to impose on woman. It depends on how much he has been obeyed and mythologized by women, who each should convince herself that she has done it for her own good, and she is grateful to him. We can understand that man does not retreat from our moments of subjectivity that ask for approval: it is evident that our claim is not really a claim of subjects. As long as we leave him the faculty to judge the right to our own space, man will not be able to not occupy it, since it is not a physical space that we are talking about— although we are also deprived of a private space—but a historical, psychological, and mental space.

We of Rivolta Femminile occupy it little by little with *autocoscienza* (consciousness raising) in women's groups. The mirage of demonstrating to man our right to subjectivity is a contradiction that he does not fail to notice and exploit. We also recognize that this is his business. But we, in trying to gain his collaboration for an autonomy that he cannot want, respond to the conditioning of vaginality within a sexual culture that has deluded us in a reciprocal goal that was only ever our one-sided slavery. Trusting in the role assigned to those who have been defined as vaginal, complementary, lacking, man resorts to the patriarchal threat: "Excluded!"—from his culture, his creativity, his revolution, his utopia, his days, his nights. He awaits the effects of our panic.

But now he cannot do anything to prevent us from becoming aware [*prendere coscienza*]: and that is the first space we lack.[1] Man's proclaimed investiture in our redemption is a farce of male power, a farce as tragic or more so than any other colonization. It is here that the feminist groups of *autocoscienza* acquire their true physiognomy as nuclei that transform the spirituality of the patriarchal age: they work for the clawed-at subject [*scatto a soggetto*] of women who recognize each other as complete human beings, no longer in need of men's approval.[2]

Feminist *autocoscienza* differs from any other form of self-awareness, in particular from that proposed by psychoanalysis, because it returns to the problem of personal dependence within the female species, as a dependent species itself. Realizing that any attachment to the male world is the real obstacle to one's liberation triggers self-awareness among women, and the surprise of this situation reveals unknown horizons for their expansion. It is in this passage that the possibility of feminist creativity emerges: it is through the affirmation of herself, without the warrant of man's understanding, that woman reaches that stage of freedom that makes the myth of the couple decay, inasmuch as that myth was drawing her toward a being on which her own fate depends.

If man, his culture, deceives woman by guiding her toward the freedom he desires, it is only to condition her to become aware of his domination and reconfirm it from within. He accustoms her and reinforces her habit (ancestral vaginality) to take the licence of human beingness from the hands of man, to whom she dedicates the most absolute portion of her exchange with others. In this sense, the male sexual revolution was the last act with which the patriarchy tried to make oppression revolutionary. "Sex is beautiful! Coitus is beautiful!" once again deceives woman about what is good for her.

The mechanism is always the same: gratify her in order to confuse her, and echo her in a new conquest, a new patriarchal enterprise. By recalling woman to coitus, man recalls her to the bond with himself, to complementarity as her only true essence, to pleasure as her only goal, once again passive witness to the ideological verb of the man who does and undoes his interpretations of the world. He will continue to divide his interests between men and women, between subject and object, between sublimations and pleasures, between equality and supremacy. But he will pretend to envy woman's wonderful sexuality, one invented by him, while he blaming himself for being so alienated that he cannot render woman and sex but a part of his dramatic life as a civilized and unhappy individual.

Feminism begins when a woman seeks self-resonance in another woman's authenticity because she understands that her only means of finding herself is in her own species.[3] And she does so not to exclude men but because she realizes that the exclusion that men subject women to backfires on them while only expressing a problem of man—a frustration that is his, an inability that is his, a habit that is his of conceiving woman to sustain his own patriarchal equilibrium.

Feminism is the discovery and actualization of the subject-birth of the singular member of a species that has been subjugated by the myth of self-realization through loving union with the species in power.

Milan, June 1972

This translation of "Significato dell' autocoscienza nei gruppi femministi" is from Rivolta Femminile's original six-page cyclostile handout that circulated to various feminist groups in 1972. It was republished in Carla Lonzi, *Sputiamo su Hegel. La donna clitoridea e la donna vaginale e altri scritti* [Let's Spit on Hegel: The Clitoridean Woman and the Vaginal Woman and Other Writings] (Milan: Scritti di Rivolta Femminile, 1974), 141–47. The text charts the direction of Lonzi's feminism in the years to come, notably describing the relationship between two women as the key to mutual resonance and authenticity. The balance of the Rivolta Femminile group, already precarious in its unity, was at this point sacrificed to "the discovery of a process of revelation, of manifestation of the self." Carla Lonzi, *Scacco Ragionato: Poesie dal '58 al '63* (Milan: Scritti di Rivolta Femminile Prototipi), 35. Less prescriptive and full of anger than earlier Rivolta Femminile texts, this text has formal similarities with the writings of Lonzi's second feminist period and serves as a bridge between theoretical feminist texts and her *scrittura autocoscienziale*.

1. We translate this passage as "becoming aware," although, as mentioned in earlier footnotes, readers should keep in mind that the original *prendere coscienza* is closely associated with the process of *autocoscienza* engaged by the group.

2. "*Scatto a soggetto*" is a typically untranslatable Lonzian phrase. "*Scatto*" in this context can mean both a "shot" and "trigger," but also a "sudden jump"; something like a bike's gear that helps the rider move forward by dramatically shifting the pace of the movement. Another possible translation would be as the "trigger" for the new feminist subject Lonzi defines.

3. Rivolta Femminile uses the term "*specie*" here in the context "*di ritrovare se stessa è nella sua specie*." Using the biological term "*specie*" could be interpreted as a critical reference to the concept of "species being" (*Gattungswesen*) in the 1844 manuscripts of Karl Marx, which was largely translated into Italian as "*essenza-specie*" or "*essere-specie*."

For the Identification of Rivolta Femminile

In print journals and other media, the name of Elvira Banotti has been continuously repeated with the appellation of "leader" of our groups.

With this text, Rivolta Femminile of Rome, together with the groups of Milan, Turin, and Genoa, wishes to reiterate and make known as widely as possible the following:

1) Rivolta Femminile has no leader and never has had one.

2) Rivolta Femminile has never intended to provoke or accept dialogue with the male world, even on those occasions when other feminists participate in such a dialogue.

In Italy, and around the world, women now work toward the birth of a feminist situation that we believe is the most important event occurring in the history of the present. The awareness of this global rise of an abundance of feminist groups opens the possibility, and even the guarantee, of experimenting with many forms of expression such that any ideological levelling is avoided, and each individual group has the calm and space required to manifest its discoveries in its own temporality in a climate of authenticity, sheltered from those who, not being similarly inclined, might distort their meaning. We thus try to defend ourselves from the naivety of speedy operations.

We realistically assess the enormous difficulty of affirming women in a male civilization. Rivolta Femminile is not a party and does not aspire to become one: it expresses itself without sacrificing anything, neither of the moments of individual quality achieved nor of the points in which woman is traditionally rendered inferior. This is knowledge that the chapters of Rivolta Femminile sense, without doing cultural operation[1] to understand it. We do not want to do feminism that uses just any behaviour or any action: we do accept the risk that can derive from a misunderstood diffusion. We have the writings of Rivolta Femminile to communicate, and they are an example of a form of expression using outsider language that corresponds to our pride.

The women of Rivolta Femminile therefore consider neither part of their group nor a leader a feminist who operates with initiatives and presentations of herself in official circumstances of debate in the male world, which cause the above-mentioned misunderstanding.

For the same reason we do not provide objective data on our composition or our functioning outside of feminism: not even to those young women who prepare "theses" for the university.

The relationship of feminism with the institutions of male culture is not that of making available to man news that allows him to monitor our movements as we make them, through a service that facilitates scholarly operations regarding our work. We ask young women not for a "thesis" that exploits the work of feminists but for a point of pause and reflection in contact with feminism from which to derive a new critical energy to undermine the certainties of man within the heritage of his culture.

At this moment, a year and a half after the first Rivolta Femminile meetings and the publication of our Manifesto (July 1970), we wish not to leave our identification in doubt: the groups formed after Rivolta Femminile that have given themselves the name Collettivi di Lotta Femminista are not our continuation, as R. Spagnoletti states in her book on Feminist Movements in Italy. Rivolta

Femminile exists through its *autocoscienza* (consciousness raising) groups and its premises have always had a continuity of development. With this we do not deny the fact that, at the birth of feminism, we join in enthusiasm with so many diverse groups that then must be separated in order to leave each its specific field of implementation. We do not want to burden this problem with an unnecessary dramatic weight, and therefore we would clarify: the existence of myriad feminist groups is for us confirmation that each group's differences are not a negative because this corresponds to the discovery of the multiplicities that make up the female world.

Rome, February 4, 1972

Roma, via del Babuino 164, 672359
Milano, via Monte di Pietà 1, 898240
Torino, via S. Francesco d'Assisi 11, 540896
Genova, via Fabrizi 9, 331318

"Per l'identificazione di Rivolta Femminile" was a two-page cyclostyle memo released in 1972, signed RIVOLTA FEMMINILE. The letters and unpublished documents held in the Carla Lonzi Archive, at La Galleria Nazionale in Rome, Italy, help to clarify the many steps of the drawn-out disintegration of the original group—composed of Carla Accardi, Elvira Banotti, and Carla Lonzi—of which this particular document is a precious testimony. The relationship between Lonzi and Banotti, named in this document as the alleged leader of Rivolta Femminile, had been tense since the drafting of *Sputiamo su Hegel* (*Let's Spit on Hegel*) in the summer of 1970. Shortly after this statement's release, the long-standing friendship between Accardi and Lonzi also dramatically come to an end. This testimony highlights Rivolta Femminile's intention to distinguish itself from new feminist groups that were a continuation of Lotta Femminista (Feminist Struggle) and once again affirms the group's nonnegotiable distance from and refusal of "institutions of male culture."

1. "Cultural operation" (*operazione culturale*) refers to a process of liberation from patriarchal structures that Lonzi

and the women of Rivolta Femminile theorize as a deep understanding of one's own self-imposed biases, followed by a rejection of any ideology or thought developed by men (what Lonzi refers to as "culture"), including, for example, psychoanalysis, Marxism, and Catholicism. A related concept in Lonzi's feminism is the "ground zero of culture" (*la tabula rasa della cultura*), a necessary step for any woman who wants to achieve authenticity and self-consciousness.

Carla Lonzi

Selection from
"An Itinerary of Reflections"

I've always liked autobiographical books of saints of what one might call "nuns," but really of those who are not recognized by the church and, if they wrote, have not been published. I read them in boarding school[1] between the ages of ten and thirteen, and I continued to have a fondness for them later in life: in particular I have been drawn to them in moments of crisis, when I had to admit an illusion and find inner peace from which to begin anew.

I returned several times to Thérèse Martin's [Thérèse of Lisieux's] *Story of a Soul*, that is, "Saint Teresa of the Child Jesus," together with Teresa of Ávila's *The Book of My Life*. Both were written on request out of obedience to a church superior; they are in the first person and express phenomena and inner states natural to me and that I could not find expressed elsewhere. It was a comfort that other women had felt and talked about these states simply: their words addressed a phenomenon that I otherwise would have felt compelled to reject as a consequence of morbid and unreal emotion. I discovered these states earlier in the religious language of the two Thérèses, rather than in the literary analyses of female writers. Although very different personalities, I saw no limits to their ability to inquire and doubt: they sought these resources within themselves, even with the awareness that there are no adequate resources.

With the exception of my schooldays, because I lived in a nonpracticing environment and, later, in decidedly secular circles where people either ignored the existence of these women or would have considered them with all sorts of prejudices, I identified with them through that part of me that was ignored or withdrew from expectations of various kinds, ranging from the most traditional to the most emancipated; standards against which I was called to measure myself. I liked them because they were engaged in an invisible and unnegotiable venture as abstract as love, as concrete as suffering. I didn't see how you could do without it. I have found no obstacles toward them; even their edifying aspects are secondary: they enlighten me on identity, they precede me on this path, and—although it seems that they give up everything—it is clear to me that they have not given up the essential. On the contrary, they revealed to me what this essential is. I was waiting for a confirmation.

When I read in [American feminist writer and artist] Kate Millett's *The Prostitution Papers* that prostitution is the extreme position that lays bare the general condition of women in this society, I wondered whether or not this observation was true. Instead of an answer, I was reminded of the place toward which, by contrast, I was pushed as a more congenial symbol of such a condition, if not of my own way of being and feeling by my nature, certainly my way of feeling and reacting to this society: the cloister and the Carmel.[2] A place of deprivation, but not of destruction, managed by women buried alive, a place that exists even outside of History, a place of inefficiency, but not sterile, that I knew with all the reclusive intensity of my life as a woman.

There has been much emphasis on the nuns' poor mental health, on the hysterical and melancholic origins of their personalities, on masochism and the father complex. But what I saw of women considered "normal" was that they were companions of men considered "normal," which made me think that the tyranny of an internalized image left greater margins of freedom than the wear and tear of regular physical contact with an individual in flesh and blood, often tyrannical in its mediocrity and presumption.

A loving and omnipotent Lord and master who lived thanks to a need [for a higher power], an unleashing, that took those women very far, whereas the routine of family life, the waste of oneself, the continuous interference, a real being with whom to agree to please and placate, ended up producing self-forgetting or self-annulment. The fact is that we know little of the expressive potential of women who have entered the machinery of marriage and children.

One of the three remaining poems of the first known female Italian poet, the Florentine Compiuta Donzella of the thirteenth century, is on this theme: salvation is seen in the convent as opposed to in the marriage demanded by the father, as was the custom. But, more generally, then as now, marriage meant remaining in a violent world, suffering from it and risking being overcome; not even the literary institution sheltered women: there was nothing left but the convent, whose tortures, by comparison, seemed less definitive, if they were chosen.

I wish to abandon the world and serve God
and distance myself from all vanity,
because I see insanity and villainy
and falsity growing and flourishing,
and I see wisdom and courtesy dying,
along with fine honors and all goodness;
for I wish to have neither husband nor lord,
nor to stay in the world of my own will.
Recalling that all men adorn themselves with evil,
I am strongly disdainful of all of them,
and my person turns instead toward God.
My father makes me be melancholy,
for he wishes to turn me from serving Christ:
I don't know to whom he wants to give me as bride.[3]

Feminism presented itself to me as the possible outlet between the symbolic alternatives of the female condition, prostitution and seclusion: being able to live without selling one's body and without forfeiting it. Without getting lost and without getting to safety. Finding again a completeness, an identity opposed to a male civilization that had made it unattainable.

When I left boarding school, the world appeared to me within reach: setting aside the religious digressions, I began to respond to the stimuli to which I gradually found myself sensitive. I felt the desire to participate.

I started looking for the points of contact between myself and others, between me and reality. I thought I caught it on various occasions (the university, Marxism and political activity, art criticism). They were exhausted, one after the other. I found consideration in them, but neither resonance nor an atmosphere favourable to the unfolding of myself. I had to admit that the point of encounter remained elusive to me. The conjunction of two incomparable entities could not be entrusted to my individual will alone.

When, with the emergence of feminism, I searched for my origins, among those women who could help me—less deluded than others, less compromised, more secure in personal experience and in the way of conducting it, with an indestructible core of fragility—Thérèse Martin and Teresa of Ávila appeared again. Even before this, at the end of my period dedicated to art criticism, while I was putting together a book of conversations with some artists accompanied by my and their photographs, I was seized by the desire, sudden and unjustified, to include a photo of Thérèse Martin.[4] I had learned of a volume of portraits of her made by one of her sisters, a Carmelite herself, who had entered the Carmel of Lisieux with a 13×18 camera, a Darlot lens, and used it to capture some moments of that community. But since reproduction of the images wasn't allowed, I was forced to resort to a stratagem: one of the artists in the book proposed making a painting using the portrait of Thérèse, which was lawful, such that it was possible, by reproducing the painting, to include the portrait. So we did: the work in question is reproduced in the first pages of *Autoritratto* [*Self-portrait*] (1959), where I speak of myself, and the actual work is in my bedroom. Encouraged by this solution, I proposed to the publisher to put on the cover another photo of Thérèse dressed as Joan of Arc in chains for a thearer performance in the Carmel. I had no arguments to advocate for this choice in a book on art and artists: the proposal was rejected as a typically feminine bit of clumsiness. I was seized with vomiting, sick from disappointment and helplessness.

This is why, when I read in an interview with the anthropologist Ida Magli the claim that feminists did not understand the importance of the saints, and in particular the despised Saint Thérèse of the Child Jesus, I felt the same feeling of abuse. Of course no one could know my background in this regard, but an interest in nuns was shared in the Rivolta Femminile group to such an extent that one of the volumes of our writings that we published was dedicated to Thérèse Martin, and this anyone could know.[5] I replied to the interview with a polemical denial; the provocation had awakened my competitiveness: if there were an indication that I believe in Thérèse Martin, I could not bear that it could be denied to us. The anthropologist in the shadow of her interest as a scholar, I in the shadow of my participation in feminism, clashed: beyond right or wrong, with an analogous need to affirm ourselves. But why had she cleared the field of alleged rivals in order to assert herself? Who was the recipient of this confrontation?

I wonder, seeing the frenzy that surrounds the question of feminism's areas of intervention, what would have become of Rivolta Femminile if we had taken man as our cultural model. Not in a palingenesis of the future, but in the possibilities at our disposal in the present. Would anyone continue to waste their time in "studying" the female question with the illusion of curtailing the work of feminists? I take the case of [philosopher and semiotician] Julia Kristeva, who stimulated me in the introduction to the volume *About Chinese Women* (1974): I recognized intuitions and subtleties, concerns that I share. They enter to the extent that they are compatible with the presuppositions of her culture; but at the same time, it is precisely these same presuppositions that push her to obligatory conclusions. To pre-feminist conclusions.

There is no culture, however prestigious, that is not misleading for woman; there is no woman of culture for whom one can deny that, to a greater or lesser extent, she brings vases to Samos.[6]

Kristeva's reasoning is flawless: man is phallus, word, because he has established himself by denying the existence of the other sex, of the woman, that is, of the vagina, which has been removed, becoming the mute place of enjoyment. Thus Electra, the unmarried daughter of the dead father of whom she is the spokesperson, is non-vaginated (because she is incredulous of the enjoyments of the mother), as opposed to the stammering sister Chrysothemis, daughter of the mother (and ultimately the mother herself), who is vaginated.

Woman's space would be between these two poles: between silence (the lack of a symbol) and the word of the Father, the Law, Value. In Electra, Kristeva recognizes the antecedent of the figure of the saint, of the revolutionary, of the feminist.

Now, I don't recognize myself in the figure of Electra, just as I don't see her in the friends of Rivolta or the saints I prefer, though I do recognize a good number of feminists as emancipated women, among the totality of revolutionaries and the militant ranks of culture. Furthermore, I note that, considering the need for them to be non-vaginated, they are certainly vaginal, should the state of "virginity" be "transgressed," so to speak. So what? This analytical scheme, although apparently unassailable, does not convince me; it is in fact a scheme whose crucial points are presuppositions that were born not to clarify my ideas but to confuse them, that is, they are of male origin. If I abandon these assumptions, I rediscover my life, where the mute daughter and the daughter as spokesperson are interchangeable, and in fact equivalent in that they are both identified not in themselves but in a functional relation to patriarchy. These are just instances of roles.

As long as the *aut-aut* [either/or] is either "identification with the vagina" or "refusal of the vagina," then we are inside the logic of vaginality, which means inside the logic of an identification of the woman who supports the identification of the man (dead or alive father) in the phallus. The path to the research of the self and of one's own autonomy cannot but exclude that *aut-aut* for women. And, in fact, the women who have tried out this exclusion have been excluded by men. Both Electra and Chrysothemis are the two female entities in which the culture has congratulated itself for the work done—the work of erasing the woman on the two fronts; vaginal pleasure confirms the pleasure of the other as much as the quoted word of the father confirms the absolute identity of the other.

Kristeva attempts to salvage the feminine from out of these various roles by recognizing in the woman "the eternal irony of the community" (the same phrase I quoted from [Georg Wilhelm Friedrich] Hegel in "Let's Spit on Hegel" by trying to suggest a form of behaviour that realizes such eternal irony). Thus, there is ultimately no Electra and no Chrysothemis but only a continuous work of the woman who illuminates the shadowy part, the repressed element, of every masculine formulation. Whereas I saw in the woman figured as "the eternal irony of the community" only traces of the emergence of the feminist singularity across time, Kristeva sees an axiom that commands us to never stop trying to realize, through a masochistic effort of Sisyphus, a collaboration/struggle that continually undermines the claim of a masculine absolute. A subaltern destiny gratified merely in knowing a lot about the illusions of the dominant destiny. Which remains dominant, and indeed is gradually made more enlightened and more self-conscious.

This is what authenticity advised us to do, nonrepayable, before feminism—what I was doing "then." "Now," individual consciousness has intervened, leading to the constitution of a very different ego both from man's (phallic) ego and from the female pseudo-ego understood as a complementary structure, one that reaches its maximum potential in improving the male reality in every field without ever provoking self-affirmation. As long as female identification is determined on the basis of the vagina and nothing else, instead of the woman's self-discovery, of individual women, an indistinct movement of female dissidence will continue to operate in society ("the irony of the community"). Hegel had already understood how the cunning of reason would not fail to make it functional to patriarchy.

I recognize myself in an identification elsewhere.

It has been said that with the theses of "The Clitoridean Woman and the Vaginal Woman," I entered into lesbianism in that I posed the clitoris as the female sex. But the clitoris, if it is an organ nonfunctional to heterosexual intercourse, is no more inherently functional to homosexual intercourse. In fact, among women there is no further facilitation toward clitoridean intercourse than the removal of an obstacle, the phallus (not the penis), and therefore the removal of a concept. The clitoris counts as sex for both the man not identified in the phallus and for the woman not identified in the vagina. It is beyond the categories of homo- and heterosexuality. The distinction of complementarity and subordination between the two sexes falls away. And it is woman—revealing and at the same time removing the support of the vagina and her vaginal identification—who undermines the myth of the phallus and the phallic identification of man.

Many feminists say: "We rediscover our body, we rediscover the vagina," and they try to take possession, through knowledge, of this anatomical part of their body. But the impediment to feeling it as one's own is not of a sensorial nature, due to repression, but of a cultural and structural nature: How can it be rediscovered if it does not first return to being neutral ground? Now it is a marked area of our body that we accept, to allow man his culture and his ego. That marked area prevents our culture and the establishment of our I. As [the American feminist Valerie] Solanas rightly says, our "I" has become what his "I" does not want to be, and this operation has been possible for him thanks to the fact that "our" vagina is part of "his" culture. In this culture, loving it is loving the identity that subtends and implies it.

The identity that springs from the clitoris starts from a nothingness, from a cultural void, and is gradually constituted by an acceptance of oneself that becomes one's destiny, but cannot be fixed in a role, because it would fall into vaginality. And it cannot reveal itself in the cultural word, but in that which derives directly from the assumption of a nonconforming sexual identity, which, unique, allows one to pronounce authentically and in its entirety: "I." It is this "I" as a cultural void that constitutes the prerequisite for a rediscovery of our body, that is, of our culture. All preceding stages are undertaken in vain. But every woman is alone in facing this void, in measuring it: it is barely bearable; it is the risk of losing reason that [Rivolta Femminile member] Maria Grazia Chinese refers to. There is a risk in which I have made sure I am capable of living, now that I know that I have shared it: feminism has given me this; from feminism I wanted this. This risk is my sense of femininity.

The saints, too, often appeared to me characterized by that cultural void that allowed them to live their own identities on the verge of madness. By voluntarily and consciously renouncing their sexuality, they renounced not only the vagina (like Electra) but above all the vaginal identity. Since they lived an erotic emotionality, it is rightly defined as mystical; in fact, it no longer has a basis in sexual identity but in a different identity. In relation to them, and contrary to mysticism, I am interested in a sexual identity because I see an outlet in it, because I guessed it and it corresponds to me. To be myself, not to have an alienated destiny, I must not abdicate my body; on the contrary, I find in it the element on which to base my autonomy. This is the first act that I recognized in myself as creative.

If all this seems excessive, at least it doesn't transform this risk into ideology. After writing "The Clitoridean Woman and the Vaginal Woman," I was confused to see that it was taken both in the sense of a positing a new sexual norm and in the sense of programmatic homosexuality. But it is evident that an ideological adherence to homosexuality reconfirms ideology instead of opening love between women: by reconfirming subjection to a male value, it reveals that it stems from a vaginal identity, in fact, it implies a distrust that eroticism between women can take place through authentic and personal impulses.

I would like to quote some passages that were not included and that seemed to me to already contain a warning:

"We do not make a pronouncement on heterosexuality: we are not so blind as not to see that it is a pillar of the patriarchy, we are not so ideological as to reject it *a priori*."

"The clitoridean woman is not the liberated woman, nor the woman who has escaped from suffering the male myth—these women do not exist in the civilization in which we find ourselves—but the one who faced this myth moment by moment and was not captured by it. Her operation was not ideological, but lived."

"The clitoridean woman has nothing essential to offer man and expects nothing essential from him. She does not suffer from duality and does not want to become singular. She does not aspire to matriarchy, which is a mythical age of the glorified vaginal women.… Life between the sexes begins outside the indissoluble bond. It is no longer heterosexuality at any price, but heterosexuality if it is priceless."

"We want to affirm clitoridean love as a mode of female sexuality in the heterosexual relationship, since it is not enough for us to have the clitoris as a conscious reference point during sex, nor do we want the official clitoris to belong to the lesbian relationship. But we are convinced that as long as heterosexuality remains a dogma, woman will in some way remain the complement of man."

"Having remained for a long time in that condition of unrealization—that is, of loss of personality without resorting to alternative solutions of identification—constituted an existential process of the clitoridean woman, whose unforeseen outcome was establishing her autonomy. In fact, it was not defined in gestures that deviated from the norm but was consolidated in authentic gestures of concentration on oneself. This clarification allowed her to observe that her conduct did not arise only from rebellion or negative participation but from something else that was not possible to identify before feminism. Indeed, feminism in some of its points is triggered precisely by the self-awareness of the woman who leads her fight against patriarchy on her own ground. The lack of humanity that the patriarchal point of view discerns in her becomes, alternately, a need for humanity as a presence of oneself."

"The affirmation of the clitoris as sex in its own right is the current phase of liberation of the woman who discovers her identity in the course of the species, in history and in the present."

"Hers is a conquest of self and of her own femininity that is not concentrated in a space complementary to that of man but extends beyond patriarchal heterosexuality."

At the time of writing "The Clitoridean Woman and the Vaginal Woman," while relying on myself, I was not yet aware that it was precisely at that point that everything was decided. It was not easy to realize that that lack of identity I have always felt as typically mine, and from which I have drawn satisfaction and despair, was myself—my only chance to be. Some of my poems written between '58 and '63 under the title *Scacco ragionato* [Thoughtful check] helped me to understand how I managed to keep at bay the first moment this was revealed to me as an irrefutable fact. I never wanted to publish them because I couldn't see who would read them; I only knew that they would suffer a foreign fate in the culture. It was useless for me to address those who could not give me resonance; I took other paths. Now I am aware that they have been the means to train me to resist in a condition that pushed me to deny and be resolved in the adaptation.

Those were the same years in which Sylvia Plath wrote her verses and became familiar with death. She was looking for an outlet in poetry; I was looking for an outlet in reality through poetry. I made it to feminism, that was what I wanted; she managed to reveal herself in the poem, which was what she wanted. I didn't ask myself to be anything other than what I was (neither writer, nor poet, nor anything else), and I was making bets with myself if I would be able to accept myself as such. The lack of identity that gnawed at me was also the only link to keeping the faith.

Plath I sense floating free, free on the verge of suicide. I can find a sister in her now; before, I don't know if I could have: it would have dragged me too low, it would have lifted me too high. Whereas she accepted being alive by chance ("by accident"),[7] I discovered myself alive miraculously. Since I didn't want to die and I counted on the miracle, I had one more reason to doubt myself. I believe that Plath found a solution to her identity by entering the no-man's-land of death (of pre-death, of the return from the dead), which has become her land. She had believed in the culture, but she had found that casual way out, which would have involved the latest myth in consideration of the vanity of everything.

The oldest poem I found in the notebooks from when I was in middle school I dedicate to Sylvia Plath. The call to which she replied was also part of my voice, and perhaps those of each of us. It reminded me that, for me too, living seemed to stem from a decision to live.

1977

From "Itinerario di riflessioni," in *È già politica* [It is already politics], by Maria Grazia Chinese, Carla Lonzi, Marta Lonzi, and Anna Jaquinta (Milan: Scritti di Rivolta Femminile, 1977), 13–26. Pages 26 to 50 not included.

1. The religious period mentioned here is described in the biography of Lonzi by her sister: "At nine years old, after a summer spent with her sister Lidia at the castle of Rignalla, the summer venue of the boarding school in Badia a Ripoli, Carla decides to continue her study there and she remains there until the age of thirteen" Carla Lonzi, *Scacco Ragionato: poesie dal '58 al '63* [Thoughtful check: Poems from '58 to '63] (Milan: Scritti di Rivolta Femminile, 1985), 11. The boarding school was a Catholic school run by nuns, formally called Istituto delle Suore della Provvidenza e dell'Immacolata Concezione.

2. Lonzi uses "Carmel" here in reference to the Carmel of Lisieux, the chapel and cloister of Saint Thérèse of Lisieux referenced above.
3. Compiuta Donzella, "La Compiuta Donzella of Florence (ca. 1260): The Complete Poetry," trans. Fabian Alfie, *Medieval Feminist Forum* 55.3 (2019): 1–42.
4. Lonzi is here referring to *Autoritratto*. See Carla Lonzi, *Self-portrait*, trans. Allison Grimaldi Donahue (New York: Dia Art Foundation, 2021).
5. Alice Martinelli, *Autocoscienza* (Milan: Scritti di Rivolta Femminile, 1975), 6.
6. The expression "*portare vasi a Samo*" means to needlessly bring something of value to a place where it is already abundant, as in bringing vases to Samos, the Aegean island renowned in antiquity for its pottery.
7. "By accident" is written in English and placed in parenthesis in the original.

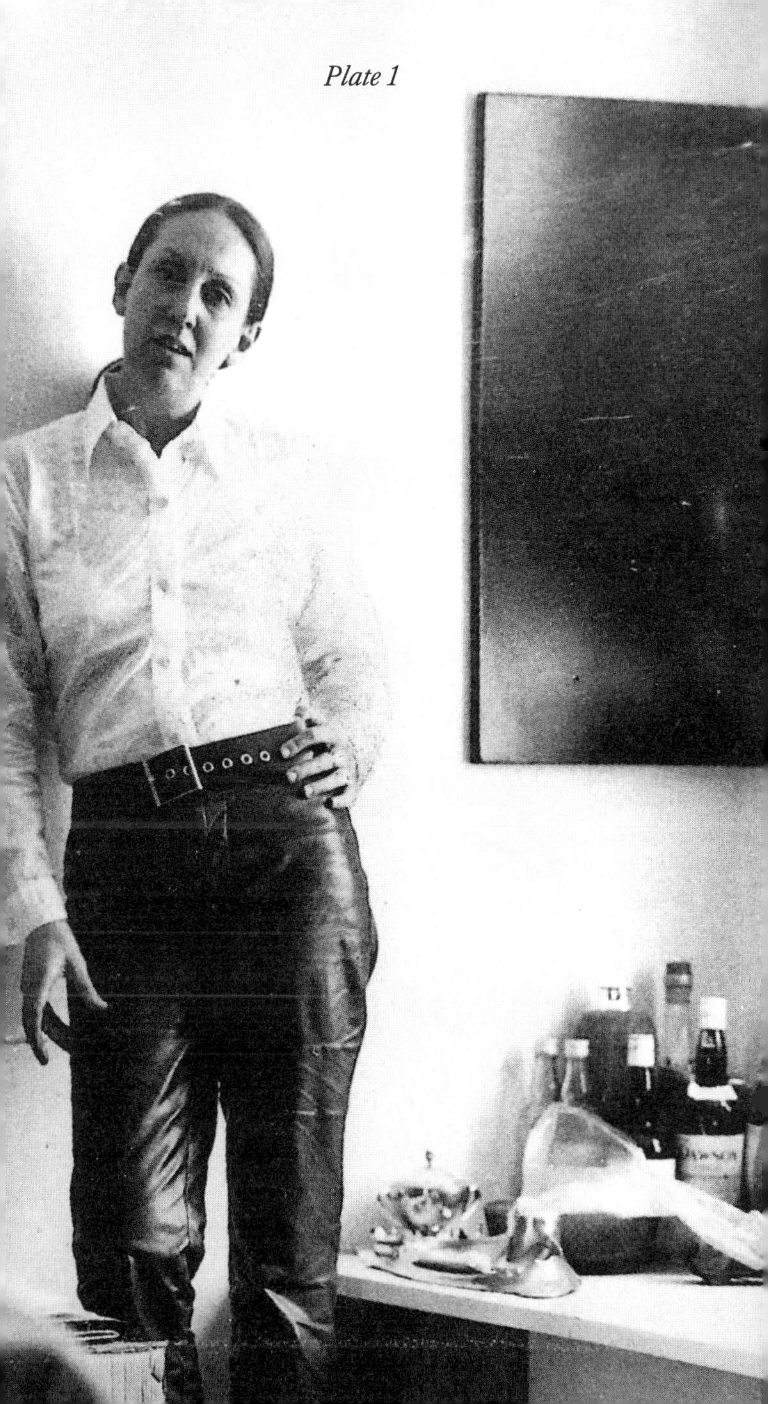

Plate 1

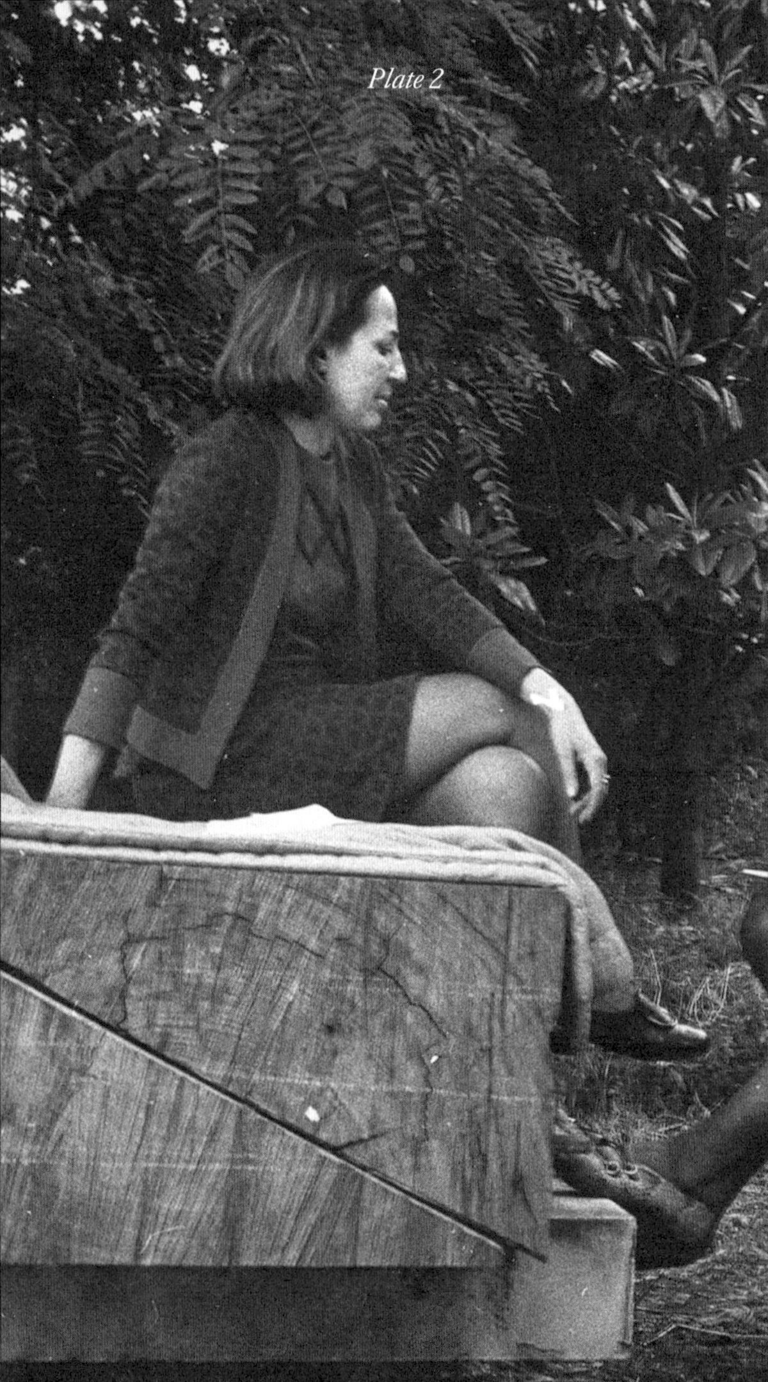

Plate 2

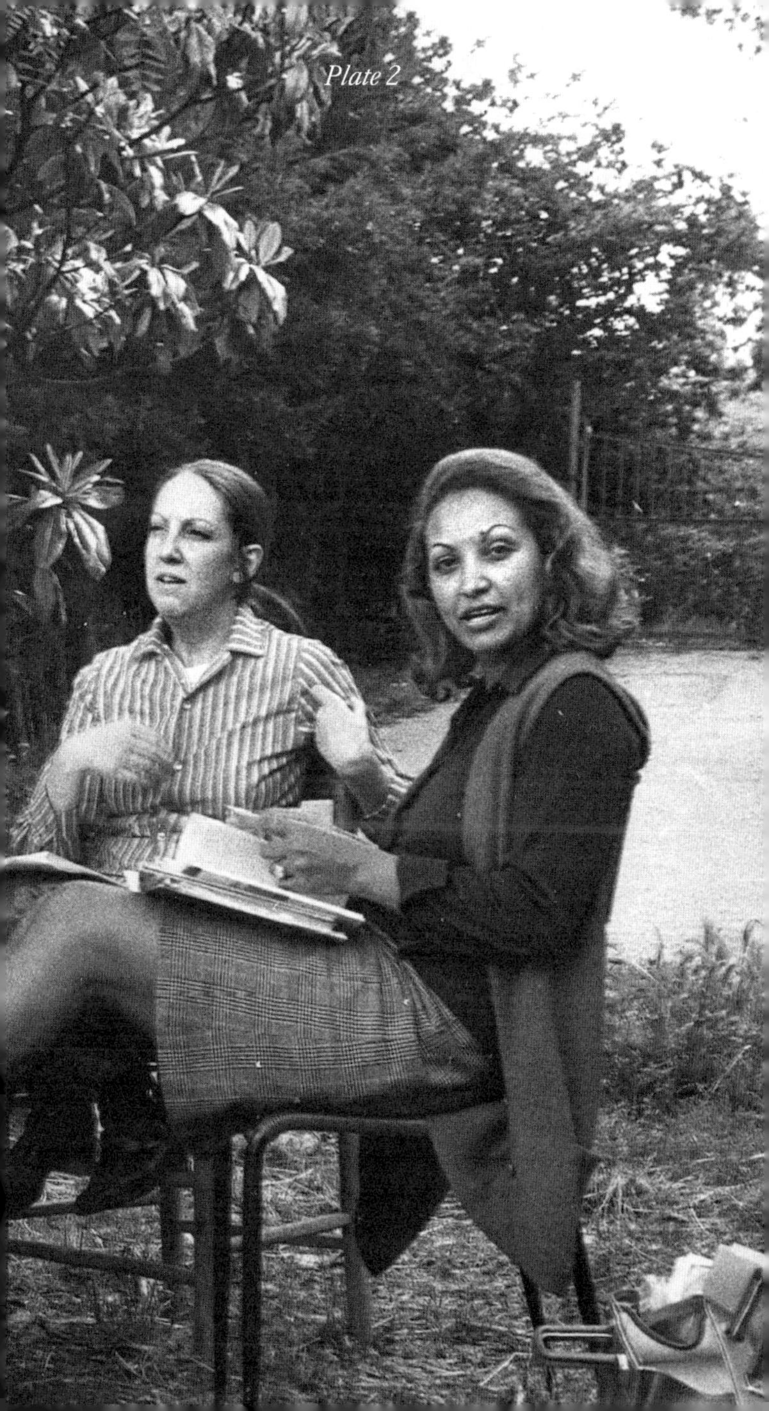
Plate 2

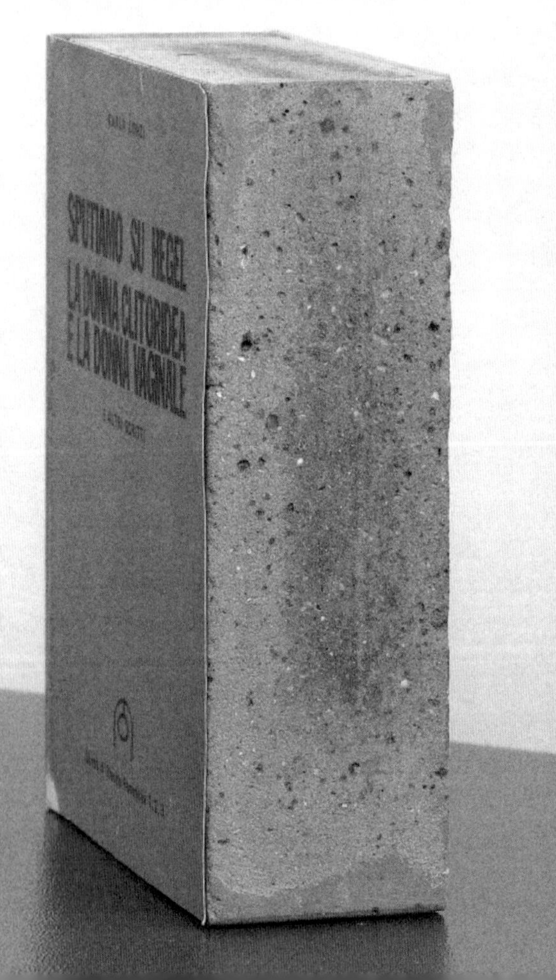

CARLA LONZI
SPUTIAMO SU HEGEL
LA DONNA CLITORIDEA
E LA DONNA VAGINALE
E ALTRI SCRITTI

CARLA LONZI
SPUTIAMO SU HEGEL
LA DONNA CLITORIDEA
E LA DONNA VAGINALE
E ALTRI SCRITTI
Scritti di Rivolta Femminile 1, 2, 3

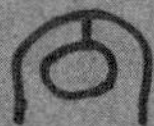

Plate 4

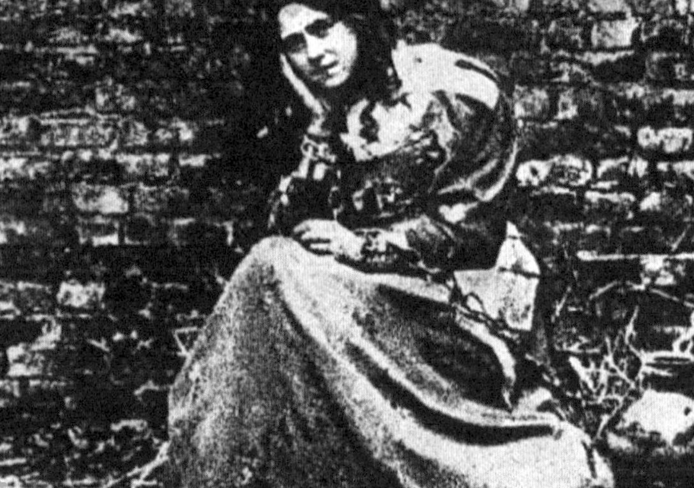

Plate 5

Plate 1
Carla Lonzi.

Plate 2
Carla Accardi, Carla Lonzi, and Elvira Banotti in Rome, 1970. Photo by Pietro Consagra.

Plates 3 & 4
Claire Fontaine, *Sputiamo su Hegel: La donna clitoridea e la donna vaginale brickbat*, 2015. Brick, brick fragments, glue, archival digital print, 169 × 122 × 60 mm. Courtesy of Claire Fontaine. This work comes from Claire Fontaine's series of "brickbat" works, in which the covers of radical texts are wrapped around bricks and pavement stones. Many of the covers come from the Scritti di Rivolta Femminile series.

Plate 5
Photo of Thérèse of Lisieux (born Marie Françoise-Thérèse Martin), the popular nineteenth-century saint, in costume as Joan of Arc. The writings of Saint Thérèse and this photograph are discussed in Carla Lonzi, "Itinerario di riflessioni" ("An Itinerary of Reflections"), in Maria Grazia Chinese, Carla Lonzi, Marta Lonzi, and Anna Jaquinta, *È già politica* [It is already politics] (Milan: Scritti di Rivolta Femminile, 1977), 13–26.

Plate 6 (p. 70)
Diagram from the Italian edition of Masters and Johnson's *Human Sexual Response* diagramming the sexual response cycle in male and female test subjects, published as William H. Masters and Virginia E. Johnson, *L'atto sessuale nell'uomo e nella donna. Indagine sugli aspetti anatomici e fisiologici* (Milan: Feltrinelli Editore, 1977). Lonzi reproduced this diagram as an illustration to "La donna clitoridea e la donna vaginale" ["The Clitoridean Woman and the Vaginal Woman"].

Claire Fontaine
On the Illegible

I am not recorded anywhere, I am talking air. If you deny me I will go back to being air, if you say "no, she doesn't speak" how can I say "no, I have spoken"? If you don't witness for me, who can witness for words that haven't been heard?
—Carla Lonzi, *Vai pure* (*Go Then*, 1980)[1]

Carla Lonzi gave up her work as an art critic shortly after '68 to fully invest herself in feminist liberation. Her vitalism is the key to understanding her abandonment of the posture of the critic, which she interprets as a position of presumed intellectual and academic authority abusively giving value to artistic expressions. The production of hierarchies in the name of criteria established to separate and exclude seems an aberration to Lonzi. In fact, any strategy oriented toward self-preservation and affirmation of oneself is courageously discarded by her, even if the price to pay is political illegibility and nonexistence on a social level. In *Autoritratto* (*Self-portrait*), Lonzi still finds the position of the artist politically more honourable than the one of the critic, mainly more sincere, as at the time the market's deformation of the reception of the artwork seemed less harmful than the one caused by critique, making artworks say things they are not meant to say.

Her opinion of artists and art would radicalize with the passing of time. Exemplary of this is her 1971 text "Assenza della donna dai momenti celebrativi della manifestazione creativa maschile" ("The Absence of Woman from Occasions Celebrating the Manifestation of Male Creativity").[2] In her diary, we can read an entry from 1975 that clarifies her concerns: *I wake up troubled: the myth of creativity is barring the road. It is like the myth of infantile innocence, created by adults and their sense of guilt. The myth of creativity has been invented by the excluded. Mankind bows to the man who nominates himself as a candidate to the myth, as if bowing to someone touched by grace. Even psychoanalysis has backed off in front of the myth of the artist. The category of the artist is the only untouchable one within the contemporary destruction of every category. The artist persecutes mankind through the continuous display of a self-assurance that from the existential level has been elevated by culture to the rank of ontological assurance.... The myth of art will continue to crush mankind, who produced it, because of its need of idealizing and seducing its persecutor.*

I would like a world where every expression remained at an existential level: writing, playing an instrument, painting, making all sorts of operations and with all sorts of mediums. For this to happen, everybody should accept the need of expressing themselves. If only one person remained inhibited, blocked, Art would plant its roots in his mind.[3]

The roots of words said with capital letters in people's souls do have terrible consequences. Lonzi's research through and within a language of a "minor literature"[4] to express the feminist form of life was shared by other members of Rivolta Femminile (Women's Revolt) and other subjectivities from that time.

Reciprocating recognition, legibility, wasn't a priority, because there was no aim of establishing a dogma or finding a leader to follow. It wasn't a matter of reducing the incomprehension but more faithfully enhancing the complexity.

If subjectivities are legible it is because the language of domination has written things about them that they don't themselves agree with or believe in.[5] Lonzi's feminism is a journey into ignoring or erasing the text of power and exploring confusion and transformation: in her perspective, dismantling authority isn't a voluntary action; it is the result of work on one's desires.

As long as man remains the desirable interlocutor, he will spread rivalry among women, she writes. Feminist culture must fight this problem, but another option is available: living through insecurity without institutionalizing roles or competences that will limit it from the outside; but recognizing the difficulties and the impulses that derive from them; distinguishing inner peace from passivity, the moment of action from activism; accepting one's own limitations without considering them insurmountable—that's how freedom could be experienced and shared.

After quitting her role of art critic (because it imposed too heavy of limitations on her self-expression), she describes being in a group of women that had been kept secluded from culture. "I experienced," she writes, "a real regret for the original integrity from which I felt I had taken my distance: in the disorientation of desiring the resonance of another lost woman, I became aware of myself." She goes on: "The cultural void with which one must identify isn't the original integrity but the continuous consumption of the subconscious ties with the masculine world by living through them and becoming aware of them."[6]

Not fearing this blurred area, in which the categories that define subjectivities are rejected and not yet recreated, is the precondition for this journey. Describing a dinner with people who weren't familiar with feminism or any of her activities, Lonzi writes the following memorable lines in her journal, entitled *Taci, anzi parla* (Speak not, no, speak): *What I am is pathetically invisible and inaudible and I can't use it. Now I am sure that I am not making a drama of it, because it is in fact a drama; my decision of not falling into the trap anymore is taken.... I, who doesn't exist socially, can recognize another woman who doesn't exist socially and so on. But my consciousness isn't recognized by culture, so this chain of recognition between nonexisting is valid only between us. I don't see the possibility of a different man because it is unthinkable that one can give up a social identity that he has for one that doesn't exist.*[7]

The awareness of this fact—that nonexistence confounds recognition—renders social relationships, even the most banal and common, totally unbearable, because it unmasks their complicity with the forces at work within the current situation. Lonzi perfectly understands that the reward given to masculine subjectivities is valueless for women and doesn't allow them to buy anything but the sadness of separation. Here lies, in fact, the bitter truth of the reformist emancipation and the dead end of its illusions. The nonexistence, the result of the refusal of the path of "equality with men," so painful in the banal violence of daily life—as much as in the absurdity of an evening spent with people who aren't even unpleasant—manifests itself with all its power in Lonzi's position, which becomes illegible, a weapon impossible to use. This situation also makes clear that the dialectic paradigm of master/slave of the Hegelian matrix is a useless tool to interpret the man/woman problem, which is the other name for the human relationship in general.[8]

That's why Lonzi's attack on culture as a patriarchal institution is extraordinarily violent and pertinent. It is a point of view created within a blind spot of a language that includes not only its silence but also the very cause of it.

That the subalterns should be the victims of such paradoxes can be reversed—and in fact is—in many of her writings, like in the "Mito della proposta culturale" (The Myth of Cultural Proposal): *I ask myself why shouldn't a worker in the Bovisa know what the hatred of a woman is? Why shelter him from expression? Is it that in other fields one uses special precautions with people who must become conscious of the fact that they are prevaricating? Why are direct attacks silenced until they can be placed between two quotes of Marx? Why do we need to approach men as if they were children to whom one has to present truth in the language of their ABC's? Why such seriousness and heartache? To make them understand, in other words, to not lose the connection with culture. If this is true, then, which one is the practice that withers away Politics? (and capitalized ideas, more in general)? Is it the one that "asks questions that challenge the instituted power-knowledge,"? Is it the one that makes all the gestures of expression of oneself and all the gestures of recognizing the other woman, so that the doors to the limbo where women look for (without finding it) a real incarnation can be kept open? The blockade needs to be forced piece by piece: this is the necessary step for the birth of one's individuality, the prerequisite for any change.*[9]

The necessity of submitting to men because they are the owners of all criteria of recognition and legibility, political and intellectual—and therefore controllers of the processes of subjectivization—is mercilessly stigmatized by Lonzi, but in a way totally deprived of resentment and simply pragmatic. It isn't in fact a matter of defending a theoretical point of view but of forcing the blockade so that women's bodies can exit the silence and begin to speak, even if this happens in the realm of illegibility, even if this gesture isn't codified or understood by the existing feminism: it's a vital necessity; the world needs it.

But plunging into this exciting fog in order to pursue the quest for an identity not indebted to power and its logics is also dangerous, because the outcome might still be misunderstandable, easy to dismiss, or remain unexplored.

Looking at the question of illegibility in Lonzi's thinking brings us to her refusal of Marxism as a device of optical legibility for society and conflict. In *Sputiamo su Hegel* (*Let's Spit on Hegel*)—which, as she explicitly states, means "let's spit on *Marx*"[10]—she makes the essential point that the blindness of interpreting society on the basis of the pure category of class leaves invisible and submerged domestic and emotional exploitation, basically the reproductive work without which society simply wouldn't exist. This reproductive work has a particularly "human" and artisanal quality, possibly because, as the sociologist and Lotta Femminista (Feminist Struggle) member Giovanna Franca Dalla Costa writes,[11] nobody cares how long the work takes or how taxing it is for the worker when the work is unpaid.

Reproductive work is also the hardest to quantify and to artificially separate from daily life. Its omnipresence and endlessness questions the very idea of remuneration of work and implicitly puts into crisis the whole wage economy.[12] Requesting remuneration for this inestimable service is obviously a way of stating the failure of capitalism, or its parasitical nature. As capitalism not only thrives on primitive accumulation, theft of land, privatization, and slavery—it also thrives first and foremost on reproductive labour, which means not only the actual labour of giving birth and raising humans who will become the future workforce but also the love labour that keeps us fed, healthy, and not depressed, sick, or mentally impaired.

The skills demanded for this kind of labour are extremely complex and their reproduction totally taxing. In fact, capitalism not only parasitizes this work but also negates its value by paying women who work outside their homes lower salaries than men, because they have to perform their double duty and this supposedly will reflect negatively on their professional achievements.

This form of illiteracy translates into the "sentimental retardation" typical of patriarchy that has taken us to the place we find ourselves today. That sexual and social relationships between women and men over the past years have needed continuous scrutiny in light of the meaning that was given to the concepts of violence and abuse, and that consent can still be seen as a grey area defined as confusing and ambiguous, shows that the illegible is the result of the voluntary illiteracy of power. Institutions and the men that rule them have yet to fully master the foreign language within the language of women's freedom, but very soon everyone will be able to read it.

This text was first published in Ilse Lafer, ed., *Deculturalize* (Bolzano, Italy: Museion; Milan: Mousse, 2020).

1. Carla Lonzi, *Vai pure. Dialogo con Pietro Consagra* [*Go Then: A Dialogue between the Author and Pietro Consagra*] (Milan: Scritti di Rivolta Femminile, 1980), 106.
2. Carla Lonzi, "Assenza della donna dai momenti celebrativi della manifestazione creativa maschile" ["The Absence of Woman from Occasions Celebrating the Manifestation of Male Creativity"], in *Sputiamo su Hegel. La donna clitoridea e la donna vaginale e altri scritti* [*Let's Spit on Hegel: The Clitoridean Woman and the Vaginal Woman and Other Writings*] (Milan: Scritti di Rivolta Femminile, 1974), 63–65. See also the translation beginning on p. 59 in this volume.
3. Carla Lonzi, *Taci, anzi parla. Diario di una femminista* [Speak not, no, speak: Diary of a feminist] (Milan: Scritti di Rivolta Femminile, 1978), 1, 173–74. All translations from Italian to English are the authors', with amendments by Sara Colantuono, unless otherwise indicated.
4. The concept of minor literature comes from Gilles Deleuze and Félix Guattari's *Kafka: Toward a Minor Literature* (Minneapolis: University of Minnesota Press, 1986). There we can read the description of the process of finding the foreign language within language, finding one's inner third world. "How to become a nomad and an immigrant and a gypsy in relation to one's own language?," Deleuze and Guattari write. "Kafka answers: steal the baby from its crib, walk the tightrope" (p. 19).
5. This concept comes from the work of Michel Foucault but can be found in some feminists' works, such as that of Gayatri C. Spivak.
6. Carla Lonzi, *È già politica* [It is already politics] (Milan: Scritti di Rivolta Femminile, 1977), 36.
7. Lonzi, *Taci, anzi parla*, 1,172–73.
8. See Maria Luisa Boccia, *Con Carla Lonzi. La mia opera è la mia vita* (Rome: Ediesse, 2014), 20–21.
9. Carla Lonzi, "Mito della proposta culturale" ["The Myth of Cultural Proposal"], in *La presenza dell'uomo nel femminismo* [Male presence in feminism], by Carla Lonzi, Marta Lonzi, and Anna Jaquinta (Milan: Scritti di Rivolta Femminile, 1978), 141–42.
10. Lonzi, *Vai pure*, 110.
11. Giovanna Franca Dalla Costa, *The Work of Love: Unpaid Housework, Poverty and Sexual Violence at the Dawn of the 21st Century* (New York: Autonomedia, 2006).
12. For more on this subject, see Silvia Federici, *Wages against Housework* (Bristol, UK: Falling Wall Press and Power of Women Collective, 1975).

Sara Colantuono

"Writing is a public gesture"[1]

*On Interlocution and Recognition
in Carla Lonzi's Feminist Practice*

Writing, for Carla Lonzi, is a form of expression diametrically opposed to art making, which is for her incompatible with feminist practice.[2] If we look within her thought for an explanation for the differentiation between art and writing, we find a coherent argument developed throughout her oeuvre. The relationship between writer and reader can be direct, reciprocal, and interchangeable, and it can be liberating. Writing, and especially autobiographical writing, is natural: "the form of expression to which almost every woman spontaneously resorts to in order to reflect on her own life."[3] The relationship between artist and spectator is, by contrast, mediated by the art critic, and it cannot be reciprocal and interchangeable. She further develops this argument through the idea of the "interlocutor," which Lonzi opposes to that of the "spectator." In other words: "everyone is a reader and potentially a writer," while not everyone can be an artist.[4]

Carla Lonzi (1931–82) was an Italian art critic and feminist best known for her work with the separatist group Rivolta Femminile (Women's Revolt) and for developing the practice of *autocoscienza*.[5] A successful art critic and curator in the 1960s, Lonzi progressively distanced herself from the art world through a series of articles and books—notably *Autoritratto* (*Self-portrait*, 1969) and "La critica è potere" (Art criticism is power, 1970)—that question the legitimacy and truthfulness of the profession. Lonzi considered her "period as an art critic" essential to her feminist theorizations, but she also unequivocally deemed it a closed chapter of her life.[6] Italian writer and politician Maria Luisa Boccia effectively summarizes this relationship: "Once her own initiation to conscience through art has failed, the estrangement from cultural structures becomes total for her."[7] In a fascinating essay published in 1977, "Itinerario di riflessioni" ("An Itinerary of Reflections"), Lonzi reflects on her withdrawal from art criticism by comparing herself to the American feminist activist Valerie Solanas: *At the beginning of feminism, when I became conscious of the sacrifices I had been making at the expense of the expression of my true self that were implicit in my work as an art critic, I could not foresee any possibility other than retiring and focusing on liberation. While Solanas dismissed her affiliation with the art world by firing three gunshots, I abandoned the same world, but without denying anything. The experience I made did not deserve to be annulled with such a self-destructive gesture.*[8]

While the withdrawal came without rejection, and the experiences made as an art critic still had value for Lonzi, the abandonment was total. Refusing the cultural structures of art, including art making and art criticism, was for Lonzi the first step toward feminism, because she realized that the impossibility of finding answers within that culture was inherent to her gender. In the essay "Assenza della donna dai momenti celebrativi della creatività maschile" ("The Absence of Woman from Occasions Celebrating the Manifestation of Male Creativity," 1971), Lonzi outlines the correspondence she had come to realize between artist-spectator and man-woman: *By becoming conscious of their condition in relation to male creativity, women have two possibilities: on the one hand, they can reach equality on the creative plane, which is historically defined by man, alienating for her and granted to her with indulgence by man; the other, the one that the feminist movement seeks, the autonomous liberation of women who restore their own creativity, nurtured in the repression imposed by the models of the dominant sex.*[9] For Lonzi, equality was never really a possibility, neither in theory nor in practice. In this 1971 essay, she elaborates on how, in seeking equality and thus participating in the celebration of men's creativity, women unconsciously perpetrate the myth of the artistic genius, in the double role of passive spectator and object of artistic expression. To "restore their creativity," they must abandon the mythologization of art and thus reject any participation in or celebration of art made by male artists. What emerges here is the idea of the cultural void or "tabula rasa," which is central for Lonzi in all the different stages of her critique and became more and more important as autobiographical writing developed into the core of her feminist practice.[10] For Lonzi, it is not possible to achieve liberation in the realm of art, because women always will be relegated to the role of spectator. On the contrary, the practice of writing "allows us to change the way we read and takes away from the act of writing much of its mythical value, which is the value attributed to a thing by those who do not make it."[11]

Throughout her life, Lonzi developed *scrittura autocoscienziale* as a specific form of autobiographical writing embedded in the collective practice of *autocoscienza*.[12] She wrote consistently during her lifetime, in the form of notes, diaries, poems, and letters. In her diary, she calls this ongoing project "the single romance of my life" and dwells on the possibility of publishing everything she has ever written: "With Rivolta [publishing press] I want to publish everything about myself, from the diaries of when I was a little girl to the letters, notes, poems, everything, the single romance of my life."[13] Lonzi conceived of the gesture of sharing one's writing with other women as a process that must accompany the collective, oral work done during the meetings of Rivolta Femminile. Much like a collective session of *autocoscienza*, writing about (or recording) herself, and then sharing what she wrote (or said) publicly, allowed Lonzi to find her place within the cultural extraneousness she deems essential in the quest toward an authentic form of self. One of the ways this testimonial gesture is achieved is through the individuation of an interlocutor, a figure radically different from the spectator; this is key to the differentiation Lonzi makes between art making and writing. She defines the interlocutor as "someone you can listen to without letting them determine who you are. It happens when you are grounded, of course still subjected to a weave of suggestions, but you are grounded in yourself. When this happens, I do not call it 'culture' anymore—I call it interlocution."[14] The difference lies in the element of reciprocity. As opposed to spectatorship, a role Lonzi largely criticizes in relation to art, interlocution operates within mutual recognition and implies a mirroring response: "Another woman, clitoridean, recognized me as a woman, clitoridean, while I was recognizing her in the same terms. This happened during the spring of 1972. Now I know who I am and I can consciously be myself."[15] These words open Lonzi's diary, *Taci, anzi parla. Diario di una femminista* (Speak not, no, speak: Diary of a feminist, 1978), which, as she states, "is all about relationships, and not at all about people."[16] By marking the beginning of her book with a reciprocal recognition, she sets the terms of the agreement with the reader: she must be available to lose herself "in the trick [*tranello*] of finding that she is mirrored in an image of herself that includes all her illusions and her ambitions."[17] From Lonzi's perspective, publishing her own diary meant making herself available for that mutual recognition.

In the preface of *Taci, anzi parla*, Lonzi describes what writing a diary after ten years of art criticism (1960–70) and two years of feminist activism and writing (1970–72) meant for her: "I feel like I have come to the form of the diary with the necessity to present myself to myself and of finding motivation for doing what I do.… I needed to draw out all my dissent on the image through which others saw me, and wherein I felt constricted."[18] The six-year-long diary—spanning from the summer of 1972 to January 1977—is an in-depth testimony of a voyage into "past present future," where daily reports of events and relationships are integrated with poems, letters, photographs, and accounts of dreams.[19] These years, spent "in the strongest state of concentration," constitute for Lonzi a crucial moment of self-reflection and self-critique and establish once and for all the primacy of autobiographical writing in her feminist practice. The gesture of publishing her diary was as important as writing it, and it forms part of her programmatic demolition of social impositions based on gender, and of social fabric more generally: "Somewhere we must begin to demolish the false identities that are stuck to women like a shroud. It is a surprise then to realize that when one does this, they risk breaking the house of cards of false identities that hold the social fabric together."[20] In demolishing "the false identities" that constitute women, Lonzi operates in the realm of authenticity—a key concept established in the essays of her first feminist season and then developed later in conjunction with her autobiographical writing practice within the process of *autocoscienza*.

Published in 1978, *Taci, anzi parla* is part of a constellation of texts that mark Lonzi's second feminist season (1973–80). This period began with the disintegration of the original Rivolta Femminile group, led by Lonzi along with the Italian *arte povera* artist Carla Accardi and Italian Eritrean journalist Elvira Banotti, and with the end of the long-standing friendship between Lonzi and Accardi, in

February 1973. The original group published the *Manifesto di Rivolta Femminile* in 1970, and then a series of essays collected in the volume *Sputiamo su Hegel. La donna clitoridea e la donna vaginale e altri scritti* (*Let's Spit on Hegel: The Clitoridean Woman and the Vaginal Woman and Other Writings*, 1974). The feminist militancy they foresaw was not directly political or institutionalized but rather intimate and active at the level of individual consciousness, gained through the collective practice of *autocoscienza*. This point is crucial when approaching Lonzi's writing practice, because writing and sharing one's own writing, and especially one's own diary, gradually becomes the bedrock of the collective practice of *autocoscienza*. The urgency of autonomy and difference, rather than equality, was Lonzi's priority, and for her autonomy was accomplished primarily on the level of expression: orally in her first period, then, in her second, in written form. The association between the orally based practice of *autocoscienza* and writing as the privileged forms of female expression was a peculiarity of Rivolta Femminile. But writing (*la scrittura*) was, for Lonzi, a form of expression different from literature, a category that often seemed too similar to art. Her models were not romances or philosophical texts but rather diaries and autobiographies: *I've always liked autobiographical books of saints.... I read them in boarding school between the ages of ten and thirteen, and I continued to have a fondness for them later in life: in particular I have been drawn to them in moments of crisis, when I had to admit an illusion and find inner peace from which to begin anew. I returned several times to Thérèse Martin's* Story of a Soul, *that is, "Saint Teresa of the Child Jesus," together with Teresa of Ávila's* The Book of My Life. *Both were written on request out of obedience to a church superior; they are in the first person and express phenomena and inner states natural to me and that I could not find expressed elsewhere. It was a comfort that other women had felt and talked about these states simply:* their words addressed a phenomenon that I otherwise would have felt compelled to reject as a consequence of morbid and unreal emotion. *I discovered these states earlier in the religious language of the two Thérèses,* rather than in the literary analyses of female writers.[21] This passage comes from a text Lonzi published in February 1977, probably written while she was concluding her diary. The importance of the two "autobiographical books of saints" is highlighted more than once in *Taci, anzi parla*, where Thérèse of Lisieux and occasionally Teresa of Ávila emerge as models of authenticity and "comrade(s) of liberation."[22]

While literature, and more specifically literature by women, became the main form of expression and reference for many Italian feminist groups, Lonzi always privileged what was, for her, the most unmediated and authentic kind of writing. In a rare interview granted to French feminist activist Michèle Causse in 1976, Lonzi touched upon the different functions of writing within Rivolta Femminile's work: "Our writings are born from the need to communicate, communicate with oneself and with other women. They are born in the form of diary (at least so far), which is the mode of expression used spontaneously by any woman to reflect on her own life."[23] Autobiographical writing and diaries gradually became central in Lonzi's second feminist period. In her diary, Lonzi describes women like Moderata Fonte, Thérèse of Lisieux, Teresa of Ávila, Sylvia Plath, and Virginia Woolf as models of self-discovery, brave pioneers of *scrittura autocoscienziale*.[24] But what interested Lonzi was neither the foundation of a new language for women nor the quest for a canon of women's literature; rather, she sought the authentic and direct experience of writing about oneself. She emphasized the difference between literary invention and diaries multiple times over the years: *While watching a movie about Woolf, I remembered that I read when I was a young girl* Diary of a Writer, *which together with [Cesare] Pavese's and [Franz] Kafka's diaries forms the diaristic trilogy at the base of my youth. I actually never read much of these three authors: after entering the private dimension,* the literary invention interested me much less. [25]

Uninterested in the "literary invention" of romances and novels, what Lonzi looked for is the disintegration of the border between private and public. It is this dynamic she seeks to reproduce with the publication of many of her texts, from *Autoritratto* to *Taci, anzi parla* to *Vai pure* (*Go Then*, 1980). [26] In an undated, unpublished manuscript, Lonzi reflects on the effects of and premises for the publication of *Taci, anzi parla: To publish a diary is to unveil oneself outside of conventions…a diary written, and not published, is only a materialization of impotence and of defeat.… For me, the diary was a temporary secret: once I had constructed the right circumstances, I would reveal it.… A new situation had to be created in which the expectation was of reciprocal revelation.* [27] For Lonzi, writing is meaningless if it isn't shared, and shared with the purpose of mutual recognition and interlocution. Here, and elsewhere, she gives writing a salvific and therapeutic capacity, situating it as an urgent need, one that distinguishes this practice above everything else. Lonzi's language in these excerpts—*unveil, materialization of impotence, revelation*—points to an almost mystical experience embedded in the process of writing about oneself.

Between 1973 and 1977, the years that *Taci, anzi parla* covers, the practice of *scrittura autocoscienziale* in the form of autobiographical diary became almost mandatory among the women of Rivolta Femminile. More importantly, perhaps, the act of giving one's diary to another woman in the group also became mandatory. Writing one's own and simultaneously reading other women's diaries developed as a process necessary to acquire and mutually share *autocoscienza*. Lonzi recorded this experience of reading other women's diaries many times, always speaking of it as a pivotal moment in the relationship between the reader and the writer. In May 1974, in a letter included in *Taci, anzi parla*, Lonzi wrote to a friend whose diary she was reading: *Dear Valeria, I hope I really did* autocoscienza.... *I am on page 179.* Autocoscienza *is the most exciting thing in the world, or at least yours is. It is overwhelming, it is relentless. I recognize it from the pace. I know I am infallible there, like John the Baptist.... Through reading your diary, I have discovered* autocoscienza *again. In every phase of our lives it reveals itself as a different combination of personal energy, sense of existence, acceptance of reality, consciousness of oneself and of the other.*[28] Reading another woman's experience of *autocoscienza*, "the most exciting thing in the world," is what triggers the same experience in Lonzi. This mirroring dynamic, now embedded in the process of writing and reading, is the core of Lonzi's feminist practice. It is the most intimate form of *risonanza*, which Lonzi described in the summer of 1976 as "the improvement and deepening of relationships, of mutual understanding rather than punctual feedback."[29]

---

1. Carla Lonzi, "Mito della proposta culturale" ["The Myth of Cultural Proposal"], in *La presenza dell'uomo nel femminismo* [Male presence in feminism], by Carla Lonzi, Marta Lonzi, and Anna Jaquinta (Milan: Scritti di Rivolta Femminile, 1978), 137.

2. I use the term "feminist practice," rather than "feminist theory," in accordance with Lonzi's statement that "feminism is not an idea, it is a practice." Carla Lonzi, "Itinerario di riflessioni" ["An Itinerary of Reflections"], in *È già politica* [It is already politics], by Maria Grazia Chinese, Carla Lonzi, Marta Lonzi, and Anna Jaquinta (Milan: Scritti di Rivolta Femminile, 1977), 33. All translations

are mine, unless otherwise noted.

3. Carla Lonzi, *Taci, anzi parla. Diario di una femminista* [Speak not, no, speak: Diary of a feminist] (Milan: Scritti di Rivolta Femminile, 1978), 106.

4. Lonzi, *Taci, anzi parla*, 107.

5. *Autocoscienza* is often translated as "consciousness raising" or "self-consciousness." To mark its originality and its difference from other second-wave feminist practices with which it is often conflated, such as North American consciousness-raising groups, I use the original Italian term.

6. Lonzi, *Taci, anzi parla*, 40. For an in-depth analysis of Lonzi's art critical work see, among others, Ventrella Francesco and Giovanna Zapperi, *Feminism and Art in Postwar Italy: The Legacy of Carla Lonzi* (London: Bloomsbury Publishing, 2020).

7. Lonzi, *Taci, anzi parla*, 59.

8. Lonzi, "Itinerario di riflessioni," 35. Lonzi here refers to an event that took place on June 3, 1968, when feminist author Valerie Solanas attempted to murder Andy Warhol by shooting him three times, thinking that he wanted to steal her script for the play *Up Your Ass.* Solanas, who in 1967 self-published her now well-known *SCUM Manifesto* (SCUM is an acronym for Society for Cutting Up Men), was at the time occasionally working for Warhol as an actress. After the shooting, Solanas was charged with attempted murder and diagnosed with paranoid schizophrenia. She served a three-year prison sentence.

9. Carla Lonzi, *Sputiamo su Hegel. La donna clitoridea e la donna vaginale e altri scritti* [Let's Spit on Hegel: The Clitoridean Woman and the Vaginal Woman and Other Writings] (Milan: Scritti di Rivolta Femminile, 1974), 66.

10. For an elaboration of the term "tabula rasa," see the manifesto-type text Rivolta Femminile, "Primati dell'intuizione nella tabula rasa della cultura" [Primacy of intuition in the ground zero of culture], in Lonzi et al., *È già politica*, 65.

11. Carla Lonzi, "Intervista di Michèle Causse a Carla Lonzi," interview by and Michèle Causse, in *È già politica*, 107.

12. Maria Luisa Boccia, *L'io in rivolta: vissuto e pensiero di Carla Lonzi* (Milan: La Tartaruga, 1990), 32.

13. Lonzi, *Taci, anzi parla*, 503.

14. Lonzi, "Intervista di Michèle Causse a Carla Lonzi," interview by Causse, 105.

15. Lonzi, *Taci, anzi parla*, 13.

16. Lonzi, *Taci, anzi parla*, 7.

17. Lonzi, *Taci, anzi parla*, 2

18. Lonzi, *Taci, anzi parla*, 9.

19. Lonzi, *Taci, anzi parla*, 9.

20. Carla Lonzi, *Scacco Ragionato: poesie dal '58 al '63* [Thoughtful check: Poems from '58 to '63] (Milan: Scritti di Rivolta Femminile, 1985), 51.

21. Lonzi, "Itinerario di riflessioni," 13. My emphasis. See also the translation beginning on p. 109 of this volume.

22. Lonzi, *Taci, anzi parla*, 223. Teresa of Ávila was a sixteenth-century Spanish Carmelite nun and prominent mystic and religious reformer. Active during the Counter-Reformation, she reformed the Carmelite Orders of both women and men. Thérèse of Lisieux was also a Carmelite nun who lived in France (1873–1889), canonized in 1925. She is one of the most popular saints of the twentieth century. I explore the religious element within and beyond Lonzi's thought in my dissertation, "The Catholic Matrix of Italian Feminism:

From Carla Lonzi to Michela Murgia" (PhD diss., Brown University, 2024), https://fillip.ca/7s68.

23. Lonzi, "Intervista di Michèle Causse a Carla Lonzi," interview by Causse, 107.

24. Further references include, among many others, Anne Frank, Anaïs Nin, and a young Viennese girl who was a patient of Sigmund Freud, whom Lonzi calls "Anonima Viennese" and who is the alleged author of *A Young Girl's Diary*. Eden Paul, Cedar Paul, and Sigmund Freud, *A Young Girl's Diary* (New York: T. Seltzer, 1923).

25. Lonzi, *Taci, anzi parla*, 617. My emphasis.

26. Carla Lonzi, *Vai pure. Dialogo con Pietro Consagra* [*Go Then: A Dialogue between the Author and Pietro Consagra*] (Milan: Scritti di Rivolta Femminile, 1980).

27. Lonzi, *Taci, anzi parla*, 51.

28. Lonzi, *Taci, anzi parla*, 535.

29. Lonzi, *Taci, anzi parla*, 1,005.

Jaleh Mansoor

The Hidden Abode
Beneath/Behind/Beyond the Factory Floor, Gendered Labour, and the Human Strike

Fire in the Nail Salon

The phrase "hidden abode" in the title of this text, in a particular manifestation of Feminist art of the late twentieth and early twenty-first century (formulated in response to an equally specific current of twentieth-century feminism), is drawn from a nineteenth-century classic on which both art practice and feminist theory depend: Karl Marx's *Capital*, specifically volume one, chapter six: "The Buying and Selling of Labour-Power." Marx writes: *Accompanied by Mr. Moneybags and by the possessor of labour-power, we therefore take leave for a time of this noisy sphere [the market], where everything takes place on the surface and in view of all men, and follow them both into the hidden abode of production, on whose threshold there stares us in the face "No admittance except on business." Here we shall see, not only how capital produces, but how capital is produced. We shall at last force the secret of profit making.*[1] There, the "hidden abode" is a way to articulate the site where the capitalist mode of production actually takes place, given the way in which it is usually occluded from the marketplace and ideology alike, hidden under the shrouds of bourgeois mystification. This hidden site is where value is limned from the labour power of embodied workers in exchange for enough remuneration for those workers to replicate their own lives while the results of their labour is valorized on the market.

Now, to get to feminism from Marx may seem like crossing a wide abyss due to the entrenchment of sexism, despite the numerous foundational feminist texts that generously engaged Marxism, among which psychoanalyst Juliet Mitchell's and radical feminist Shulamith Firestone's writings come at once to mind.[2] Yet Italian feminism of the last quarter of the twentieth century elaborated a theory of gendered everyday life, of the motivation behind the production and replication of sexual difference within modernity, around a theory of the wage by arguing that women's unpaid labour provides its own "hidden abode" under Marx's value-productive one, thereby bridging this abyss. Italian feminism of the 1960s and '70s noted that men do not show up to the factory or to work without the daily care provided by women, unpaid, in the guise of naturalized family relations. They mediated the space between home and factory, indeed created an analogy of the home to the factory, a domestic "factory" operative beneath the factory—supported by the unremunerated, the naturalized, work of women. The present text retraces that feminist Marxist analytic's suturing of the economics of everyday capital within the capitalist mode of production to the specifically gendered reproduction of everyday life under it, through a monographic exploration of the work of the art collective Claire Fontaine. Here, the notion of the "general strike," as a strike under a specific work-related strike, will take on resonance as a specifically feminist tactic of resistance and integrity. But first I'll begin with a description.

In February 2013, at the Queen's Nails Gallery salon in San Francisco, California, an installation by Claire Fontaine caught fire. The walls of the space in turn caught fire, turning the exhibition into a public emergency. The piece, entitled *America Burnt/Unburnt* (2011), was composed of matches arranged to form the shape of the United

States' contour on a world map. While the bas-relief sculpture had appeared in numerous earlier exhibitions, none of the previous versions had caught aflame. In this instance, the fire destroyed the interior of the gallery.

Not least because Claire Fontaine's installation just some months before at the Audain Gallery at Simon Fraser University in Vancouver, British Columbia, was titled *Carelessness Causes Fire*, there was some speculation that the mishap may have been vaguely predetermined. Demonstrating the unstable criteria by which media distinguishes among spectacle, accident, and willed violence, the occurrence stood at the intersection of probable cause, innocent synchronicity, and irony. Made of matches after all, the shape of the United States as depicted on a world map also paid fairly innocent homage to the modernist painter Jasper Johns and to an American history of pop art.

The uncanny *timing* of the incident, just after the exhibition *Carelessness Causes Fire* in Vancouver, insinuated a horizon of *intention*, also because it took its place within a frame of reference elaborated in Claire Fontaine's previous work. Who is Claire Fontaine? According to the publicly available description on their website: *Claire Fontaine is a Paris-based collective artist, founded in 2004. After lifting her name from a popular brand of school notebooks, Claire Fontaine declared herself a "readymade artist" and began to elaborate a version of neo-conceptual art that often looks like other people's work. Working in neon, video, sculpture, painting and text, her practice can be described as an ongoing interrogation of the political impotence and the crisis of singularity that seem to define contemporary art today. But if the artist herself is the subjective equivalent of a urinal or a Brillo box—as displaced, deprived of its use value, and exchangeable as the products she makes—there is always the possibility of what she calls the "human strike." Claire Fontaine uses her freshness and youth to make herself a whatever-singularity and an existential terrorist in search of subjective emancipation. She grows up among the ruins of the notion of authorship, experimenting with collective protocols of production, détournements, and the production of various devices for the sharing of intellectual and private property.*[3]

Claire Fontaine's practice is in part founded on the shoulders of the Situationists and at the junction of the French and Italian post–World War II avant-garde, movements that explicitly situated the work of art at the intersection of chance, unconscious desire, and conscious intention. As such, *America Burnt/Unburnt* tested the limits of where art and life came together in the most embarrassingly banal way possible: an accidental fire! Claire Fontaine cite Situationist founder Guy Debord's work in their writing. "Ready-Made Artist and Human Strike: A Few Clarifications"[4] opens with a citation of Debord's film *In girum imus nocte et consumimur igni* (1956). This particular occurrence, the fire resulting from the *America Burnt/Unburnt* show in San Francisco, hangs suspended between accident and a horizon of intention as evoked in thesis 91 in Debord's *The Society of the Spectacle*: "The critical position later elaborated by the Situationists has shown that the suppression and the realization of art are inseparable aspects of a single supersession of art."[5] For the work of art to have succeeded is to no longer recognize it as a work of art but to be living inside its economy. *America Burnt/Unburnt* feigns ambivalence about violence; does violence issue from forms of resistance, or from the state itself? Compounded by the "dialogue" with *The Society of the Spectacle* at the level of (art) objects, which Claire Fontaine illustrate by wrapping the jacket for *Society of the Spectacle* around a brick, suggesting that direct action might resonate with words, the artist collective take their reference from the

Italian feminist analysis of labour and gender, also evoked in the just cited text, "Ready-Made Artist and Human Strike."

In what follows, I trace the way in which Claire Fontaine re-pose the questions of feminist agency, feminist determination, feminist autonomy, and chance in relation to economic determination in the face of the total administration of everyday life through the lens of Italian Marxist feminism. I describe a handful of the collective's objects made in homage to a key figure of Italian feminism, in order to also present the histories and theories that constitute this particular matrix of feminist politics.

To begin, and to supplement the artist's self-description cited above, Claire Fontaine is an artist that is in fact a collective comprised of two people who identify as one, notable above all for their explicit, indeed insistent, feminist and anticapitalist position. Founding herself (or itself or themselves) in 2004, after the anticapitalist anti-G8 uprisings in Genoa in 2002, and growing partly in the ashes of another radical-left collective in Italy and France that wrote and disseminated text under the name Tiqqun,[6] Claire Fontaine have come to cast a wide and long shadow over the art world. While they show in galleries, that shadow is felt most at commercial art fairs and biennials—showcases of contemporaneity that are marked by historical contradictions of their own: art fairs like Art Basel and Art Basel Miami Beach, and those historically legitimate World's Fair–like displays that bask in the glow of historical sanctimony, including the Venice Biennale of 2005, Istanbul Biennial of 2011, and Manifesta of 2012, held in Palermo. These are sites offered as the cultural vehicles of new counterhegemonic developments, which could more accurately be described as barely mediated vehicles for the most hegemonic social forces of all: the market-state nexus.

The art fair in particular finds its motivation in the grey indeterminate area between academic cultural discourse, on the one hand, and advertising and product positioning that marks the high-end market of the art world, on the other. Claire Fontaine's position finds traction through their antagonistic relationship to these environments.

Claire Fontaine locate their intellectual roots in the originary matrix of Rivolta Femminile (Women's Revolt), a group founded by two feminists, art historian Carla Lonzi and artist Carla Accardi, in Rome in 1970. Rivolta Femminile marked their activity with the publication of a body of manifestos, among which "Sputiamo su Hegel" ("Let's Spit on Hegel," 1970) is perhaps the most familiar in the Anglophone world.[7] Rivolta Femminile's formation contributed to both the Movimento di Liberazione Della Donna (Women's Liberation Movement) in 1972 and Lotta Femminista (Feminist Struggle), also in 1972.[8]

In 2015, Claire Fontaine produced a handful of works dedicated to Lonzi: art critic, feminist theorist, and "leading figure of Italy's first consciously separatist collective Rivolta Femminile."[9] The first of the five works in Claire Fontaine's Lonzi series that I will describe here is a silkscreen image of Marilyn Monroe, or rather, Andy Warhol's iconic and idiomatic presentation of her face in his own practice in the medium of silkscreen. Claire Fontaine have taken this canonized image and stencilled in spray paint across it the words "we are all clitoridian women." These words, in turn, are drawn from Lonzi's essay "La donna clitoridea e la donna vaginale" ("The Clitoridean Woman and the Vaginal Woman"),[10] which occasioned Claire Fontaine's own essay "We Are All Clitoridian Women: Notes on Carla Lonzi's Legacy," written and published in 2013, two years before the objects in question were made.[11] Lonzi's words overwriting Warhol's image of the American movie star is charged with contradiction, addressing the historicity of the *miracolo italiano* (the Italian economic miracle). These years cross 1949–69, when Italy experienced a late and accelerated modernity characterized by the mass exodus of labouring bodies from the rural south to fuel the factories of the industrial north, which were financed by American capital under the auspices of the Bretton Woods program and Marshall Plan. These Cold War–era American programs and plans were explicitly designed to keep communism at bay by enabling a flourishing economy through forms of financial assistance, loans, and gifts. Lonzi's own politics—although critical of both the Communist Party for its failure to address patriarchal structures of property in the form of women and what she called the proletariat's reformist tendencies when it came to women—had emerged from her historical affiliation with the left and with the Communist Party, with which many in the Italian left broke in the 1950s and '60s in protest of its ultimate complicity with American capital and with the postwar boss class of the *miracolo*. Lonzi's words form a dynamic dialectical relation with Warhol's image, suggesting a kind of sexuality of the surface in keeping with the superficiality of American pop art associated with American capital, forging its cultural arm such that pop came to be synonymous with capitalist realism. Notably, the stencilled letters composing words are arranged, spaced, and distributed such that "women" is divided into "wo" and "men," with the latter fragment becoming its own word, "men," over the entire last line, suggesting a kind of indeterminacy in which "women" does not break from "men" without compromise, without possible inscription into the very economy from which it wishes to break: "men."

But of course it's much more complicated than that. As Claire Fontaine point out in their essay, Lonzi's project came to focus on the problem of women's autonomy within the narrow twin parameters of, on the one hand, patriarchy and, on the other, the new postwar capitalism of the *miracolo*, oriented to American culture and ultimately funded by American dollars—a problem she came to formulate as one of resistant, independent consciousness, or *autocoscienza*.[12] To make this move, Lonzi had to have already accepted that not only was the personal political but indeed that the political was personal, such that collective determinations of state and market would come to impinge on the intimate qualities of women's everyday lives, insofar as women were relegated to the domain of the private and intimate by a state-to-market axis interested in placing women there. Claire Fontaine note that, in "The Clitoridean Woman and the Vaginal Woman": *Lonzi demolishes psychoanalytic fallacies regarding women's pleasure. She reveals how an autonomous feminine sexuality, one that dissociates the sex act from reproduction—even within heterosexual relationships—can be the starting point for a different type of subjectivization for women. For Lonzi, being a clitoridian woman has not only sexual connotations, but* existential and political *connotations as well.*[13] Lonzi's work comes to stand in for a form of autonomy against a compound masculinist determination: not state or market but rather the state-to-market relationship enabling the labour-to-capital relationship in which women are doubly captured. Sexuality, and sexual pleasure, are noted as those interstices of everyday life through which women are socialized and submitted to the rational disciplinary order of the reproduction of social life, of "things as they are," namely, of counterrevolutionary tendencies to maintain the status quo. In this sense, sexual and political autonomy are interlaced. Lonzi says of the clitoridean woman: "Finally, in full possession of her sexuality, no one can convince her that her efforts will be rewarded and that the pleasure of a moment will be worth a life of slavery."[14]

This "slavery," in turn, is the economy where women, women's work, and women's time are devalued in order to remain unremunerated while enabling the conditions for the possibility of men's work to be "counted" as value productive, and to thereby be awarded and remunerated.[15]

The next objects in Claire Fontaine's Lonzi series offer a way to actually act against this economy of gendered slavery. The collective take Lonzi's books' covers and wraps them around bricks (Plates 3 & 4). The joke here may be the relationship between text and action in the age-old conundrum among Marxists about the relation between theory and praxis, wherein Marx was to have taken the idealist dialectic of Georg Wilhelm Friedrich Hegel and turned it on its feet to make concrete changes in the political social field. Here, Claire Fontaine suggest that Lonzi's books can be efficacious in the world of direct action—as weapons. The collective made four "brickbats," all in 2015, using Lonzi's book covers and titles: *Taci, anzi parla*; *La presenza dell'uomo nel femminismo*; *È già politica*; and, of course, *Sputiamo su Hegel: La donna clitoridea e la donna vaginale*. The last, while offering the titles for which Lonzi is best known, returns to the usual bind between theory and praxis. Again, if Marxism and the workers' struggle aimed to turn dialectics into an effective mode of historical struggle, then the revolutionary struggle populated by men missed the boat. It failed to locate the source of value—that which was being contested after all in the dialectics of distribution and abolishing of labour—in women's (feminized) daily labour. Ostensibly, the book included in Claire Fontaine's artwork could be read, were the viewer to look up the title elsewhere, and could thereby serve as a weapon to destroy the actual limits and barriers that enslave women.

Or, even more immediately, the book itself could be weaponized—thrown like a brick.

While the collective's work, especially the idiom they have worked out with book covers and bricks, returns to this limit and spur that is the interval or interstice between knowledge and action, Lonzi's name and voice situate the divide as a problem specific to women's political self-realization as individuals and as a class. "Let's Spit on Hegel" is especially passionate about the need to overcome the masculinist fetish for authors, theories, and ideas, in the expectation that words might finally be used to *do* something about the master-slave dialectic Hegel was so keen to expound.

Lonzi's Legacy

In 1970, Lonzi wrote the manifesto-like statement "Let's Spit on Hegel," in which she dialectically traces back women's subordination to the master of dialectics, Hegel. She thereafter founded Rivolta Femminile with painter Carla Accardi, with whom she ran a publishing house and space for the presentation of artwork (1970–75). While continually resonant in relation to both the Italian art movement of the 1960s and '70s, including *arte povera* and its reception, and to Italian Marxist revisions of Marxian theories of labour and revolutionary praxis (in particular its feminist iteration), Lonzi's work has more recently been revived in an Anglophone context, including as part of Claire Fontaine's project. On the face of it a bibliographic reference, Lonzi's work rather operates as a plinth to the collective's diagnosis of the present in a corpus of art founded on text as much as object. While "Ready-Made Artist and Human Strike" avows its debt to Italian feminism, the collective has focused on Lonzi's work on occasion to emphasize her role in forging a bridge to discussions outside the debate on labour, to women across class yet nonetheless bound to the logic of labour, as described by another Italian feminist scholar, Leopoldina Fortunati: occluded, unremunerated, foundational to the social reproduction of everyday life in capitalism. In a 2013 essay on Lonzi, Claire Fontaine emphasize Lonzi's attention to the way power is structured through time and task performance: "In the preface to her journal, Lonzi gives her final word on the feminine skill of multitasking: 'For me, doing one thing has a value because it prevents me from doing two.'"[16]

At first glance, the statement reads as almost elitist in its dismissal of maintenance work, multitasking, and "women's work." However, its quiddity in articulating the degree to which changes in labour determine all social relations outside the immediate space of production rests on two entwined but ultimately autonomous lines of argumentation drawn from *operaismo* (workerism):[17] that in the de- and recomposition of labour required by the factories in the post–World War II *miracolo*, deskilled labour wasn't the vehicle of workers' self-realization that Vladimir Lenin promised it would be, but rather a way for capital to extract more value from the working day. The Italian feminists' analysis of the working day was tightly entwined with the Italian ultra-left (those rethinking Marxism against the Italian Communist Party or state communisms understood to be counterintuitively allied with capitalism through emphasis on value-productive labour over workers' own interests), which analyzed skill as that manipulatively divested of the modern worker in the interest of capital.

Romano Alquati, part of a group rethinking labour in relation to capital, noted the strange emerging dynamic between skill, discipline, and professionalization. He described the way in which rationalized work creates hierarchies and evacuates the creative agency of workers on all levels. He writes of factory labour directly observed on Fiat's and Olivetti's production floors: *The fundamental contradiction seems to be precisely that internal to technical productive rationalization, which creates mere executants and then in order to proceed must give them "responsibility" which systematically separates and counterposes levels and then has to join them all together again in a rigid system that annuls both the individuals and groups that comprise it, posing shops, teams etc as minimum technological units. This promotes a professional career and annuls professions.*[18] But the observation was already dialectical. If labour in the late twentieth century was organized by managerial discipline engineered to squeeze the most value from the least possible amount of labour, surely there would be ways to turn that discipline against the system. This drew Alquati and his peers into a fundamental disagreement with Lenin and Leninist communism. While within communism the worker was historically understood to realize themselves *as* a worker, Alquati et al. saw organized work as the very problem, insofar as disciplinary labour would only ever function against the worker and in the interest of the capitalist classes, with work and communism essentially being antithetical. This required a re-reading of Marx. In the process of this re-reading, the faction of the Italian left that parted with the Italian Communist Party inverted the Bolsheviks' understanding of discipline. Alquati saw discipline as that which separates the worker from themselves, weakening agency, while Lenin advocated for organizational forms, believing that industrial production would impress discipline on an unruly agrarian mass. Alquati theorized that spontaneity and indiscipline was what capital feared most, despite the granular hold it had on individual and collective labouring psyches and bodies through the very structure of task performance itself. On the topic of skill as that which is to be differentiated from value-productive task performance, and its relationship to labour and discipline, the Italian Marxists critical of the Italian Communist Party's acquiescence to American capital could not have located themselves at a greater distance from Leninism and Bolshevism, indeed from historical communism.

Enter the politics of the strike, of interruption and sabotage, against the capitalist extraction of value from disciplinary, often unskilled or deskilled, task performance.

The Human Strike and the Feminist Movement in Italy, 1970

Claire Fontaine's frequent evocation of the term "strike" in both their object production and textual production, and specifically "the human strike" of their text "Ready-Made Artist and Human Strike," emerges from the struggles characterizing the fraught labour-to-capital relationship of the *miracolo italiano*. While profits were soaring and seemingly buying Italy out of the devastation of World War II—Italy being the terrain over which the Allied and Axis powers enacted the most brutal aerial attacks—labour was beginning to understand that it had received the raw end of the deal. The exodus from the agrarian south to the industrial north to lubricate the factories and provide labour had done much for national industry and banking, but little for the worker. In 1962, workers rioted in Turin. The event, known as the Piazza Statuto riots, initiated fifteen years of struggle, of class war, ending with the suppression of protest under the rubric of "terror" in 1977.[19] In that time, the Italian far left formed, elaborating an informal movement comprising many movements, running through the period associated with *operaismo* to Autonomia (Workers' Autonomy), so named for the split within the historical Italian workers' movement that precipitated a proportionately large exodus from the Communist Party that they felt had betrayed them and from union representation (indeed, from representation in general), as well as external constraints issued by the state-market nexus associated with the misnamed *miracolo*.

Arte povera (1968–75) is the art movement most frequently associated with the era and with the dramatic struggles specific to that geopolitical arena. But those same years also saw the proliferation of a dynamic, rich, and complex spectrum of feminisms. While most of these feminisms interrogated the wage and "primitive accumulation" of the unremunerated women's work that enabled the worker to produce value on the factory floor, Lonzi herself veered to an exploration of the intersubjective, social, psychosexual, and collective existential dynamics structuring everyday life along the axis of the primary gender binary. Claire Fontaine have explored the central importance of this aspect of Lonzi's thinking in the aforementioned "We Are All Clitoridian Women" text.[20]

The present analysis will focus on Claire Fontaine's essay "Ready-Made Artist and Human Strike: A Few Clarifications" for this reason, for shifting the parameters of feminism from the psychoanalytically theorized sexual difference (drawing upon Jacques Lacan, also indebted to Hegel via Alexandre Kojève et al.) to a materialist analysis of the social field revolving around the wage relation. This exploration necessarily entails stepping back to address the history of class struggle from which Italian feminism derived, in distinction from other feminisms, due to its preoccupation with wage relations.

"Ready-Made Artist and Human Strike" looks to the Bolognian women's collective's writings of 1976 for its key point. That year, the Bolognian collective for a domestic salary wrote: "If we strike, we won't leave unfinished products or untransformed raw materials; by interrupting our work we won't paralyze production, but rather the reproduction of the working class. And this would be a real strike even for those who normally go on strike without us."[21] Claire Fontaine gloss this assertion as follows: *This type of strike that interrupts the total mobilization to which we are all submitted and that allows us to transform ourselves, might be called a human strike, for it is the most general of general strikes and its goal is the transformation of the informal social relations on which domination is founded. The radical character of this type of revolt lies in its ignorance of any kind of reformist result with which it might have to satisfy itself. By its light, the rationality of the behaviors we adopt in our everyday life would appear to be entirely dictated by the acceptance of the economic relationships that regulate them. Each gesture and each constructive activity in which we invest ourselves has a counterpart within the monetary economy or the libidinal economy. The human strike decrees the bankruptcy of these two principles and installs other affective and material fluxes. Human strike proposes no brilliant solution to the problems produced by those who govern us if it is not Bartleby's maxim: "I would prefer not to."*[22]

Readymade

Claire Fontaine refer to themselves as "a ready-made artist stripped of use-value who intervenes in a world." What might this mean? Having taken part in numerous art world conventions, such as the aforementioned Venice and

Istanbul biennials, and having made some witty objects that function as biting retorts to canonized objects of official contemporary art, Claire Fontaine's strength lies in their textual production. Their best known, well-circulated texts offer a lucid history of twentieth-century art on the one hand, and radical politics of the 1960s and '70s on the other, to recast the cultural matrix of the present. They begin by locating symptoms of the historical unconscious in the present and its seeming impasse: "The dispossession that we thus feel with regard to our presumed identity is the same as that, which we feel when facing history, now that we no longer know how to somehow take part in it."[23]

As signalled in the title of the collective's most frequently circulated piece of writing, and equally indicated by the objects displayed in the spaces of art reception as art (often banal objects of quotidian and practical use available in hardware shops, such as tools to fix and/or break locks), Claire Fontaine pick up the legacy of the Duchampian readymade. They rehearse the ways in which skill, originality, creativity, and authorial intention are displaced and dissolved in the expanded field of capitalist reproduction. The circuitry and processes of production, distribution, and consumption create a seamless feedback system that, resonating in the social field, disciplines all aspects of social life to support, enable, and service the extraction of value from the worker through labour—regardless of however widely dispersed production sites and distribution chains are in the present global financial order. Rather than collapsing into either melancholic or nihilistic rhetoric, the collective's text turns to recent history to suggest the possible continuity of revolutionary time in the present.

Claire Fontaine draw on a falsified—falsified by official history—sense of the failure of the revolutionary past in order to suggest that the recovery of revolutionary, explicitly feminist, history is in itself a way to *recognize*, to become perceptive of and alert to nascent struggles in the present, an operation to which I will return. They turn, then, to the period marked by the fight for autonomy on the part of the *expanded* working class of the 1960s and '70s in Italy. They take on the Italian expression "*gli anni di piombo*" or "the years of lead," used to describe the volatile struggle between labour and capital marking—sometimes erupting—into full blown class war in the streets. As labour scholar Steve Wright notes of this moniker: "The fact that these years of unheard-of collective creative fertility, both in terms of life forms and intellectual production, passed into the history books as 'the years of lead' tells us a lot about what we are supposed to forget."[24] And what we are supposed to forget are the two revolutionary developments of this era in Italy: feminism and forms of independent expression on the part of the working class and those dispossessed by capital, and then that element of the demographic that included both: women.

Italy's "Hot Autumn" of 1969 commenced with strikes at Fiat factories and developed into the "Creeping May" of 1969–77— "creeping" because of its duration and referring to France's May '68— spilling out of factories and into demographics with no immediate experience of the assembly line (students, the unemployed). Writers associated with the Italian ultra-left have on occasion tried to map Italy's radical years against the better-known (to the Anglophone world) radical years of France in the 1960s. Mario Tronti, for example, has attempted to differentiate Italy's Creeping May from France's May 1968 by emphasizing the fundamental economic revolution at stake in Italy in contradistinction to France's cultural revolution, characterizing the latter as "a *cultural* transition and a [merely] generational changing of the guard rather than a movement of politicized class struggle."[25] In Tronti's words, the issue in Italy was not "anti-authoritarianism, but anti-capitalism, [which] made a substantive criticism of 1968 in advance."[26]

Italy's May '68: A Creeping May, 1969–77

Tronti and politician and Marxist theorist Raniero Panzieri, who together began the journal *Quaderni Rossi* (Red Notebooks) in 1961, attempted a re-reading of Marxist theory and reimagining of Marxist praxis responsive to the particular contingencies of Italy throughout the 1950s and '60s. This praxis came to involve a form of low-grade civil war in the arena of waged labour, on the factory floor. Rather than emphasizing work as a site of potential emancipation and self-realization for the worker, the ultra-left, declaring its autonomy from the Italian Communist Party, came to call for direct forms of sabotage on the factory floor while also theorizing the conditions for the possibility of dismantling forms of valorization beyond the factory floor. Tronti's hope was to radicalize the "potential" of the Paris barricades.

Those accounts of the *anni di piombo* struggles, such as those of philosopher Antonio Negri,[27] now dominant in Anglophone accounts also place emphasis on rethinking the potential political role of the unwaged. Negri shifted the problem onto ontological questions about the political subject. Autonomia, as Negri and later other theorists (such as Paolo Virno and Franco "Bifo" Berardi) presented it, thus incorporated aspects of the Situationist International, the Frankfurt School, and a workerist class critique with anarchist praxis. As a theoretical formation, Autonomia departed from *operaismo*'s emphasis on the factory floor as a site of value production informing the *totality* of life under capital (and not just on the factory floor) by extending its analysis to include both the waged and the unwaged. Political theory was thereby finally motivated to rethink the source of capital not only in labour but also in gender, the latter understood to be determinative and determined by nonremunerated work enabling remunerated work. Tronti theorizes the "social factory" of work in the expanded social field, locating both the results and the conditions for the possibility of the labour-to-capital system outside the immediate process of production and the commodity itself.[28]

Turning once again to "Ready-Made Artist and Human Strike," Claire Fontaine confronts the crisis of democracy reflected in the art "world" with startling frankness by going to the source of value: production. They register the foreclosure of a historical model of value production in which the artist could still claim autonomy from fully subsumed industrial production at the level of object making. Tracing the present to the charged relationship between value and (non-)workers (in keeping with Leopoldina Fortunati and others working in the context of Italian feminism), they conclude that at this historical moment "the only way of assisting creation is to protect those who create nothing and are not even interested in art."[29] Claire Fontaine's statement recalls philosopher Theodor W. Adorno's anguished, dialectically motivated proclamation that there could be no lyric poetry after Auschwitz.[30] He, however, made the case for why literature has to resist this verdict, and concluded by insisting that it is all the more imperative to practice a form of lyricism to push against cynicism.

In 1972, Fortunati elaborated and radicalized Tronti's work by arguing that primary social reproduction serves *already*—and prior to value extraction through labour on the factory floor—as a form of daily primitive accumulation silently operating behind the wage and enabling it: the hidden abode beneath Marx's hidden abode.[31] She posits this as a feminist problem, one at once hinging on gender and reproducing its order in the interest of capitalism. For the worker does not show up at the factory door without being "produced" by the domestic sphere in which women are set to task making babies and keeping males, workers and potential workers, fit for work by meeting their immediate embodied needs. The male worker is the "product" of his mother's, and then his wife's, replication of his daily well-being, his comforts, his labour capacity.

Two texts in particular formulate the way in which "women's work" undergirds capitalist productive labour (value) by being unaccounted for within its systems of measure, that is to say, by the wage. These are feminist activists Mariarosa Dalla Costa and Selma James's *Potere femminile e sovversione sociale* (*The Power of Women and the Subversion of the Community*, 1975)[32] and Fortunati's *L'arcano della riproduzione* (*The Arcane of Reproduction*, 1981). Both locate the seat of revolutionary struggle in a *negative* relation to power and to capital. They turn to those whose survival is fully structured and determined by capital but who are nonetheless excluded from it. The contradiction in the labour-to-capital relationship originates in the nonrelationship, mediated negatively and negatively mediating capitalist reproduction. *The Power of Women and the Subversion of the Community* circumscribes the problem thus: "What has been neither clear nor assumed by the organizations of the working class movement is that precisely through the wage has the exploitation of the non-wage laborer been organized.... This exploitation has been even more effective because the lack of a wage hid it."[33] The statement, from a text first distributed as a pamphlet then published as a book (yet still making its rounds as a pamphlet at book fairs and online over the last decade or so), is striking for how it uses a kind of double negative to describe an empirical condition. While Dalla Costa and James (unlike Negri) preserve the wage as the anchoring point of their position, they emphasize the way it structures disenfranchisement from the wage as much as workers' discipline within it. The traditional terms through which to understand exploitation by the wage are turned inside out. Notably, James and Dalla Costa defer to metaphors of vision to articulate hidden conditions of actual labour: "Her role in the cycle of social production remained invisible because only the product of her labor, the laborer, was visible there."[34]

Dalla Costa and James generalize "the housewife" as the condition basic to all those occupying a position of vexed autonomy in relationship to capital yet foundational to its self-reproduction, a position replacing the historical role of an organized class. Their position is predicated on the absence of quantification in calculating the value of domestic labour that allows it to be all the more violently usurped. Women in this position live by the clock of waged time without receiving the wage or the social freedoms it buys: *That is, on a world level, it is precisely what is particular to domestic work, not only measured as number of hours and nature of work, but as quality of life and quality of relationships which it generates, that determines a woman's place wherever she is and to whichever class she belongs.*[35] Dalla Costa and James effectively replace the parameters of solidarity understood through class relation alone (class consciousness) with the position women fill by being the link between the value-productive domains of the wage on the one hand and the unwaged domain on the other—tasked with facilitating social *re*-production. One might call this "maintenance" rather than "creative work" in the parlance of the American feminist artist Mierle Laderman-Ukeles, who notes that task performance seems to be divided into "creative" or "reproductive" depending on the gender of the executor.[36] Fortunati and Dalla Costa in collaboration with James turn those terms around to excavate the relationship between labour and capital, as well as the form that relationship takes from within, in order to find the locus of gendered identity.

Gendered identity turns out to be an unstable variable. Under capitalism, gendered identity is coercively stabilized as a variable around which capital recreates itself daily beyond the factory floor. Fortunati as well as Dalla Costa and James note the way in which *she* is the very ground for the daily reproduction of *he*, who is to appear at the factory door each day ready to sell his labour power to generate surplus value in which he will not partake. To facilitate the extraction of value from labour, capital must also produce producers and consumers. It turns out that what constitutes gender in capitalism is not a quality or substance but rather a (negative) relation to market mediation on the one hand and surplus value on the other. *She* is capitalism's unseen foundation, and as such in the clearest position from which to interrupt it. In a circular process characteristic of the feedback mechanism between manufacture, consumption, and social reproduction of labour power, this structured relationship gradually heightens the gender polarization it requires: because of the way women are indirectly mediated by capitalism, they are *at once* disciplined and marginalized, however conceptually incompatible these terms may be.

Dalla Costa and James mark the shift from patriarchy to *capitalist* patriarchy in the recomposition of the labour-to-capital relation that accomplished a qualitative and quantitative change in the power dynamic, a transition they describe as moving from oppression to exploitation:

"The unfree patriarch was transformed into the 'free' wage earner, and upon the contradictory experience of the sexes and the generations was built a more profound estrangement and therefore a more subversive relation."[37] Folding the situation inside out, Dalla Costa and James see the very site of capitalist structuring—the place of production of labour power in the sphere formative of, yet hidden by, the wage form—as the place from which to launch a counterattack, a class war organized around the false binary of public and private. That binary is capitalism's most operative myth, so totalizing and pervasive as to have been unnoted by Marx. Activist and philosopher Silvia Federici, who in 1975 founded the International Wages for Housework movement in Padua with Selma James (also within the context of Automatist feminism and Lotta Feminista), notes the degree to which capitalism and its Marxist critique share a common logic vis-á-vis women: *No difference is made between commodity production and the production of the workforce. One assembly line produces both. Accordingly, the value of labor power is measured by the value of the commodities (food, clothing, housing) that have to be supplied to the worker, to "the man," so that he can renew his life process.*[38] Again, this seeming political paradox results directly from contradiction within capitalism. Insight into this apparently paradoxical condition became an entry point to extrapolate a notion of feminized work, which in turn became one way of disarticulating class struggle from its exclusive dependence on the wage.[39] Claire Fontaine explicitly acknowledge Leopoldina Fortunati, Carla Lonzi, and Mariarosa Dalla Costa as the framework for their own writing, in pamphlets frequently disseminated at international art fairs, book fairs, and online throughout the 2000s.[40] As Claire Fontaine make clear in "Ready-Made Artist and Human Strike," the vanishing point of their project is the two-faced problem: concealed labour, and the specific way in which the labour-to-capital relationship structures subjectivities as it decomposes and recomposes to render autonomous resistance newly possible or impossible.

Claire Fontaine build their prognosis of the present and its potential for the future around this logic of inverse power relations, picking up on the concrete potential of the "negative," as Fortunati formulated it in a metaphor wherein she evokes the relationship of a film negative to the photographic image (those captured in a wage relation without being recipients of the wage or part of value-productive work). The problem, then, is not only one of latency but of dependency on a hidden, originary matrix structured by the wage.

What Claire Fontaine frames in their own practice and is articulated in "Ready-Made Artist and Human Strike" is the fundamental insight of Italian feminism, historically elaborated in the context of proletarian struggles in which the traditional understanding of class *could no longer inhere*. In particular, the collective's text resurfaces the question of the revolutionary subject and of class consciousness in a way foreclosed by postmodern theories of aporia (the question of authorship and identity Claire Fontaine raise to argue against—a rhetorical strategy they share with the better-known Tiqqun collective).

The part of Claire Fontaine's oeuvre to date that is not rooted exclusively in textual strategies revolves around the exploration of the term "general strike." Through the decade 2005–15, Claire Fontaine staged numerous projects, including constructed objects, often including the word "strike" presented in the collective's idiomatic fluorescent tubing.[41] This preoccupation with the strike situates itself in the institutionalized context of the art fair. Given the metabolic rate of late capital in general and the velocity of circulation in its cultural arm in particular, the "general strike" has come up in the numerous clearing houses of cultural production: the biennials, the art fairs, the convention-type exhibitions modelled on the World's Fairs of the late nineteenth century, when Paris and London were undergoing rapid modernization, or recomposition, of labour pools.

Human Strike

Claire Fontaine's implicit conclusion that there can be no art under capitalism nonetheless fails to echo so many modernist prohibitions. Unlike Adorno's pronouncement that there can be no lyric poetry after Auschwitz, Claire Fontaine's claim is not that art is impossible due to ethical or existential questions, as though protest is to withhold one's artistic genius. Rather, the collective notes a much more practical problem, namely that the condition under which the making of a work is even possible is itself under extreme duress. It is simply not possible to *make* a work outside the parameters determined by the vicissitudes of market determination at any given moment. The collective reframes the problem by turning its angle of analysis to the point of view of the artist who is expected to deliver expressive or alert consciousness within the determinations of a support that is itself the index of subsumption, a readymade. Be it canvas, video, digital media, or even performance, happenings, and participatory events, the artist must on some level acknowledge (self-reflexively) the labouring bodies of others elsewhere that produce the materials that constitute the artist's material support (digital device, neon lighting, commodity object resituated as "art") through the fact of its manufacture. Claire Fontaine write: *Located in the forced intimacy between human beings and all sorts of vulgar and odious objects, which constitute the daily life of the majority under advanced capitalism, this continuity has produced effects on our subjectivities far more pernicious than those Marx was able to describe. Reification, real subsumption, and alienation say nothing to us of the lack of words afflicting us when faced with our evident familiarity with commodities and their language, as well as our simultaneous incapacity to name the most simple facts of life, such as political events, for a start.*[42]

Against this the collective poses the term "strike": *This type of strike that interrupts the total mobilization to which we are all submitted and that allows us to transform ourselves might be called a human strike, for it is the most general of general strikes and its goal is the transformation of the informal social relations on which domination is founded. By its light, the rationality of the behaviors we adopt in our everyday life would appear to be entirely dictated by the acceptance of the economic relationships that regulate them. Each gesture and each constructive activity in which we invest ourselves has a counterpart within the monetary economy or the libidinal economy. The human strike decrees the bankruptcy of these two principles and installs other affective and material fluxes.*[43]

Outside the culture sector, a general strike is an organized refusal to work on the part of a critical mass of labourers. It is a tactic attendant upon and responsive to the specific capitalist form of accumulation, in which lives are reduced to "congealed" labour measured in clock time and conjugated with currency. Salient to the logic of the strike is the recognition that violent and inhumane conditions for workers who produce value for others are not a matter of ethical social choices but an inherent function of capitalist means irrespective of human agency. Having variously emerged and receded as a broadly recognized means of resistance since the mid-nineteenth century, a general strike has the potential to precipitate capitalism's *inherent tendency to crisis.*

Divorcing wages from work (calibrated against the clock, that metaphor of rationalization), Italian Marxist feminism sought to disable not only the system of primitive accumulation daily rehearsed in the private sphere that makes capital possible but also, fundamentally, the logic of quantification subtending general equivalence. It had become clear to the generation coming of age to be the supply of workers to the factory—or to be the supply of managers to its social mediator, the university—that work had nothing to do with choices, with ethics, or with individual will, much less self-realization. It was simply part of a system of value in which the human itself was a disposable by-product. But the insight was arrived at, and acted on, first by feminists in Italy associated with Wages for Housework.

Without its *invisible* structural support, there would be no labour-to-capital relationship to speak of, no labour power, and therefore no value source; there would be no capitalism. Artist and writer Maya Gonzalez finds the quasi-totalizing relationship between women's work (e.g., indirectly market mediated and not necessary value productive but formative of the value relation) and value in Dalla Costa's dialectical articulation: "As Dalla Costa bluntly put it: '*there has never been a general strike.*'"[44] The prognosis is all the more blunt for being posited negatively. A strike—a refusal to produce value, in the private as well as the public sphere, "women's work" as well as waged work—has never in fact occurred. Were a general strike to (have) happen(ed), the entire capitalist fabric would come undone, would be unravelled.

To conclude: How might the question of authorship, that question that preoccupied a generation (structuralism;

poststructuralism) be a historical problem specific only to advanced capitalism? Claire Fontaine reorients the familiar questions back to the obfuscated hidden abode. The structuralist and new historicist query into the subject in language, variously crystallized by Michel Foucault's "What Is an Author" (1969) and Roland Barthes's "The Death of the Author" (1967), acknowledges the artwork's split condition. Both essays present the speaker as making a set of seeming choices of speech (*langue*) in a predetermined field of language (*parole*). While "Ready-Made Artist and Human Strike: A Few Clarifications" certainly avows its debt to this discursive legacy, it breaks the limits set by that legacy. Claire Fontaine's text insists on the historical facts *and* historicity of production to argue that authorship, far from a category to be cleverly dismantled, is itself the fetish to abolish, is already historically obsolete in the face of capitalist subsumption. This reopens the path to the hidden abode, intimate and elsewhere, the anonymous toil constitutive of the material support beneath the author function. Quite literally, who produced the woven fabric of the canvas support under so many masterpieces of modernism? How is this form of labour itself gendered as much as it is dependent on the division of gender within capitalism? Finally, drawing the question of authorship back through that of reification at the level of real abstraction, Claire Fontaine's work asks how the question of real abstraction is also a question of gender in the age of "repressive tolerance."

This text was first published in Hilary Robinson and Maria Elena Buszek, eds., *A Companion to Feminist Art* (Hoboken, NJ: Wiley-Blackwell, 2019).

1. Karl Marx, "The Buying and Selling of Labour-Power," chapter 6 in *Capital, Volume 1* (1867), https://fillip.ca/1xmk.
2. Nancy Fraser, "Behind Marx's Hidden Abode," *New Left Review*, no. 86 (March–April 2014), 55–72.
3. "Bio," Claire Fontaine's website, https://fillip.ca/81tp, accessed November 16, 2018.
4. Claire Fontaine, "Ready-Made Artist and Human Strike: A Few Clarifications," https://fillip.ca/jhg0, accessed November 16, 2018.
5. Guy Debord, *The Society of the Spectacle* (Detroit: Black and Red, 1970), 191. For a sense of Debord's interest in the Italian context and the "Italian Question," see Guy Debord, "The State of Spectacle," trans. Wendy Greenberg and John Johnston, in *Autonomia: Post-Political Politics*, ed. Sylvère Lotringer and Christian Marazzi (Los Angeles: Semiotext(e), 2007).
6. One "issue" of *Tiqqun*, divided, translated, and disseminated as short books in English, situates the historical conditions for the emergence of the collective in Italy's Creeping May. See *Introduction to Civil War*, trans. Alexander R. Galloway and Jason E Smith (Los Angeles: Semiotext(e), 2010) and *This Is Not a Program*, trans. Joshua David Jordon (Los Angeles: Semiotext(e), 2011). Both appeared (in French) as *Tiqqun*, no. 2 (2001). See also Jason E. Smith. "The Politics of Incivility: Autonomia and Tiqqun," *Minnesota Review*, no. 75 (Fall 2010): 119–32.
7. Carla Lonzi, "Let's Spit on Hegel" (1970), in *Italian Feminist Thought: A Reader*, ed. Paola Bono and Sandra Kemp (Oxford: Blackwell, 1991).
8. Claire Fontaine, in conversation with the author, September 2012. For an overview of the class struggle of 1962–77 from which Italian Marxist Feminism emerged, see Steve Wright, "Potere Operaio," in *Storming Heaven* (London: Pluto, 2002), 134. The authoritative source on Italian Feminism remains Bono and Sandra, *Italian Feminist Thought: A Reader*.
9. Maude Anne Bracke, introduction to *Women and the Reinvention of the Political: Feminism in Italy, 1968–1983* (New York: Routledge, 2014), 5.
10. Carla Lonzi, "La donna clitoridea e la donna vaginale" ["The Clitoridean Woman and the Vaginal Woman"], in *Sputiamo su Hegel. La donna clitoridea e la donna vaginale e altri scritti* [*Let's Spit on Hegel: The Clitoridean Woman and the Vaginal Woman and Other Writings*] (Milan: Scritti di Rivolta Femminile, 1974), 19.
11. Claire Fontaine, "We Are All Clitoridian Women: Notes on Carla Lonzi's Legacy," *e-flux journal*, no. 47 (September 2013), https://fillip.ca/97wm.
12. Claire Fontaine, "We Are All Clitoridian Women."
13. Claire Fontaine, "We Are All Clitoridian Women."
14. Lonzi, "La donna clitoridea e la donna vaginale," 19. Cited in Claire Fontaine, "We Are All Clitoridian Women."
15. Leopoldina Fortunati, "Learning to Struggle: My Story between Workerism and Feminism," in

"Workers' Inquiry," ed. Asad Haider and Salar Mohandesi, special issue, *Viewpoint*, no. 3 (September 30, 2013), viewpointmag.com.

16. Claire Fontaine. "We Are All Clitoridian Women."

17. See Wright, *Storming Heaven*.

18. Romano Alquati, *Scritti Sulla Fiat* (Milan: Feltrinelli, 1975), 69. Translation taken from Evan Calder Williams, "Reading Romano Alquati," in "Workers' Inquiry," ed. Asad Haider and Salar Mohandesi, special issue, *Viewpoint*, no. 3 (September 30, 2013).

19. See Wright, *Storming Heaven*.

20. See also Carla Lonzi, "Let's Spit on Hegel" (1970), in Bono and Kemp, *Italian Feminist Thought: A Reader.*

21. Bolognian women's collective, quoted in Claire Fontaine, "Ready-Made Artist and Human Strike."

22. Claire Fontaine, "Ready-Made Artist and Human Strike." See also Claire Fontaine, "Human Strike in the Field of the Libidinal Economy," https://fillip.ca/23pw.

23. Claire Fontaine, "Ready-Made Artist and Human Strike."

24. Claire Fontaine, "Ready-Made Artist and Human Strike."

25. Mario Tronti, "Our Operaismo," trans. Eleanor Chiari, *New Left Review*, no 73 (January–February 2012), 127.

26. Tronti, "Our Operaismo," 136.

27. For a thorough account of the way in which Negri's position came to "represent Italy" in the most interesting post-1968 discourse in France, see François Dosse, *Gilles Deleuze and Felix Guattari: Intersecting Lives*, trans. Deborah Glassman (New York: Columbia University Press, 2010). See also Adam Schatz, "Desire Was Everywhere," *London Review of Books*, December 16, 2010.

28. Mario Tronti, "Social Factory," in *Workers and Capital* (1966), available online as a chapter of *Operaio e Capitale*, https://fillip.ca/hn48; and Mario Tronti, "The Strategy of Refusal," in Lotringer and Marazzi, *Autonomia: Post-Political Politics*.

29. Claire Fontaine, "Ready-Made Artist and Human Strike."

30. Theodor W. Adorno, *Notes to Literature,* Trans. Shierry Weber Nicholson (New York: Columbia University Press, 1991).

31. Leopoldina Fortunati, *The Arcane of Reproduction: Housework, Prostitution, Labour, and Capital* (Oakland, CA: AK Press, 1996).

32. Mariarosa Dalla Costa and Selma James, *Potere femminile e sovversione sociale* (Padova: Marsilio Editori, 1972), published in English as *The Power of Women and the Subversion of the Community* (London: Falling Wall, 1975). This text has appeared as both a book and as a pamphlet distributed on the street, at book fairs, and online. See in particular its dissemination format on Petroleuse Press's website: https://fillip.ca/k9hu.

33. Dalla Costa and James, *The Power of Women.*

34. Dalla Costa and James, *The Power of Women.*

35. Dalla Costa and James, *The Power of Women.*

36. Mierle Laderman-Ukeles, "Maintenance Art: Manifesto!" (1969), in *Feminism-Art-Theory: An Anthology (1968–2014)*, ed. Hilary Robinson. (London: Blackwell, 2015), 88–90.

37. Dalla Costa and James, *The Power of Women.*

38. Silvia Federici, "Wages against Housework" (1975), in *Revolution*

at Point Zero: Housework, Reproduction and Feminist Struggle (Common Notions, PM Press, 2012). Cited in Maya Gonzalez, "The Gendered Circuit: Reading *The Arcane of Reproduction*," *View Point Magazine. Special Issue on The Workers' Inquiry* (September 28 2013), https://fillip.ca/ltgo.

39. Selma James and Silvia Federici founded Wages for Housework in London in 1975. See *Revolution at Point Zero: Housework, Reproduction and Feminist Struggle* (New York: Common Notions; Oakland, CA: PM Press, 2012).

40. Fulvia Carnevale, in discussion with the author, September, 2012.

41. See the many, various, and consistent permutations and reiterations of the collective's production of signage declaring "Strike": *STRIKE (K. font V.I.)* (2005); *Strike V. !!*, 2005–07; *Greve Humaine* (2004–).

42. Claire Fontaine, "Ready-Made Artist and Human Strike."

43. Claire Fontaine, "Ready-Made Artist and Human Strike."

44. See in this volume: Maya Gonzalez, "The Gendered Circuit: (Re)reading *The Arcane of Reproduction*," 235.

Leopoldina Fortunati
Selected Texts (1981)

Contents

Translated by Arlen Austin
and Sara Colantuono

The following selections are drawn from Leopoldina Fortunati's text *L'arcano della riproduzione: Casalinghe, prostitute, operai e capitale* (*The Arcane of Reproduction: Housewives, Prostitutes, Workers and Capital*, 1981). Composed throughout the 1970s, during a period of the author's involvement with the feminist collective Lotta Femminsita (Feminist Struggle), the work's initial publication in Italian was delayed by the crackdown on the extraparliamentary left in Italy in the late 1970s.[1] Subsequently, the political climate and intricacies of rendering the text into English caused long delays with an abridged version not published until 1995.[2] The selections collected here are new translations drafted by Sara Colantuono and Arlen Austin, which come from the first full-length presentation of Fortunati's key work in English, scheduled for release by Verso in 2025.

We have attempted to choose passages that both complement and provoke dialogue with those drawn from Carla

Lonzi and Rivolta Femminile (Women's Revolt), published elsewhere in this Folio. The projects of Fortunati and Lonzi and their respective collective engagements can be considered "incompatible" on a certain level, even as they must be read dialectically as co-constitutive of a feminist revolutionary process. Indeed, Fortunati seems to derive a certain pleasure in (mis)using Marxist categories, particularly as they were understood by the *operaisti*, in a fashion that Lonzi and her cohort repeatedly condemn as always already compromised.

We have chosen to include three passages newly translated from chapters 1, 3, and 10 of *L'arcano della riproduzione*. Selecting excerpts was a difficult task given that the whole unfolds with an extreme rigour akin to a series of musical exercises—playing through Marxian themes in a feminist key. These excerpts should serve rather as a primer than a substitute for reading the work in its entirety, and, furthermore, to truly engage with *L'arcano*, one must consider it in the context of Fortunati's entire oeuvre and her interventions in a broader theoretical, political, and historical context.[3]

However, we hope that the translations of these chapter segments offer some sense of the urgency, excitement, and feminist agency conveyed in Fortunati's original text. The first chapter, "Produzione e riproduzione: l'antitesi apparente del modo di produzione" ("Production and Reproduction: The Apparent Antithesis of the Capitalist Mode of Production"), engages in a delightful détournement of traditional Marxist narratives of the transition between pre-capitalist and capitalist modes of production, insisting that reproduction comes to be presented as a naturalized realm of freely given labour while in fact becoming newly essential to value production itself. The third chapter, "La forma capitalistica del rapporto uomo/donna" ("The Capitalist

Form of the Man-Woman Relationship") presents what is perhaps Fortunati's most scathing condemnation of what would come to be referred to, in queer and feminist theory, as "heteronormativity." Her analysis zeros in on the relation between the subject positions of men and women in familial-sexual relations in the Fordist household. The final set of excerpts, from chapter 10, "Quella strana forma di plusvalore assoluto…" ("That Strange Form of Absolute Surplus Value"), soundly critiques the tendencies of a historicist Marxist narrative by describing a "new" form of the extraction of value. Here, value is extracted not in terms of the intricacies of relative surplus value enabled by technological innovations or an innovative new organization of labour on the factory floor but in terms of the unquantifiable temporal and spatial dimensions of reproductive labour (women's work, specifically) under capitalism.

—Arlen Austin
and Sara Colantuono

1. The Lotta Femminista collective, formed in the Veneto region of northeast Italy in 1971, would divide into two groups in 1972, one of which affiliated with the International Wages for Housework movement. For a history of the group, see Louis Toupin, *Wages for Housework: A History of an International Feminist Movement, 1972–1977* (Vancouver: UBC Press; London: Pluto, 2018), 83–130.

2. Leopoldina Fortunati, *L'arcano della riproduzione: Casalinghe, prostitute, operai e capital* (Venice: Marsilio Editori, 1981). Published in English as Leopoldina Fortunati, *The Arcane of Reproduction: Housework, Prostitution,* *Labor and Capital* (Brooklyn: Autonomedia, 1995).

3. An important complement to the work, composed in the same era, and a more explicitly historical genealogy of the emergence of a distinctly capitalist form of gendered hierarchy is Fortunati's work on the witch hunts and transition to capitalism co-authored with Silvia Federici. See Silvia Federici and Leopoldina Fortunati, *Il Grande Calibano. Storia del corpo sociale ribelle nella prima fase del capitale* [The Great Caliban. History of the rebellious social body in the first phase of capital] (Milan: Franco Angeli, 1984).

Leopoldina Fortunati

Production and Reproduction

The Apparent Antithesis of the
Capitalist Mode of Production

We begin our analysis of reproduction by examining the transition from precapitalist to capitalist modes of production. This examination is crucial not only to understanding the destiny of reproduction in the new mode of production—the privileged object of our analysis—but ultimately to understanding how the entire cycle of capitalist production is articulated. The transition from precapitalist to capitalist modes of production is characterized by the fact that the economic purpose in capitalism is radically different from that of previous modes of production. If in previous modes of production the economic purpose was "the production of use values, i.e., the reproduction of the individual within the specific relation to the community in which he is its basis,"[1] in capitalism it becomes the production of exchange values, the creation of value. This means that "production appears as the aim of mankind and wealth as the aim of production" such that the "unhappiness of society," and no longer the reproduction of the individual, becomes "the purpose of political economy."[2]

Obviously, this upheaval of economic purpose has precise consequences both for the premises and conditions of the existence of capitalist accumulation and for reproduction. In the first place, this means that the individual as a commodity with exchange value comes to take precedence over the individual in their capacity as a use value. This process occurs despite the fact that the individual is the sole source capable of creating value. Indeed, it happens precisely because of this fact. Because it is only by positioning individuals as devoid of value, as pure use value, that capital is able to transform their labour power into exchange value, to force them to sell their capacity to work and thus to realize their exchange value. But the devaluation of the free worker is not merely an effect of the new mode of production. The devaluation of the free worker is also the premise and the condition of existence of the new mode of production. Capital cannot exist, it cannot become a social relationship, if it cannot confront an individual devoid of any value, and who is thus forced to sell the only commodity they possess—their labour power.

The second consequence of the transition to capitalism is that *reproduction is separated from production*. The unity existing in precapitalist modes of production between the production of use values and the reproduction of the individual—in which production is not production of use values subordinate to exchange value—has disappeared. The general process of commodity production is now separated, by the dividing line of value, from the process of reproduction, and it is now opposed to it. While the first process (production of value) appears as *creation of value*, the second (reproduction) becomes *creation of nonvalue*.[3] The production of commodities becomes *the site par excellence of capitalist production* and the laws that govern it become *the laws that characterize* capitalist production itself. On the other hand, *reproduction*, which has become the creation of "nonvalue," becomes the site of *"natural" production*. This shift corresponds to the fact that the individual has been devalued. In production, work is paid for with a wage and performed in the factory, the quintessential capitalist structure. Its organization specifically involves developing cooperation and the division of labour, as well as high levels of technological development. In reproduction, work is not paid work, it is done in the house, a structure organized in a very different fashion, one opposed to that of the factory. Its organization requires neither the development of cooperation nor the division of labour, and it demands only limited technological development. In other words, reproduction is governed *by laws that are very different*, if not opposed, to those that govern production. *Reproduction* appears as *the mirror image*, the photographic negative, of *production*.[4]

This difference between production and reproduction has been previously interpreted in multiple ways. First, as the insufficiency of development within reproduction, which is to say as the persistence of strong precapitalist vestiges in its structure. Secondly, it has been considered as a mode of production in its own right—an interpretation that would characterize reproduction as a noncapitalist realm persisting at the heart of capital. Third, it is regarded as a "natural" form of production, albeit one that is recognized as increasingly incorporated into the overall accumulation cycle or at least increasingly organized in a manner compatible with capitalist development in accordance with the rules of production. The contradictions opened by these interpretations are many: above all, that reproduction turns out not to produce value, even though it is a sector that produces commodities (the commodity of labour power specifically). Leaving aside for the moment such contradictions, let's ask ourselves: What does this separation through the dividing line of value mean? Does it really mean that reproduction is relegated to the realm of nonvalue such that it is not invested in by the laws of the new mode of production? In our opinion, it does not. This "separation" concerns only the formal plane and not the real one. In this context, by the term "formal plane" we mean how things appear, while with the term "real plane" we refer to the intrinsic nature of things.[5] Our first argument is that although *reproduction* presents itself as *creation of nonvalue*, as "natural" production, it works, as we will demonstrate below, as *creation of value*, and thus as an integral and crucial part of the capitalist accumulation process. The difference between the two is that while production is value creation and is presented as value creation, reproduction is value creation but is presented as its opposite.

In spite of the apparent separation between production and reproduction, the capitalist mode of production persists in both as a process of valorization. As we will see later, production and reproduction are indissolubly linked and interdependent, with each being the presupposition and condition of the other. Reproduction operates with more complexity when compared to production. Production is what it appears to be: it is "production of commodities." Reproduction—or, more precisely, reproduction of the commodity that is labour power—is instead forced to appear as reproduction of individuals devoid of value. This greater complexity of reproduction concerns all its aspects and elements. While productive labour is presented as the waged production of commodities, reproductive work presents itself as a natural force of social labour.[6] Although reproduction is represented as an unwaged personal service, it is, in reality, the indirectly waged labour of reproducing labour power.

In the realm of production, the exchange between worker and capital is twofold. On the formal plane, their exchange is represented as an exchange of equivalents between equals, while on that of the real, it is an exchange of nonequivalents between unequal parties. In the realm of reproduction, the exchange between worker and capital operates on *three* different levels. This splitting occurs so that these exchanges can simultaneously exist as exchanges of nonequivalents between unequal parties while, at the same time, they can avoid appearing as organized in a capitalist fashion. While an exchange appears to take place between the waged worker and the woman, in reality the exchange occurs between the woman and capital as mediated by the waged worker. In terms of the objects exchanged in this labour process, while they appear as reproductive work on the one hand and the wage on the other, in reality they consist of the relation between labour power and money operating as capital.[7]

The extreme complexity of the organization of reproduction has greatly weakened the possibility of struggle in this arena. Moreover, this complexity of organization is accompanied by an *ideological orchestration* far more richly articulated and vast than that which accompanies production. In the realm of production, organized workers' struggles soon demystified the formal arrangement that claimed equal exchange between workers and capital, making evident the real level of exploitation. In the realm of reproduction, however, women's struggles have faced more difficulty in revealing the mechanisms of exploitation because of the particular complexity of their relationship with capital.

Now if, on the level of the real, reproduction is an integral part of the capitalist production process—that is to say, the fact that the dividing line of value marks a separation between production and reproduction does not mean that both realms do not produce surplus value—then the question remains: How does capitalism really work? Our second thesis is that the *capitalist mode of production* is *formally* characterized by its dual character: production/value, reproduction/nonvalue. However, on the level of the real, the capitalist mode of production operates as creation of value throughout its entire production cycle, including that of reproduction. The capitalist mode of production formally operates on two different tracks with determinate laws governing the production cycle, and different laws governing the cycle of reproduction, while on the level of the real these two cycles share a single character. The fact that capital formally assumes a twofold nature is the very condition that allows it to work in a unified fashion, with a single logic, with a unified direction and purpose. Its twofold nature is the condition that allows capital to make use of both production and reproduction as two sides of the valorization process; to exploit both the waged worker and the unwaged woman for the creation of value.

One can understand how capital works only by starting from the hypothesis of its duplicity. Capital operates in production and in reproduction as the valorization of value by requiring each element to assume a twofold nature. This duplicity of value/nonvalue affects the entire ground of reproduction, starting from the individual. It is not only assumed by the labour of commodity production, as Marx discovered. This *doppelcharakter* is also assumed by reproduction, but in a different fashion. In the realm of reproduction such duplicity operates on the status of reproductive labour as both a commodity and a natural force of social labour. Once the sphere of reproduction has been established as creating nonvalue, it becomes possible to understand production as the site of value production. At the same time, once reproduction is established as a site for the creation of nonvalue, reproduction itself can in turn operate for the production of value.

This duplicity is played out by capital in relation to value. To be precise, this duplicity not only allows the capitalist mode of production to exist and function but allows it to function *far more productively than previous modes of production*. The capitalist mode of production is made more productive not only by lengthening the working day to the limit of human resistance in the production process but also by framing reproduction as a *natural* form of production....

…Within individuals there exists a commodity—their labour power as productive capacity—that has exchange value. The individual is thus established as *value*, even if this is true only in the moment when he exchanges such a commodity with capital. The time limitation of the individual's role as value derives from the fact that "for capital, the worker is not a condition of production, only work is," and it is not the worker that is appropriated but only work "not directly, but mediated through exchange."[8] And therefore labour, when it appears before capital, does so as a "pure use value, which is offered by its possessor himself in exchange for it, for its exchange value."[9]

The specific contradictory character of this co-presence of value and nonvalue within the individual must be understood in the context in which each characteristic seamlessly opposes itself to the other. Individuals in their status as nonvalue are opposed to themselves by capital as the commodity labour power and as exchange value. This contrast is inherent in the fact that individuals exist both in relation to their own *reproduction* and to the production of commodities. While, as the subjects/objects of reproductive labour, individuals have no value, as the subjects of productive work, they have a determined value.…

Capital does not appropriate labour through a direct exchange with the individual. As noted above, if this exchange took place directly, the individual would have inherent value. Rather, capital appropriates the use value of labour power in a more mediated fashion: indirectly, through the exchange with the individual in their capacity for production. For capital, therefore, it is the individual that creates value. The appropriation of this value by capital occurs indirectly because it is individuals themselves who self-expropriate their own value. How does this occur? At first, this value formally belongs to the worker, as the owner of labour power as productive capacity. But, since workers can only sell their capacity of production as a use value to capital, every time workers sell such capacity, they expropriate themselves of the product of their own reproductive labour, and thus of the value of such labour power as a capacity of production.…

This is the twofold nature that reproduction assumes within capitalism. Reproduction represents itself as a creation without value, but only for the individual and not for capital. For capital, reproduction is just creation of value. In other words, it is only by positioning the process of reproduction as a natural process and therefore the labour of reproduction as a natural force of social labour that reproduction costs nothing and capital can self-valorize. It is only by opposing, within the individual, the capacity of reproduction, as pure use value, to the capacity of production, as exchange value, that capital is able to simultaneously oppose labour power as use value and thus devalue the individual.

The twofold nature of capitalist individuals ultimately arises from the co-presence within them of labour power as a capacity for production and as a capacity for reproduction. Thus, as Marx realized, there is no direct correspondence between labour power and the capacity to produce commodities. Rather, there are two opposed faces of labour power: the first the capacity of commodity production, and the other that of reproduction of individuals as labour power. Divided one from the other by the line of value, the first face confronts capital as commodity, as exchange value. The second face confronts capital as non-commodity, as pure use value, as a natural force of social labour. The duplicity of the capitalist mode of production also affects labour power. It affects labour power as reproductive capacity. On the one hand, in relation to capital, reproductive capacity appears as a natural force of social labour. On the other hand, in relation to labour power as capacity of production, reproductive capacity appears as a commodity—and therefore as exchange value....

We talked above about the separation, created by the dividing line of value, between labour power as productive capacity and its reproductive capacity. Let us now consider another aspect of this separation: its sexual connotation. Productive capacity is in fact developed primarily in male workers and reproductive capacity primarily in working women. On the one hand, in fact, the liberation of labour power implies that, for the male worker, the possession of productive capacity is accompanied by the expropriation of his labour power as a capacity of reproduction. In other words, masculine labour power is fundamentally alienated from the objective condition of its own reproduction, constituted by its own labour power as a capacity of reproduction. On the other hand, the liberation of labour power implies that, for working women, possession of the capacity of reproduction is accompanied by that of production, but with the compulsion to primarily sell the first and, only subordinately, to sell the second. There is a precise difference between the destiny of the male worker and that of the woman. While for the former the possession of labour power involves their "liberation" (here understood in a literal sense as liberation from the labour of *self-reproduction*), *this liberation can also be seen as the alienation of male workers from the objective conditions of their reproduction as constituted by their own labour power in its capacity for reproduction*. For many men, it was extremely convenient to free themselves from domestic work during their marriage, but once they were widowered, for example, they found themselves very vulnerable because they had lost any ability to reproduce themselves. For women, by contrast, possession of labour power as reproductive capacity *does not* imply their liberation from productive labour.

In order to reproduce himself, the free male worker must confront, on the one hand, "the objective conditions of production as his *not-property*, as *alien property*, as *value* for-itself, as capital."[10] On the other hand, he must confront the objective conditions of his own reproduction—that is to say, labour power as capacity for reproduction—as the property of others but not as his own and not as having value *for* itself (for the natural force of social work has no value), but rather as having value *in* itself.[11]

Like the free male worker, the free female worker, in her productive capacity, confronts "the objective conditions of production as [her] not-property, as alien property, as value for-itself, as capital."[12] On the other hand, in her capacity for reproduction, she confronts the objective conditions of reproduction not as capital but as variable capital—the value of waged labour power as a capacity for production....

The woman, even when salaried, is obliged to exchange with the male worker for two basic reasons. First, because the extremely low salary she receives at a mass level does not allow her to reproduce herself independently from men. Second, because the possibility for the woman to reproduce herself is subordinate to the modalities of this exchange. For example, for a woman to have a "sentimental" relationship with a man, she must be willing to do domestic work for him.

Therefore, the process of "liberation" of labour power does not historically affect men and women in a *homogeneous fashion*. This process is *much more complex* than what Marx saw, even in his historical treatment, in which he considered this process of the liberation of "labour power" as he understood it in terms of its vicissitudes in production and therefore against the vicissitudes of the working class, made up predominantly of men. This is a process that runs along the gender division of labour and involves different paths of "liberation" of the worker, depending on whether that worker is a man or a woman. From a serf the man becomes a *salaried worker*: his liberation from feudalism also becomes the expropriation of any property other than labour power as the capacity of commodity production. The other side of his liberation is the compulsion to sell his labour power, to submit himself to the waged labour relationship. The woman has a more complex destiny: from servant of serfdom, she becomes primarily an *indirectly salaried worker*. She too is expropriated of the few properties she had—obviously much less substantial than those of a man—except for labour power, but in her there are two faces: reproductive and productive. The other side of the woman's liberation is the compulsion to sell these two commodities, to submit herself to the relationship of indirectly salaried work and to that of salaried work.

But the fundamental step in her liberation process is not that from a serf, "accessory of the earth," to a paid worker but rather that from serf to a natural social labour power. Therefore, the "liberation" of women is much more limited than that of men. Moreover, having suffered a liberation that only further confines her to her capacity of reproduction, she has also heavily mortgaged her potential liberation in her capacity of production. Without going into detail here, it is enough to think of the sorts of jobs women are primarily assigned to and the highly discriminatory wages they receive.

Even the history of *the exchange of labour with labour* in the capitalist mode of production is more complex than Marxist tradition has argued, because it too has a dual character. This exchange takes place in relation to the process of production as exchange of labour objectified as capital and living labour as use value. In relation to the process of reproduction, this exchange takes place in terms of objectified work: as the exchange value of labour power as capacity of production, and as living labour as use value.

Correspondingly, the transformation of the employment relationship in the capitalist mode of production is much more complex than it has appeared. The male worker, as we have seen, is freed to partake both in the waged employment relationship in the production process and in the indirectly salaried employment relationship in reproduction. The male worker's "liberation" to partake in the latter relationship (in the reproduction process) is a presupposition and condition of existence for his other "liberation" (in the salaried employment relationship).[13] *The liberation of labour power,* therefore, implies not only that man and woman workers, positioned as owners of their production capacity, are formally free to sell it, as a commodity, to the capitalist, but also that they are formally free to pose themselves as subjects of the exchange of reproductive labour and variable capital. Therefore, under capitalism, men and women as workers have not only won the right to work freely but also to marry freely. Such "freedom," however, applies only on a formal level; looking below appearances, it is clear that *the obligation to work* marches hand in hand with *the obligation to marry.*

Translated from Leopoldina Fortunati, *L'arcano della riproduzione: Casalinghe, prostitute, operai e capitale* (Venice: Marsilio Editori, 1981), 19–34.

1. Karl Marx, *Grundrisse: Foundations of the Critique of Political Economy,* trans. Martin Nicolaus, (London: Penguin, 1993), 485.

2. Karl Marx, "Economic and Political Manuscripts (1844)" in *Karl Marx Early Writings,* trans. Rodney Livingstone and Gregor Benton (New York: Penguin, 1992), 286. There is a significant difference between the Italian and English translations in this context, where Marx discusses Adam Smith's admission that new capitalist

political economies require widespread immiseration. In the Itailan, "*l'infelicità della società*," rather than the reproduction of the individual, becomes "*lo scopo dell'economia politica*." The Livingstone and Benton translation, whose page numbers are referenced here, renders the passage as simply: "society's distress is the goal of the economic system."

3. The phrase "*attraverso la linea del valore*," which is used throughout the text and which we have rendered as "by the dividing line of value," is a complex one with rich legacies in Italian Marxism. "*Attraverso*" also literally means "across" or "through," indicating not so much a strict partition as a division through a dialectical interrelation.

4. A recurring motif throughout the text, here Fortunati uses the phrase "*come l'immagine speculare, la fotografia rovesciata della produzione*" (like the mirror image, the inverted photograph of production).

5. Fortunati uses the terms "*piano formale*" (formal plane) and "*piano reale*" (real plane) in relation to the reflexive verbs *presentarsi* (to present) and *rappresentarsi* (to represent) in a rapidly shifting fashion to indicate contradictions between actual value production and its appearance or representation in the organization of a capitalist accumulation process.

6. Fortunati uses the phrase "*forza naturale del lavoro sociale*" (natural force of social labour), which recurs throughout the text to describe the naturalization of reproductive labour and its consignment under capitalism to the role of an unpaid, naturally occurring force inherent in the "social." The phrase strongly invokes

Marx's own discussions of capitalism's capacity to represent social processes and labour as natural aspects of its own "*autovalorizzazione*." The naturalization of labour as a productive force available for capitalist expropriation as distinct from simply living labour power was crucial to the analysis of the *operaisti*. For an analysis of this triangulation in the work of *operaismo* co-founder Mario Tronti, see in particular Massimiliano Tomba and Riccardo Bellofiore, "The 'Fragment on Machines' and the Grundrisse: The Workerist Reading in Question," in *Beyond Marx*, ed. Marcel van der Linden and Karl Heinz Roth (Leiden, Netherlands: Brill, 2014), 345–68.

7. Fortunati uses the phrase "*denaro che funziona come capitale*," which would be familiar to readers of Marx in Italian or German as indicating money's role in mediating social labour in a transition from a currency with metallic counterpart to a form of "coin" in increasingly abstracted and idealised form, acquiring its own specific form of "mirroring" of both value and commodity circulation. For example, the title for the second volume of *Capital* in the Italian edition (translated by Delio Canitmori) used by Fortunati and many of the operaisti is rendered as: "*Transformazione del denaro in capitale*." The greater complexity indicated in the text is one in which reproductive labour does not appear directly mediated by the money form.

8. Marx, *Grundrisse*, 498.

9. Marx, *Grundrisse*, 289.

10. Marx, *Grundrisse*, 498.

11. Here Fortunati uses "*non valore per se stante*" (not a value for itself) to describe the reproductive labour

primarily undertaken by women in the sexual division of labour and "*valore per se medesimo*" (having value in itself) to refer to the inherent value of reproductive labour for the waged worker. The passage from notebook five of Marx's *Grundrisse*, referenced in this and the next paragraph, describes the new conditions in which the worker confronts capital as labour power. It appears in the Italian edition translated by Ezio Grillo as "*alle condizioni oggettive della produzione dei valori di scambio come alla sua non proprietà, come a proprietà altrui, a valore per se stante, a capitale*." See also Karl Marx, *Lineamenti fondamentali della critica dell'economia politica*, vol. 2, trans. Enzo Grillo (Florence: La Nuova Italia, 1968) 126.

12. Marx, *Grundrisse*, 498.

13. Here Fortunati plays on Marx's account of the newfound "freedom" of the worker under capitalism most famously presented in Karl Marx, Part 8: "So-Called Primitive Accumulation," in *Capital, Volume 1* (1867), 873–942. In this context, the terms "liberation" and "freedom" are largely used ironically to describe dispossession of means of sustenance outside of the waged relationship. Fortunati amplifies the ironic usage of the terms here in discussion of the relation between productive and reproductive work.

Leopoldina Fortunati

The Capitalist Form of the Man-Woman Relationship

If the advent of capitalism signifies the reproduction of individuals as the production of value (even as it is represented as its opposite), what then of the man-woman relation?

The upheaval that the new mode of production causes throughout the sphere of reproduction determines specific transformations with respect to precapitalist forms of reproduction in the organization of the man-woman relationship.

In the history of capital, the exchange between man and woman has undergone enormous transformations as a result of the development of the sexual division of labour. In this process, it has changed radically: from *a working relationship with labour* in its immediately living form in the precapitalist societies it becomes *a relation of production* formalized between men and women themselves. However, this transformation does not become manifest, it does not appear immediately evident as such, because, just as all reproduction is organized in a dual fashion, the man-woman relationship also takes on a twofold nature. Although it is a productive relation, it is represented as a relationship between individuals. Given the radicality of the transformations involved, it would be more appropriate to speak of a leap, a clear break between its capitalist and precapitalist organization.

We will analyze the development of the sexual division of labour, with regard to the transformation of the male/female relation, examining the three primary forms of servitude that, as Engels claims, distinguish the three ages of civilization. Only in this way is it possible to address, in its essential features, the materialist history of the relationship between man and woman.

Our thesis is that:

1) The *difference in power* that emerges between the indirectly waged woman and the waged man is *incomparable* to that which existed between them both in slavery and in serfdom. The great leap caused by capital in the sexual division of labour means first and foremost a great leap in the division of men from women. Man is subjected to the waged working relationship, and he is formally positioned as woman's master. Woman has no formal relationship with capital, and she is positioned in a relationship of service to man. Given this situation, not only is his social power immeasurably greater than hers, but women and men each have antagonistic interests so far as their relationship is concerned. This division between man and woman is reflected, of course, in a stratification of power and hierarchy within the proletariat. Never before, as in capitalism, has man been divided from woman by such a deep chasm. But, at the same time, never as in this new mode of production have the possibilities of destruction of this power relationship been so great. Beyond any historical judgment of what such a relationship has represented, its persistence today is barbaric not only because this is robbery of unpaid labour from women, forced to live socially isolated and largely dependent on men, but also because it is functionally a robbery of unpaid labour from men. As women we are forced to work, through those we "love," for capital. That is why our "love" confirms their—and our—negation as individuals, their and our status as a commodity. The only alternative today is to reproduce and to be reproduced by others as individuals, no longer as commodities, to break, to interrupt this flow of love with its macabre face of exploitation. This is possible today. It is possible to destroy this power relationship between man and woman, to destroy the mediation of

men as capital and the state in relation to us. This, today, is the only realistic program of equality between men and women: the nonexploitation of both.

2) In precapitalist modes of production, the relationship between the slave and the serf with the woman was established in terms of the exchange of labour with labour in its immediately living form. This relationship does not usually include the exchange with sexual reproductive labour performed by the prostitute.[1] Under capitalism, the relationship between the male worker and the woman is an exchange with a twofold form. First, it is a relationship between the male waged worker and the female house worker based on the exchange of objectified labour with the living labour of production and reproduction of labour power. Second, it is a relationship between the male waged worker and the female sex worker, based on the exchange of objectified labour with the living labour of the sexual reproduction of male labour power....

What happens to the man-woman relationship with the advent of capitalism and the transformation of servants into free workers? *Unlike slavery and serfdom, in which men and women were fundamentally subjected to an identical relationship of production, capital establishes a relationship of production with men that is formally different from the one it establishes with women.* The sexual division of labour develops to such an extent that it leads to a sexual separation of the working subject of the production process from the working subject of the reproduction process. Here these two processes are separated through the dividing line of value. Man, as the primary working subject of production, is forced into a *waged labour relationship*. Woman, as the primary subject of reproduction, is forced into an *indirectly waged labour relationship.*

The relationship of production exists formally only between the male worker and capital. For this reason, the difference in power that exists between men and women in relation to capital *formally grows to an extent never reached by male and female slaves in relation to the master or by male and female serfs in relation to the feudal lord.* Such a difference emerges in its real amplitude if we consider that, while slaves reproduced themselves as "work machines" because they embodied such a role, and serfs reproduced themselves as "accessories of the earth" in their role as "accessories of the earth," women under capitalism do not reproduce the waged worker as waged workers themselves but as a natural force of social labour.

The freedom of the free worker to become a waged worker corresponds to the freedom of the woman to become an indirectly waged house worker and sex worker. What must be grasped is that it is precisely the formal diversity of the relations of production established by capital with the man and the woman that causes the profound inequality in the relationship they have with capital itself. *This inequality translates into a profound inequality between the man and the woman themselves* in the individual relationship between them. Such inequality is inevitable because *capital transforms the relationship between man and woman* from a relationship of exchange of labour in its immediately living form into a formal relation of production established between them.

This transformation affects many aspects of the gendered relationship. The man is formally given the right/duty to initiate relations of production with the woman. The relationship between them can now formally arise and exist as one of production only to the extent that the form of the exchange between man and woman is presented in terms of an *exchange of objectified work*, a relation between exchange value and *living labour*. The relationship between man and woman is no longer an exchange relationship in the form of the exchange of work with work in its immediately living form for the purpose of mutual consumption of the use values produced. It is no longer a *relationship based on mutual working collaboration*. It becomes a specific formal *relation of production* between the male worker and the woman in which the worker, in exchange for his wage, consumes the living labour that the woman provides. We specify this is a "formal" relation because the individual relationship between the man and the woman established as a relation of production between the two is the form of the real relations of production between capital and women. This relationship is a relationship of indirectly waged labour. The capitalist transformation of the relationship between man and woman also implies a restructuring of the consumption involved. While in precapitalist modes of production the relation between man and woman did not presuppose the separation of the working subject from the subject of consumption—because both men and women worked for each other, and both consumed the product of their labour—capitalism presupposes such a separation because it is the man in this case who buys the labour power of the woman.

Capitalism also transforms the quality of the subject that expropriates woman from the product of her reproductive labour. In precapitalist modes of production, woman was expropriated, like man, of the product of her labour of reproduction of individuals as exchange value. If she was a slave, this appropriation was performed by her master, because he possessed slaves as "work machines." If she was a serf, this appropriation was performed by the feudal lord, because he possessed serfs as "part of the feudal property…as accessory of the land, just like cattle for work."

In capitalism, woman is formally expropriated from the product of her labour to reproduce individuals as labour power. She is expropriated not by capital but by the very product of her labour power—labour power itself—which must formally belong to itself as a presupposition and condition of existence for capitalism. While in precapitalist modes of production the relationship of exchange between man and woman was subordinate to the consent of the master in the case of enslavement and to that of the feudal lord under serfdom, with the advent of capitalism this relationship of exchange became "free." *The relationship of exchange between man and woman is now configured as a "free" exchange* corresponding to the liberation of labour power. Free, in the twofold sense that man and woman become "free" both to exchange without having to depend on the consent of anyone (even the consent on the part of parents is gradually diminishing) and to choose, within certain limits, with whom to exchange.

If these are the transformations that, under capitalism, have affected the relationship between men and women at a general level, what are the changes that have taken place in the relationship between men and prostitutes? Our thesis is that the advent of the new mode of production, just as it radically transforms the relationship between man and woman at a general level, also radically changes the relationship between man and prostitute. The continuity that seems to bind precapitalist and capitalist forms of prostitution reveals all its inconsistency when subject to basic analysis.

In precapitalist modes of production, the exchange between man and woman takes the form of an exchange of labour with labour in its immediately living form. This is true except for a particular type of exchange: that between man and prostitute. The objects of this exchange are in fact basically *money* and the *living labour of sexual reproduction of the individual.* In this case, the money presents itself as money in the form of hoarded wealth. This exchange therefore implies a type of relationship that mainly includes those men who by right own themselves and can hold money, such as, for example, feudal lords and priests. This category does not totally exclude the serfs because, most likely, payment to prostitutes was, on occasion, made in kind.

Under capitalism, this type of relationship between man and woman includes above all the waged male worker. The money that is exchanged is no longer hoarded wealth, but variable capital. From a "trade," prostitution becomes *labour that is indirectly waged, even if it is paid monetarily.* The fact that the prostitute now works for the waged male worker means that the development of the waged labour relationship is also linked to the development of this specific form of exchange between man and woman. The development of capital means the development of prostitution.

Translated from Leopoldina Fortunati, *L'arcano della riproduzione: Casalinghe, prostitute, operai e capitale* (Venice: Marsilio Editori, 1981), 51–60.

1. Throughout the text, Fortunati generally uses the term "prostitute" (*prostitutes*) to designate the specific paid profession of providing sexual services rather than the (currently common) term "sex worker" (*operaia del sesso*); Fortunati generally uses this to describe the provision of indirectly paid sexual labour within marriage common to the Fordist household. As she notes in the second chapter of her book: "The term 'sex worker,' while emblematic of the content of the work of prostitution, is not the most felicitous. On the other hand, we are forced to use it, at least until another more adequate term emerges." Fortunati, *L'arcano della riproduzione*, note 49.

Leopoldina Fortunati
This Strange Form of Absolute Surplus Value

The panoramic view of production displays an inversion of that of reproduction. In production, capital accumulates workers and makes them cooperate. In reproduction, it disaccumulates house workers, atomizing them in a thousand different places: a thousand houses under the command of as many workers. Historically and conceptually, the starting point of capitalist production in both processes is different. In production it is the workshop, through the entire period of manufacturing, and subsequently the factory starting from the advent of large-scale industry. In reproduction it is the house, the atomized factory par excellence, which, despite being the factory specific to the domestic working process, appears as a non-factory. Instead, its door presents itself as that in front of which the capitalist relationship ceases; the worker is no longer a worker, the woman is only a woman, work is not work. Indeed, capital can build the factory in the production process only to the extent that it builds the apparent non-factory of reproduction.

After all, the disaccumulation of house workers in the process of domestic labour does not inhibit the determination of a socially necessary average of domestic work. The domestic labour objectified in the use value of labour power is, as we have seen, labour of an average social quality and the expression of a social average of labour power, inasmuch as it is commanded by capital in its entirety. This makes it possible to speak of the overall domestic working day and consequently of the average magnitude of this working day. This is why the disaccumulation of female domestic workers does not invalidate the determination of average socially necessary domestic labour, given that the different individual quantities of labour provided in different individual households by women cancel one another out and cause such an average to emerge.

This disaccumulation corresponds to the impossibility of both a common consumption of a part of the means of production and a corresponding impossibility of the development of cooperation. Disaccumulation does not even present such issues because, in this context, the common consumption of the means of production is intrinsically impossible. Given that the means of production are included in the means of subsistence of the individual worker, they are posited as the means of production related to a single labour process, and thus consumable only by the individual house worker. There is no buildup, no accumulation of means of production in the same place, and consequently no common consumption. There is, however, atomized dispersion, deconcentration, and individuated consumption within a single working process. Here, the means of production cannot at all be consumed in common.

This is the case for two reasons:

a) There can be no joint possession by the collective of workers (not to mention a broader community) of their means of subsistence, and there are two explanations for this. For one, the individual worker is the sole owner of the means of production of a specific house worker's domestic labour, since they are part of the means of subsistence of his family. Secondly, it is because they are a means of production of domestic labour (primarily introduced primarily starting from the advent of the Industrial Revolution), which, though not fully owned by the individual worker, cannot be consumed in common. These resources are water, electricity, gas—in a word, energy—which capital has progressively transformed from free natural resources into exchange value. Although energy is simultaneously consumed by many house workers at the same time, and therefore presupposes a collective form of consumption, it does not assume a common consumption. That is to say, it does not assume a form of consumption that would involve the development of cooperation in domestic labour.

b) There can be no common consumption of the means of production of domestic labour, because there cannot be a large enough concentration of means of production of such labour in the hands of individual capitalists. Capitalists do not have an interest in concentrating such labour on a mass level, since, to make women work side by side in the same work process, they would have to guarantee them a salary. It is much more productive for capital to posit domestic labour as a natural force of social labour. This is how it exploits two workers with a single wage.

Although no capitalist has an interest in organizing such labour, the state, in its role as collective capitalist, is obliged to do so. The state is obliged to pose itself as an owner and to build up extensive masses of means of reproduction. The terrain of individual reproduction is the fundamental moment of the overall process of reproduction, but it must be integrated through adequate levels of social reproduction of labour power. The reproduction of labour power is, however, positioned as a complementary moment to the social reproduction of labour power.

On the one hand, reproduction is complementary because it can fill only some segments of the domestic working process, with respect to which it is a far more partial working process. It is no coincidence that social reproduction can be only the reproduction and not the production of labour power. It is no coincidence that it can be the immaterial production of only certain specific use values, such as information and sex, and not others such as, for example, affection, love, care. On the other hand, reproduction is complementary because it is a moment with limited extension. This limited extension is determined by the fact that, although these are real and proper means of production (they present themselves as such) and involve a common consumption of these means by many workers, this labour must be posited here as waged labour. With the result that this "disadvantage" for capital nullifies the other advantages, so that the family system remains the most "economical."

The common consumption of the means of production of domestic labour is objectively prevented in the capitalist mode of production by the fact that one of the fundamental means of production of domestic labour is the very body of the house worker in its totality. This means that no other individual besides herself and, to a lesser extent the wage labourer who has purchased her labour power, can consume her to reproduce themselves. The same is true, albeit to a lesser extent, for the consumption of the male worker's body by the house worker. Their bodies are the only means of production that presuppose a common consumption performed by both. But this is not exactly the "common consumption" alluded to above, because it is a form of consumption that is shared not between all house workers but between a single house worker and a single waged worker, in his role as a secondary subject of reproductive labour. In any case, such common consumption transmits no value to labour power, since bodies have no intrinsic value in and of themselves, their existence being presupposed as natural.

The general lack of understanding of how reproductive labour is organized in a capitalist fashion, and thus of how it actually functions, has led to many theories and exhortations that the working class collectivize its means of subsistence or push for the collectivizing of such means by capital. These solutions, however, can only be a panacea for the emancipation from domestic slavery. Whether the proposal was to develop an organization of domestic labour that would increase cooperation and productivity (a proposal directed to capital itself), or a claim to create an alternative organization of domestic labour opposed to that of capitalism or to organize reproduction as a prefiguration of a future communist society, these proposals all failed. Their failure is the clearest demonstration that there are specific laws that regulate reproduction. To change them, the only way is struggling against capital on the very terrain of reproduction.

Finally, the dispersal of female house workers fully corresponds to the non-cooperative form assumed by their labour. In domestic labour, every single production process is isolated from the others; every female worker is isolated from the others. This non-cooperation of female house workers is the prerequisite and the condition of existence for the cooperation of male waged workers.

The fact that levels of simple cooperation do exist between members, and especially between women from the same family, does not change our discourse on cooperation. This form of cooperation is not the formal cooperation that presents itself as a historical type peculiar to the capitalist production process.

The image of the photographic negative we mentioned previously comes into focus once more. In the process of production, capital proceeds with the accumulation of workers in one place, sets average social labour into motion, causes a portion of the means of production to be consumed in common in the labour process, and develops cooperation in the process of production. In the process of reproduction, capital proceeds with the disaccumulation of female house workers, atomizes the site of production, disperses the very means of production and underdevelops cooperation even as it sets in motion a domestic social average of labour. Within the reproduction process, cooperation and common consumption of the means of production would have no benefit for capital, because they would not increase its productivity.

As for common consumption, its increase in the realm of reproduction would cause the value of its product (labour power itself) to fall. Capital, however, desires that the value produced in reproduction be as great as possible, and it is precisely the individual consumption of the means of production that raises the productivity of domestic labour: the fact that this value does not decrease leads to a greater possibility of its subsequent valorization by capital.

As for cooperation, its development in the realm of reproduction would presuppose the accumulation of house workers in a shared space. The inconvenience of such an arrangement for capital testifies to the history of the division of labour developed as a productive socialized force. In the process of production and reproduction of labour power, there is no division of labour among women house workers within a single working process. There is instead a division of every single working process from another. This is because, unlike all other commodities, labour power does not appear as the common product of many house workers but rather as the individual product of a single house worker. The woman here is not a partial worker within the division of labour but an overall one. She is able to produce the individual's labour power in its entirety, at least in relation to the process of reproduction. Of course, in this she is assisted by the other members of her family and community, other partial and secondary workers in the house. However, the cooperation existing between her and the other members is, as we have seen, a kind of simple cooperation, one that does not have much relevance with respect to our discourse.

What matters most is that there exists, using a play on words, a certain *cooperazione* (or "co-worker" arrangement) in consumption between the waged worker and the woman, in the sense that, since the means of production are also the means of subsistence, even if they are not consumed in common by more women in the domestic work process, they are however consumed in common by family members. This implies that, although in the domestic labour process there is no economy of the means of production, there is nevertheless an economy of the use of the means of subsistence. This "economy" has already been calculated in the worker's wages, that is, in the monetary representation of the value of the labour power of the entire working family.

The underdevelopment of cooperation in domestic work is accompanied, as we have seen, by the process of its division. Here again we see an inversion of the production process. While in the production process cooperation rests on the division of labour, here it is the underdevelopment of the division of domestic labour that, in turn, leads to an underdevelopment of cooperation. It is the separation, induced by capital, of the production process from that of reproduction that entails a rupture in the latter of the pre-existing cooperation of men with men, of women with women, and of men with women, and with this the "underdevelopment" in the division of labour that takes place in reproduction. A simple comparison between the development of reproduction in precapitalist societies and that determined in the capitalist mode of production testifies to this.

In precapitalist societies, each individual was constituted as a partial reproductive worker. Consequently, the individual's reproduction is a common product; the result of the work of many. But, at the same time, each individual is a partial worker with respect to the reproduction of many individuals. Everyone therefore is a partial worker of many related products. The partial nature of labour is determined not only by the sexual and generational division of labour itself but also by the further division of the labour existing in these divisions, based on the fact that there was cooperation in reproductive labour, between man and man, woman and woman, and woman and man.

In these societies, there were many partial working subjects of many common products, with respect to which each one carried out a different and independent part of the production process. This process therefore unfolded during the working time needed at many points in the working day and in diverse locations.

With the advent of capitalism, this process radically transformed. The division and cooperation of domestic labour are significantly reduced, with the consequence that the reproduction of the individual becomes the single product of the individual house worker. In other words, every house worker is now divided from the others, and in every house worker, who is now the general worker of a specific labour process, is combined what had previously been many partial labouring subjects. A concentration and accumulation of the different operations previously carried out by the many working subjects occurs. Domestic labour becomes a combination of various independent parts of the labour process, and its development is concentrated in a given time and space. In the transition to the capitalist mode of production, therefore, not only does the reproduction of the individual, once a common social product, become the individual product of a single woman, but the domestic work provided by the house worker becomes the labour of production and reproduction of the waged worker as well as the labour power of his children.

But why is the development of cooperation and the division of domestic labour inconvenient for capital? We will answer this question indirectly by demonstrating how their underdevelopment serves the interests of capital. Paradoxically, it is precisely through such underdevelopment that capital determines the increased productivity of domestic labour, forcing the house worker to produce more in less time.

How is this achieved?

a) Under capitalism the house worker carries out in less time the operations required of reproduction. Overall, this is due to the fact that the housewife performs these tasks throughout life largely in relation to a consistent form of labour power, the same worker, whereas the precapitalist worker was collectively produced and reproduced by many partial workers through common production and an alternating performance of tasks. It should also be noted that, while in precapitalist societies the work of many partial workers was not governed by an overall plan, but rather by traditions, under capitalism domestic labour came to be governed by capitalist planning.

b) Domestic labour becomes more productive because there is both a progressive decrease in the unproductive consumption of the house worker's labour power and a growing intensity of domestic labour itself. Both factors are the result of the intervention that has taken place at various levels by the capitalist mode of production to restructure the organization of reproduction.

In precapitalist societies, the alternation of the various working subjects who carry out the diverse procedures for the production and reproduction of individuals involves changes in space, since such work is dispersed and decentralized. Furthermore, it involves a temporal dispersion through various moments of the working day and a diversity of the various partial work processes, which are specific to the particular individual to be reproduced. Such passages not only from one operation to another but, above all, from one individual to another interrupt the course of work and render the working day porous. These openings are closed, however, in the working process of the capitalist housewife, who passes from one operation to another within a single working process, carrying out lifelong domestic work focused on the same individual labour power. Furthermore, the spatial separation between the different phases of the production and reproduction of labour power decreases and, with this, the time of passage from one stage to another is shortened, because domestic labour is increasingly condensed within the home. Finally, considering that the house worker must carry out the house work in a "given" time and place, in an allotted section of the workday, an increase in the expenditure of labour power in that given period of time also occurs.

c) The development of the productivity of domestic labour can be determined neither by the improvement of its instruments nor by the introduction of machinery, as it occurs for the worker in the workshop in the period of manufacture first, and then in the factory of the great industry. This difference is due to the fact that, behind factory labour, there is a different historical transformation and a different history of struggle. Any too-pronounced use of technology would run counter to capitalism's claim for reproduction as a "natural" production process. Reproduction functions, in fact, with another kind of machinery: natural machinery. This process, therefore, can only be understood as a production of labour power that is itself mediated through the consumption of labour power. In this process, these "natural machines" "work" at full speed, their functioning directly related to that of the machines in the factory.

The extraction of labour and value from the waged worker is the process that initiates the house worker's labour. Machines that, in the production process, function as the objective and systematically applied means of extorting a greater quantity of labour from the worker also "work" with respect to the process of production and reproduction of labour power. That is, they force the worker as a "natural machine" to both consume a greater quantity of domestic work and thereby to increase its intensity and productivity. It is evident that this direct interconnection of productive labour and domestic labour, as well as the direct connection of the respective workers involved, forces each individual woman to use only the "necessary labour time" for her functions. The effect is that a continuity, regularity, and, specifically, an intensity of domestic labour are generated, which are very different from the characteristics of domestic labour in precapitalist modes of production.

This "technological" discovery and its capitalist use certainly did not arise with the era of heavy industry; rather, it arose with the advent of the capitalist mode of production. However, with the development of large-scale industry, use of this human technology is perfected through the discovery that the overall productivity of labour increases if these machines can be made to function longer and more consistently in the process of domestic labour.

The massive use of natural machines for reproduction is precisely what explains the limited production of relative surplus value in this process. A simple comparison between the machinery of the factory and the tools and machines of the household (understood as the washing machine, the dishwasher, etc.) makes no sense. If one wants to compare the situation of the factory with that of the household, a comparison must be made between the heavy machinery of the former and the natural machinery of the latter.

The development of the productivity of domestic labour does not categorically exclude the use of tools and machines in this production process. On the contrary, even if such use is not of a fundamental and primary importance as in the production process, it still increases in quantitative and qualitative terms (though much more slowly and with greater significance) than in the factory.

Throughout the Industrial Revolution, a refinement and multiplication of the tools of domestic labour certainly occurred (take, for example, the history of cutlery), which undoubtedly led to a certain increase in the productivity of such labour. Relatedly, in a subsequent moment, there also occurred an increased use, however limited, of machinery in the form of household appliances.

d) The development of the productivity of domestic labour cannot even be achieved through increasing the time of surplus labour by lengthening the domestic working day. It cannot be extended, since it already coincides with the woman's lived day. There is, however, a continuous tension of this mode of production aimed at maintaining it, at reimposing its infinite extension of the time of house work against all struggles for its reduction. Indeed, this is the most productive battle for capital, even if its intervention here is difficult for two reasons: 1) The relationship between labour time and the value of labour power is based on a working day that tends to coincide with the entire lifetime of the woman, but which, for this very reason, is only imprecisely temporally determined. This can be either an advantage or a disadvantage for capital, depending on whether it succeeds in a subterranean lengthening of this workday or if women, secretly, succeed in shortening it; 2) It is an intersectoral relation, because the value of labour power is determined in the production process. The negative outcome of this is that the value of the means of subsistence of the house worker remains the same whether she works ten or eight or nine or six hours each day. Once this minimum value is established in the production process, the interest of capital is obviously that it always corresponds to the maximum amount of time for domestic labour, which coincides at least with the lifetime of the woman. The interest of women, on the other hand, is that the minimum amount of time for domestic labour corresponds to the maximum value of her labour power, and in this regard she has a better chance of success because this value is not directly related to her labour time.

Conversely, what happens in the field of prostitution with regard to the increase in the productivity of its related work? In the history of the capital, two roads have been taken to develop this productivity.

The first path is quite similar to that followed in the development of house work. It involves the organization of microprocesses of production, each separated from the other; the dispersion of sex workers; the individual consumption of the means of production; and the underdevelopment of the cooperation and division of labour. In the latter case, the division of labour inside the single working process is actually also underdeveloped, because, in reality, at the social level, there is a development of division that corresponds to the progression of the division of sexual labour. To prove this, we can see how groups of prostitutes exist who work primarily with masochistic clients, some with sadistic ones, voyeuristic, and so on.

As for the instruments and machines deployed, here too there is limited use because the fundamental machine remains the woman's body itself, reduced to its most basic sexual functions. Incidentally, it can be claimed that it is precisely the limitation of the use of machines in this sector that has caused the parallel production of films, photos, newspapers, and pornographic ephemera to expand enormously alongside it, a type of production that assumes much less living labour and more machinery. This, in turn, leads to the consumption of sex on an immaterial level.

Even in the domain of prostitution the tension of the capitalist mode of production is concentrated on both maintaining and imposing the longest possible working day and increasing the intensity of the work itself. It also seeks to reduce to a minimum the unproductive consumption of the sex worker's labour power.

The second way to increase the productivity of the labour of prostitution is much closer to the one travelled by capital in the production process. It is based on the fact that the labour of prostitution lends itself to being subject to a further leap in its productive power. The fact that the value of the sex worker's labour power is represented in monetary terms implies that her labour can be organized by capital also within a social relation of production that is strictly regulated by exchange value, that is, as a "waged" work relationship.

Throughout its history, capital has travelled both these roads and still travels both depending on how the balance of social relations of production is configured. Each has different disadvantages. In terms of the production of surplus value, the second road is undoubtedly more productive than the first, but it is not always preferable in terms of the reproduction of capital as a social relation. On the one hand, it is true that this leap obviates the structural danger inherent in the exchange between the sex worker and the pimp. Such an exchange, as has been noted, represents an inversion of roles with respect to that between the waged worker and the house worker. If in the relationship between the worker and the house worker it is the man who holds the money and purchases the woman's domestic labour, in the relationship between the sex worker and the pimp it is the sex worker who holds the money and purchases the pimp's labour. On the other hand, the factory of sex involves such contradictions for the state at the level of the social that, when faced with the emergence of countless protests, it often cannot take the second path and opts for the first.

This further leap in the productive force of prostitution takes place through the restructuring of the exchange between the sex worker and the pimp. This can happen in two directions: either this exchange is completely reversed, or an attempt is made to impose on the sex worker a forced exchange with the state itself.

In the first case, the pimp is transformed from an employee, paid by the sex worker to provide her with services, into an entrepreneur, that is, a boss who pays her to make her work for him. In this case, the exchange that takes place is one between "illegal" or "black market" capital and prostitution labour, between the pimp-capitalist and labour power as the capacity for the sexual reproduction of the waged male worker.

This step curbs the "unproductive" consumption by the pimp of the money derived from prostitution. The pimp, as an entrepreneur, makes productive use of his money, reinvesting it, to a greater or lesser extent, in this production process: in the cars, the champagne, the night clubs, and so on. These sorts of consumptions, which are very much close to those "unproductive" proletarian consumptions about which capital so much complains, thus fall within a properly capitalist framework of development.

In the second case, however, the state abolishes the pimp and presents itself as the only direct employer, as the only legitimate "entrepreneur," involved in prostitution. In this case, the exchange takes place between the state as guarantor of capital and the work of prostitution; between the pimp-state and the sex worker. In both cases, however, she is transformed into a worker once more. That is to say, the further "leap" in the productivity of prostitution consists of the fact that, already productive, it becomes increasingly productive by transforming itself into waged labour. In this case, whether we are talking about local brothels, or the German eros centres, or the brothels of Mediterranean Africa, or the *zonas rojas* (or "red light") districts of Latin America, there is an accumulation of sex workers, the common consumption of a part of the means of production, and a certain development of cooperation and division of sexual labour. However, in all these cases, we still find very low development in the level of technology.

What, then, is the form of the production of surplus value in the process of reproduction? Let us distinguish: in the process of production and reproduction of labour power, there is no development of cooperation and division of domestic labour, nor common consumption of the means of production. On the contrary, the increase in productivity here derives precisely from their underdevelopment in the first case and from the division and individuation of their consumption in the second. There is a certain use of machines, but in a context in which production fundamentally occurs through the exchange of labour power with labour power. The real battleground remains that of maintaining the domestic working day to coincide with the entirety of a woman's life.

The same thing can be concluded for the process of sexual reproduction of male labour power, whether we consider one or the other path taken by capital in developing this terrain.

To answer our questions above, surplus value in reproduction is a rather strange form of absolute surplus value, even if—starting from the historical moment of capitalist development, in which relative surplus value prevails in production—absolute and relative surplus values are intertwined in however limited a fashion.

In the future, how far we progress toward accentuating the production of relative surplus value through introducing higher levels of technology in reproduction, or how much it is restricted through opposing forces, will depend on what power relationships and mass behaviours develop between the state/capital and women. What is certain is that, while the increase or decrease in the amount of technology is certainly relevant with respect to domestic labour, it is totally irrelevant with respect to prostitution.

Here, technology can't free anyone from anything. The only thing that can free us from prostitution labour is the united struggle of housewives and prostitutes for the destruction of their unwaged work relationships. This is a radically different perspective from the aberrant one proposed by a large part of the left that reduces the problem to the forced abolition of prostitution, which translates into the violent extinction of the prostitute herself as a social figure. Hence, the most barbaric persecutions against prostitutes who do not agree to abandon the role as such or to their "re-education" and "rehabilitation" (see, for example, Vietnam, where former prostitutes were transformed into salaried workers, obviously at much lower wages).

In the process of production and reproduction of labour power, the problem of technological development is a strategic one, because the possibility of getting rid of a fairly substantial share of material domestic labour depends on how it is resolved. Whether it takes place inside the house or outside of it will depend on the directions that the behaviour of women, above all, will take. In the United States, against a decrease in the purchase of household appliances, there is an enormous increase in meals consumed outside the home, and clothes washed and ironed at the dry cleaners. This translates into the unburdening of domestic labour operations outside the home and therefore in their socialization. But there is no homogeneity in these trends, at least up to now, at an international level.

What is undeniable is that the refusal of domestic labour, expressed in a thousand forms and in the constantly increasing entry of women into waged work, has considerably lowered the levels of productivity in reproduction. Today, the domestic workday that tends toward the total twenty-four hours of the day is itself progressively disappearing: either because women use a salary to buy their way out of excessive domestic labour, or simply because they refuse to work full-time as housewives. Although women have done no official bargaining for the reduction of the domestic workday, domestic working time has incredibly, massively decreased. The turning tide in this battle indicates a fundamental defeat for capital, though simultaneously presenting a great political and organizational challenge for women.

If feminism means the struggle for liberation from unpaid domestic labour, our command over science and technology is an urgent political issue. Not only with respect to the objectives common to the whole proletariat (the problem of energy) but also with respect to our objectives, specifically concerning reproduction, which, given its particular structure and functioning, has a very low level of technological development. Just think of what antiquated contraceptive methods are still used today, how the house is cleaned.

This problem does not concern the production process to the same extent, where both capital and workers have had an interest in technological development, albeit with the opposite purpose. The aim of capital was, and remains, the contraction of its expenditure on variable capital, that of the workers was, and is, the reduction of working time. Even if, in the short term, this development has resulted in mass firings of workers, or at least in the decrease of their participation in production, nevertheless it has also represented (for them as well as for us) a step forward, because it potentially foreshadows liberation from waged labour.

In the reproduction process, not only has the level of technological development remained low, but the potential for future technological investment remains scarce given that, among other factors, interest between capital and women does not coincide. Technological advancement and investment in reproduction would not have led to the contraction of variable capital in the form of reduced wages but would only have served to reduce the time for domestic labour in the short term and to potentially prefigure the liberation of women from indirectly waged labour. In conclusion, the capitalist command over technology has progressed in very different ways in each realm.

For us, as is not the case with waged workers, the problem is that of subjectively determining, through the organization of our struggles, a technological leap such as to allow us the liberation of at least a segment of domestic labour through automation and robotization. This is undertaken of course with the awareness that the only way to preserve for ourselves the time that we free up from unwaged work is to strengthen our ability to organize and attack capital. The political initiative for the expression of a proletarian command over reproduction is ours. Let's seize it, weighing the depth of our political power as women in the struggle for our liberation.

Translated from Leopoldina Fortunati, *L'arcano della riproduzione: Casalinghe, prostitute, operai e capitale* (Venice: Marsilio Editori, 1981), 175–92. The first two pages (175–76) have been omitted here for the sake of brevity and to avoid repetition.

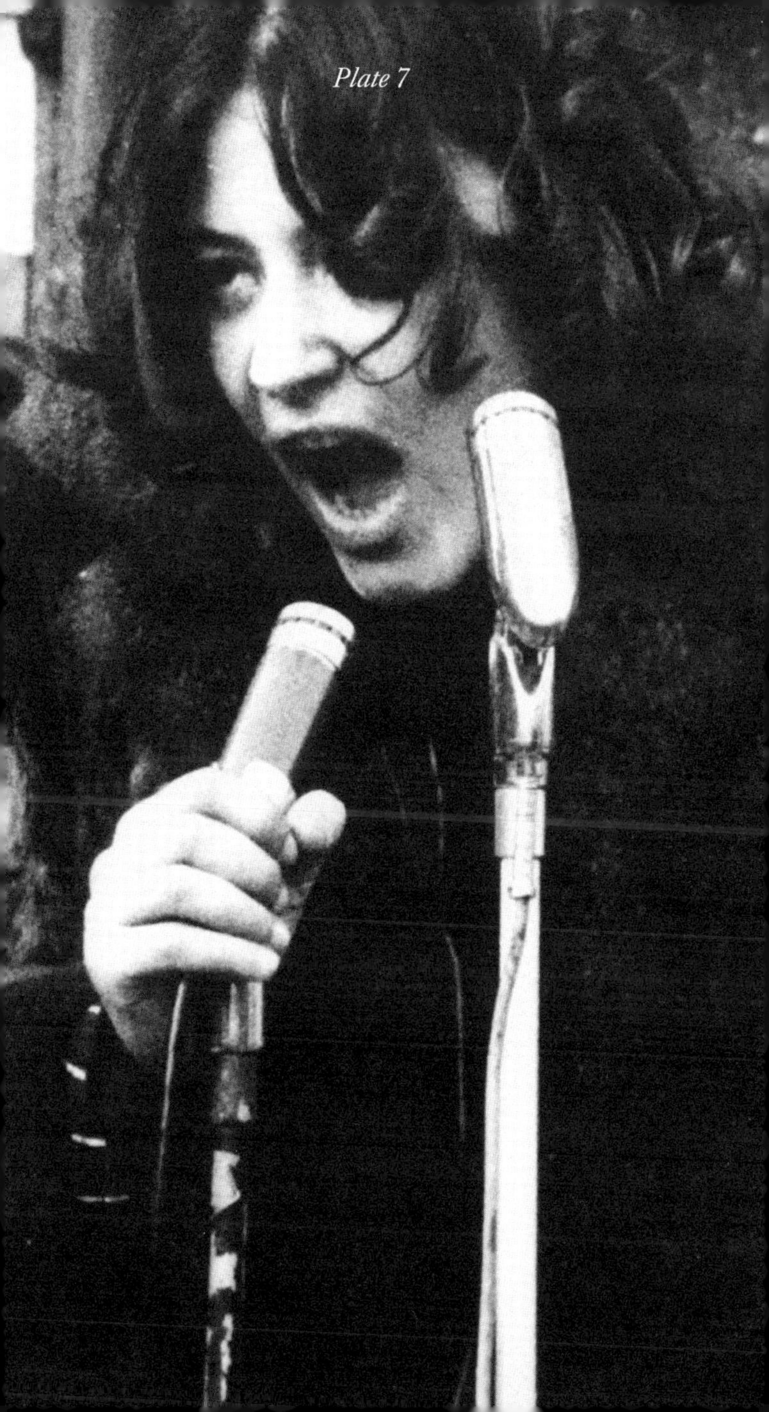
Plate 7

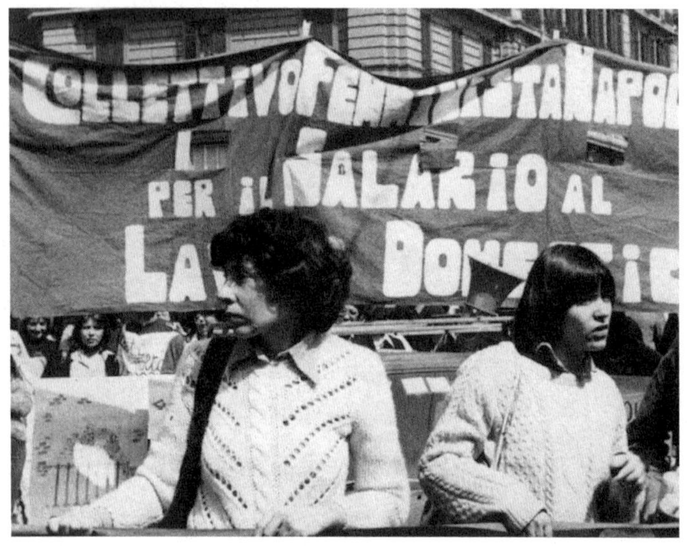
COLLETTIVO FEMMINISTA NAPOLETANO
PER IL SALARIO AL
LAVORO DOMESTICO

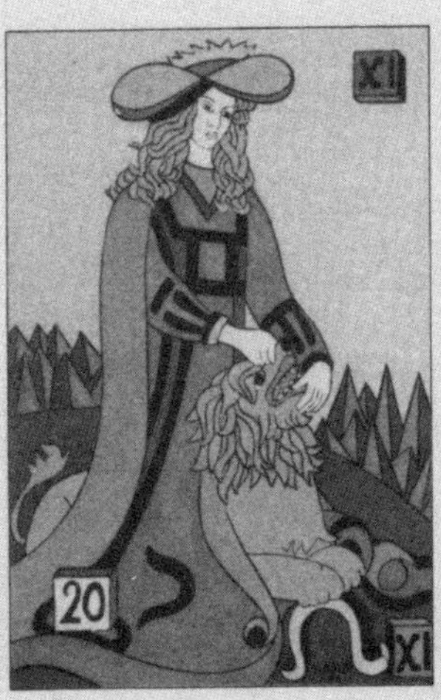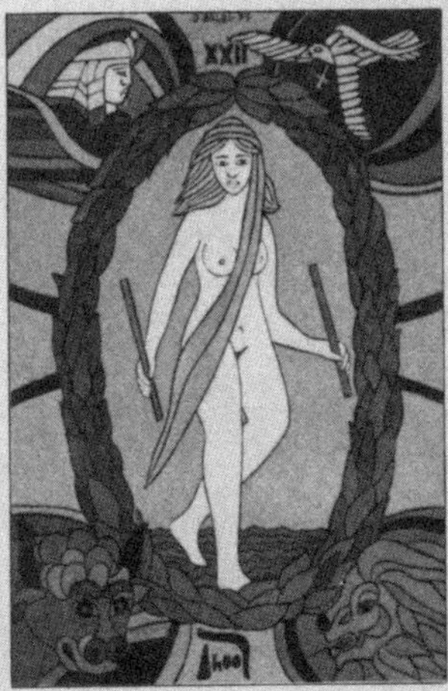
SAGGI MARSILIO
LEOPOLDINA FORTUNATI
L'ARCANO
DELLA RIPRODUZIONE
CASALINGHE, PROSTITUTE, OPERAI E CAPITALE
MARSILIO EDITORI

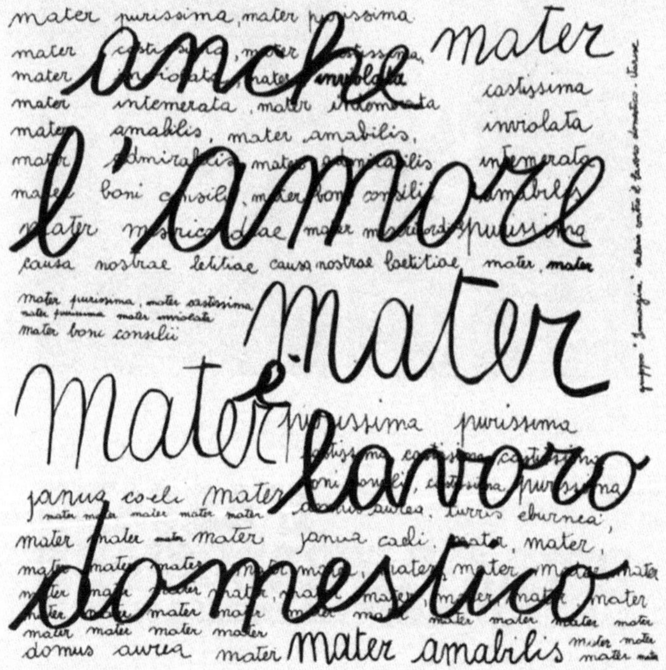
anche
l'amore
è
lavoro
domestico

Plate 7
Leopoldina Fortunati
at a demonstration in
Piazza Ferretto, Mestre,
March 1974.

Plate 8
Mariarosa Dalla Costa and
Leopoldina Fortunati at a
May Day demonstration,
Naples.

Plate 9
Original cover of
Leopoldina Fortunati,
*L'arcano della Riproduzione:
Casalinghe, prostitute, operai
e capitale* [The Arcane of
Reproduction: Housewives,
Prostitutes, Workers and
Capital] (Venice: Marsilio,
1981). The cover shows the
tarot cards XI, "Strength"
(*forza*), and XXII, "the
World" (*il mondo*).

Plate 10
"Love is also domestic
work": a poster produced by
the artist collective Gruppo
Immagine (Image Group),
whose members engaged

in Lotta Femminista and
the Wages for Housework
movement. This version
was reproduced as a back
cover for an issue of the
journal published by Lotta
Femminista, *L'operaie della
casa*, nos. 2–3, September–
Dececember 1976. The
work overlays a litany to the
Virgin Mary with the text
"Love is also housework"
(*anche l'amore è lavoro
domestico*).

Plate 11 (p. 240)
Cartoon from the final
journal published by Lotta
Femminista: "Mille fiori
sbocciano appassiti," *Le
operaie della casa*, no. spe-
ciale/documento, April
1977. The cartoon mocks
the extraparliamentary left's
claims that work could
be redistributed in a post-
revolutionary scenario
such that everyone worked
four hours a day. Here the
housewife attempts to add
four hours to her twenty-
four-hour workday.

Maya Gonzalez
The Gendered Circuit

(Re)reading The Arcane of Reproduction

Preamble

Aufheben, the left-libertarian communist collective founded in the UK in 1992, is arguably to blame for the fact that many young Marxists attracted to left communism (myself included) were overly eager to jettison "Autonomist" feminism, and with it the legacy of workerist feminism. In their eponymously named journal, Aufheben presented what, in retrospect, were overzealous attempts to discard what it had characterized heuristically as the "class struggle magnifying glass," as the Marxist theorist Harry Cleaver termed it. Aufheben humorously depicted this "magnifying glass" in an attempt to preserve its more traditional, workerist-influenced, ultra-left analysis of the logics of class struggle over a vulgar American autonomism of the antiglobalization movement.[1] What I found most overzealous in Aufheben's aspirations to transcend what they described, rather vaguely, as "autonomous Marxism" at the time was their willingness to consign a whole workerist-feminist archive to the dustbin of history—particularly Leopoldina Fortunati's *L'arcano della riproduzione: Casalinghe, prostitute, operai e capitale* (*The Arcane of Reproduction: Housewives, Prostitutes, Workers and Capital*).[2]

In some sense, the joke was on those of us self-loathing university students who eagerly read the journal—alongside the Situationist International and value-form theory—and who were craving that which went beyond the omnipresent anarchism of the era (with its antipathy toward Marxism). We were highly convinced of Aufheben's arguments even if we had never ourselves had the opportunity to read Mario Tronti's *Workers and Capital*, for instance. In accepting the collective's selective embrace of workerist traditions, we pre-emptively rejected our own potential political analysis of the "social factory," including what some consider "social reproduction." What seemed both comical, and by the same token disingenuous, about Aufheben's dismissal of "professor" Cleaver's position is that it makes no difference whether students do (or do not) "produce value" in the direct sense of commodity production: they are potentially political (or antipolitical) irrespective of their position within global production. It stands to reason that the work necessary to reproduce labour power for the market may itself be productive or unproductive depending upon its direct or indirect market mediation. Regardless, I argue that whether reproductive work is determined to be social labour in the abstract, or is directly market mediated, does not dictate its importance within political struggle. This is particularly true in the neoliberal or so-called post-Fordist era, when monetary policy and the value form dominate the political terrain of the economy and the accumulation of value through waged labour is, in some sense, "rarer" relative to the total global population and its reserve armies.

Eventually, I, along with comrades in organizing efforts, began to recognize a connection that helped us to reconsider Fortunati's work as an essential if imperfect attempt to consider the relationship between gendered labour and value production. Irrespective of whether we disagree on the productivity of housework, Fortunati does not argue that *all activity* that takes place outside of paid work is productive activity. However, rather than attempt to grasp what Fortunati might have been saying about gendered exploitation or why class oppression appears as unequal relations between the sexes, Aufheben moved quickly to a dismissal of her work, accusing it—along with the work of Cleaver and political economist Massimo De Angelis—of being engaged in a form of "autonomist Marxism." According to the collective, their theories responded to the excesses of an economistic and "objectivist" tradition with a kind of knee-jerk subjectivism, one that heedlessly attempted to claim that any of the objective categories of Marxism could be imbued with subjective experience. Moreover, against the work of Fortunati, Cleaver, and De Angelis, Aufheben affirmed the work of political philosopher Antonio Negri for taking an explicit distance from Karl Marx's theory of value. This move is supposedly justified by Negri's discovery of "an historical

change in the '70s…[when] value and its law were effectively suppressed and replaced by a political, direct, command by capital."[3]

On the one hand, Aufheben's critique of Fortunati—in addition to deploying a historically inaccurate characterization of her specific political affiliations, as I address briefly later on—fails to interrogate its own use of the categories of "subjective" and "objective" as they are mapped onto the political. Such questions were perhaps "too big to be seen," and the piece I wrote for *Viewpoint Magazine* in 2013, presented below, tacitly demonstrates that Aufheben, like many, missed two key questions: To what extent is this political fiction *generative of a powerful political force* that upholds the dominant ideology? And to what extent does the autonomy of the political performatively become the command of capital, more real in its abstraction, idealism, and fictitiousness than the economic laws governing the market (i.e., the law of value and the exchange of abstract labour)? Though the collective condescends to acknowledge that *The Arcane of Reproduction* "seems to be the most sophisticated contribution to this theme," they decry that the work of reproduction can "cover anything from playing video games, attending courses, going to a gym, watching television, looking for a job, etc." Moreover, Fortunati equates this work with the same importance as "culturally specific female activities outside the sphere of production: housework and prostitution." Aufheben writes: *Outside the workplace we are "free" to choose what to do, and how to do it. And we do what we do "for ourselves." However, this freedom hides an indirect command of capital: in a world where "what I as a man cannot do, i.e. what all my individual powers cannot do, I can do with the help of money… If we are in a position to spend time and resources in leisure and/or education…" All this is really "enjoyed" "for ourselves," and we do it without free will, but it implies out subjection to the law of value. This command is indirect in the case of the family: it is for the sake of an economic income that both husband and wife act of their own free will. Of his free will, the husband will sign a contract with an employer and will submit himself to the despotism of production for most of his active day. In the same way, of her free will, the wife will try her best to manage their home so that the husband will be able to go and earn the money they need to live. The internalization implied by commodity fetishism means that activity or work outside the sphere of production is a special "work" in a special "factory," where the "worker" is the "foreman" of himself. In this special factory the command of capital is the opposite of the despotism, organization and discipline of any other factory: it is a command based on freedom.*[4]

What is at stake here is that productivity does not necessarily determine *in any immediate or direct sense* whether or not "an activity," be it public or abjectly renaturalized as private or domestic or informal, is politically useful or valuable simply because it produces social labour in the abstract. Why confuse an economic abstraction with a politically useful technology or arena of social struggle? Moreover, whether productive labour is considered determinate of the "class struggle" will be different today than it might have been historically, in an era when the labour theory of value dominated Marxist discourse. For any reader of the work in 1974, the stakes of this debate would have been obvious.

We must give the Autonomist and the workerist-feminist moments clear credit for acknowledging that reified economic categories are split from the extended social division of necessary labour. The social factory may echo the factory, but the two are ultimately separated. And yet, necessary labour reverberates in places where it doesn't technically operate. Whether or not we believe, for instance, that university students produce value, education is absolutely necessary work done upon individuals for the reproduction of any technologically advanced society. Moreover, we all know that even working-class people are forced to compete for jobs in a market that preys on the redundancy of both skilled and unskilled labour, and individuals compete to move from one situation of precarity to another. Consequently, university students take out massive debt (trillions in fictitious human capital), even though they are subprime borrowers, and it is also true that they produce a great deal of intellectual property (again, unproductive labour in the proper sense). According to Aufheben, this positionality means that their fictions of "class struggle" politics are of less significance to anyone but students and university professors.

Perhaps the proof of their class politics (or lack thereof) is yet to be revealed. We shall see whether students' work stoppages, campus occupations, and debt strikes contribute to global class struggle. What is clear, though, is that—at least in the present conjuncture—when students misbehave it can become *political*. Since 2005, student struggles have been proven more significant than Aufheben reckoned, while remaining a trifle less "political" than Cleaver's embellishment suggested, since student movements are caught in the glitch between value production and the very social conditions necessary to keep that production and its circulation in place. Enter feminism, which afforded this broader analytic and its picture of a social field predicated on that field's occlusions. Enter Fortunati, who gave us an explanation for the mediation between immediate and diffuse relationships between value production and politics.

I argue, again, in the following, that what is productive of value is not at once political—or at least not necessarily and immediately. This is a moral (and indeed cynical or political) use of Marx's so-called law of value. Hence the criticism of productivist morality, especially when it comes to the neoliberal morality around political (sovereign) debt and its relationship to the circulation and reproduction of value. We need to look at all the ways in which that which escapes value production, including reproduction, is highly important terrain for working *class* struggle, irrespective of the economic justification. Today, rent, for instance, is highly political, even though it is *by definition* not productive. Nonetheless, for working people, the immediate relevance of unproductive categories like rent inhere in struggles over housing.

The disarticulation between the reproduction of the labour force—subject to both the historically specific law of population under capitalism and the (bio)political regime of national pro-natalist policy—and the demand for labour power by capital is directly related to the reproduction of its supply. This *indirect* relationship between the supply of labour power and its *direct* social reproduction within the circuit of capital makes the "circuit of gender" seem to exist only negatively, or domestically. This means a separate temporality may be applicable to the reproduction of those for whom the reproduction of labour power lies outside the context of the factory—in other words, within the broader "social factory," a concept not often thought of as relating to workplaces such as the household.

While it may be "one of the main contentions at the core of Autonomist Marxism" that "all human activity in either the sphere of production or in circulation and reproduction is *potentially* productive, that is, can contribute to the valorization of capital," it is not necessarily the case that all activity *as such* contributes to the creation of wealth in general in analogue to that proper site of value production: commodities.

Aufheben shares in a libertarian fantasy, basically, because it presumes a normative, liberal individual citizen, an abstraction, rather than a concretely situated racialized and gendered one, as if all have the same status, value, skills, and cost of maintenance. What of the problematic fact that it is *because* the reproduction of gendered labour power is a social cost that women are consequently *paid less*, given that, on average, they are assigned to the raising of children socially, regardless of whether they, as individuals, can or do give birth? Beyond this fact, there is also the question of rent and mobility, which affects the ability for *the bearers of labour power* to sell their commodity equally, or, more importantly, to move away from situations of gendered violence, which are, more often than not, experienced by women and children. Aufheben in some senses naturalized the inequality in property underlying internal class divisions, including the gendering of those divisions.

I argued in the article reproduced below, originally published in *Viewpoint* in 2013—as I still do today—that this internal proletarian class division exists in part because the reproduction of the labour force as such, on a national or transnational scale (i.e., population in the abstract), including migrants, refugees, and surplus citizens (and children), who are often employed informally, and the reproduction of individual or household labour power on a recurrent basis for those actively employed (but also when considering various reserve workers, which includes the retired, but also those who fall back within the former category as unemployed, disabled, and elderly), is a structural precondition for capitalist expansion that is not only ongoing but also politically relevant to Marxist analysis. All these "populations" at the level of abstract political-economic categories affect the value of labour power (if only negatively) by exerting pressure on the value of *reproducing* the commodity labour power that is exchanged with capital, and more often socially validated with some form of wages. It is worth pointing out that Aufheben, "for simplicity's sake," "avoid[s] the issue of prostitution" and therefore sex work entirely.

Nevertheless, housework and sex work—including many forms of care and domestic labour—is gendered in part because it pertains to the reproduction of populations. The impulse to denaturalize the reproduction of embodied living labour (in the form of people, or in demographic terms) is important critical work, since care, sex, and sexuality are not to be taken as neutral or natural categories or presumed to not be transformed socially. The reproduction of the population is often conflated with the reproduction of the employed sectors of the proletariat, whose labour power is exchanged directly with the value form in the form of wages. The simplifying view is to posit an either/or logic to reproductive work rather than a contradiction: *either* the reproduction of labour power (as a capacity or living labour) is that which is determined *directly* and immediately subject to the law of value, *or* reproduction is an undying vestige of another mode of production. Perhaps it is arguably both, given that the nation state and sovereign, with its territory and population, has a similarly ambiguous historical specificity reproductive of both citizens and alien populations subject to demands of capital but nevertheless dependent *indirectly* on the existence of the state. Perhaps the personal is more political than economic.

In either event, Aufheben's argument that Fortunati "comes from a tradition of Marxist feminism connected to the Autonomist area" is misleading, given that the members of Lotta Femminista (Feminist Struggle) largely engaged with Potere Operaio (Workers' Power) groups in the Triveneto region, drawing on traditions of *operaismo*, or "workerism," that were particularly vibrant. In fact, one of the most powerful arguments critical of the Autonomist factions that developed in the region was written as late as 1977 by founding members of Lotta Femminista, including Fortunati, Silvia Federici, and the Dalla Costa sisters, Mariarosa and Giovanna Franca.[5]

Since writing the article below, I have engaged in more extensive dialogue with Fortunati, and she has taken the opportunity to clarify that housework and labour sold on the market in exchange for wages is, more generally, *potentially* productive and therefore part and parcel of total social labour. It is apparent that the literature on the domestic labour debate more than clarifies, whether *incorrect or not*, that the workerist-feminist position—at least that which we find coming from Italy, up until Autonomist Marxism was reinvented in the Anglo-American sphere—consists of that "labour" (or more precisely, in Fortunati's terms, "nonvalue") that corresponds to the reproduction of the commodity labour power as the capacity sold on the market in exchange for wages more generally, and that this *is* potentially political as an articulated moment within the reproduction of the totality of social labour, even if it is never socialized but remains negatively a social cost that must be accounted for and often falls upon (even if behind) the backs of working-class women.

—March 2024

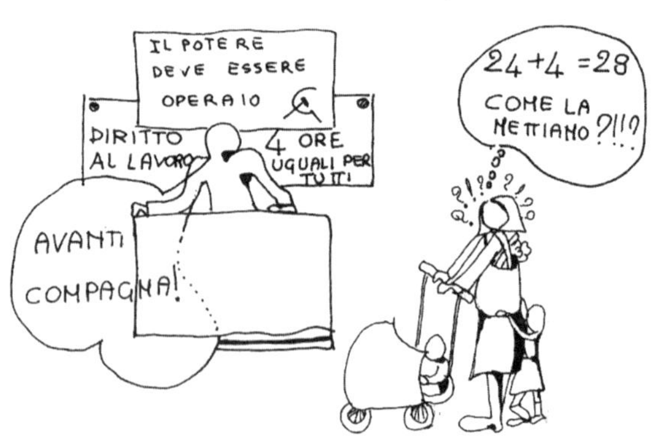

It remains to be clarified that by saying that the work we perform in the home is capitalist production, we are not expressing a wish to be legitimated as part of the "productive forces," in other words, it is not a resort to moralism. Only from a capitalist viewpoint being productive is a moral virtue, if not a moral imperative. From the viewpoint of the working class being productive simply means being exploited.... Ultimately when we say that we produce capital, we say that we can and want to destroy it, rather than engage in a losing battle to move from one form and degree of exploitation to another.
—Silvia Federici, "Counterplanning from the Kitchen"[6]

Among the most important Marxist contributions to a theory of gendered exploitation, and also one of the most widely misunderstood, is a text entitled *L'arcano della riproduzione: Casalinghe, prostitute, operai e capitale* (*The Arcane of Reproduction: Housewives, Prostitutes, Workers and Capital*). Written in 1981 by Italian theorist Leopoldina Fortunati, this rigorous account of reproductive labour under capitalism has long been underappreciated within the larger Marxist tradition. This text attempts to give it its due reappraisal, arguing for its continuing relevance not only as a necessary critique of an incomplete project begun by Karl Marx in his mature writings but also within the context of the current crisis and global struggles against austerity.

To appreciate the intervention Fortunati made—beginning over a quarter-century ago, along with the other founding members of the Lotta Femminista (Feminist Struggle) group, including Mariarosa Dalla Costa—we must first jettison some of our Marxist baggage. We might call this habit of thought "the arcane of productive labour": a privileging of value production as that which defines class exploitation. This prioritization often leads to the conclusion that the point of production is the central locus of proletarian subjectivation, as well as the foreground of revolutionary struggle and the starting place of a positive communist project. The ongoing Marxist reflex of productivism has effectively written off Fortunati's insights, along with the bulk of feminist theories of reproductive labour. The charge is that by theorizing reproductive activity as productive labour in Marx's terms, these feminist theorists have concocted a moralizing criticism, rather than a sober critique, of masculine discourses under capitalism. Of course, that sober critique would necessarily leave us with no more than "what Marx said." In any event, this reaction has framed the discussion of reproduction since the publication of *The Arcane of Reproduction*: measuring its adequacy as a theory of value rather than understanding it to reveal what a theory of value cannot immediately disclose.[7]

This reception had the consequence of *renaturalizing* the very thing Fortunati's critique was meant to *denaturalize* in the first place: reproductive labour and gendered exploitation under capitalism. It is true that if Marx's categories are stretched to incorporate reproductive labour, this can lead to further confusion. In short, if the debate revolves around whether reproductive labour is *value productive*, we are still missing the point. The point is the political, as opposed to the moral, viewpoint of the proletariat—that which arises from the wage and class relation of exploitation itself. Let us not forget that "the personal is political," which is to say, in the context of Marxist feminism, that the wage relation—not biologically but structurally—must also involve that half of the working class relegated to the hidden abode of labour power's reproduction.

This reproduction, and therefore this sphere of activity, is as relevant and historically specific a Marxist category as labour power itself—regardless of its content as social substance. Nevertheless, the fact that this activity is *feminized*, and performed by women outside the directly market-mediated sphere of capital accumulation, gives it a moral valence in the eyes of Marxist critics. To denaturalize, that is, to make political and social, the category of reproduction through the mediation of the wage was the goal of the international Wages for Housework movement, established in 1972. Whether just in the form of a demand, or through recognition won through the institution of that (perhaps impossible) demand, the movement's function was to rid gendered exploitation of its emotional connotations, and thus combat the structural devaluation of reproductive labour in capitalist social relations.

As the feminist theorist Silvia Federici had to clarify in her defence "Wages against Housework" (1975), the aim of Wages for Housework was not to win wages: "to view wages for housework as a thing rather than a perspective is to detach the end result of our struggle from the struggle itself."[8] Furthermore, she writes, this demand is "the demand by which our nature ends and our struggle begins because just to want wages for housework means to refuse that work as the expression of our nature."[9] Within the context of the feminist movement and the Wages for Housework campaign, Fortunati's achievement was not to "prove" that housework produces value. Rather, the value-theoretical analysis put forth flows directly from the revolutionary implications of the demand for wages for housework. The theorists of Wages for Housework understood the struggle could never be "won" "without at the same time revolutionizing—in the process of struggling for [the wage]—all our family and social relations."[10]

The members of Lotta Femminista were also making an appeal to their male comrades, as Federici discloses in their defence.[11] As a result, the demand for a wage was made within the traditional Marxist framework, within the assumption that the power of the proletariat is *actually measurable* in terms of socially necessary labour time. If we bracket for a moment the debate over the "productive" or "unproductive" characterization of housework, we can glimpse the political question Fortunati highlighted so well.

The Hidden Abode

Published by Autonomedia in 1995, fourteen years after its initial publication in Italian, the only available English translation of *The Arcane of Reproduction* is difficult to approach. But what becomes clear upon reading the range of paternalistic reviews it garnered is that critics who half-read the text evaluated Fortunati's analysis with a single criterion: the exactitude with which it recapitulates the central points of *Capital*. However, the book excels precisely where it diverges from the sacred tome. Especially for this reason, I hope to contribute to making this text understood, by breaking its system down into component parts and performing a brief reassembly.

Despite progressive advancements made over the course of the feminist struggle, the gendered exploitation that Fortunati described today remains a reality. This is because capitalism itself re-encloses the areas these gains have generated—which is to say, in more esoteric terms, the reproduction of capitalism daily hides the social character of necessary gendered exploitation, and it will remain *structurally* obscured unless its social character is exposed via struggle. The rolling back of social gains is precisely what restructuring under conditions of crisis renders inevitable without sustained resistance from below.

Furthermore, even to its most practical and well-meaning

critics, the actual relationship between gender and capitalist social relations remains an enigma. This is not simply because, as Marxists, we are reluctant to reproach the old man; it is also a consequence of the fact that reproductive work—still performed primarily by those assigned the fate "woman"—is extremely difficult to comprehend in the terms provided by the critique of political economy. Of course, gender is fundamentally defined by capitalism, and it should not be concluded that Marx's critique was "wrong." But *he left women out of the story*, and we need to find where he is hiding them.

Federici best summarizes this lacuna within Marx's theory: *No difference is made between commodity production and the production of the workforce. One assembly line produces both. Accordingly, the value of labor power is measured by the value of the commodities (food, clothing, housing) that have to be supplied to the worker, to "the man, so that he can renew his life process."*[12]

She rightly concludes: *The only relevant agents he recognizes in this process are male, self-reproducing workers, their wages and their means of subsistence. The production of workers is by means of the production of commodities. Nothing is said about women, domestic labor, sexuality and procreation.*[13]

What Marx leaves us with in his chapter "The Sale and Purchase of Labor-Power" is a "historical and moral element."[14] Here is the necessary structural place upon which to perform our feminist work—on the reproduction of this peculiar commodity, which Marx immediately folds, tautologically, into the factory setting: *One consequence of the peculiar nature of labor-power as a commodity is this, that it does not in reality pass straight away into the hand of the buyer on the conclusion of the contract between buyer and seller. Its value, like that of every other commodity is already determined before it enters into circulation, for a definite quantity of social labor has already been spent on the production of labor power. But its use-value consists in its subsequent exercise of that power.... The consumption of labor-power is completed, as in the case of every other commodity, outside the market or the sphere of circulation...in the hidden abode of production.*[15]

This passage makes clear that the consumption of the use value of labour power—that is, its capacity to transform the value of dead labour through living labour into a greater quantity of value—takes place in the process of production. Furthermore, this is also where the value of "his" means of subsistence are reproduced and embodied in the use values purchased through the wage, which enter the process of "his maintenance."[16] However, nowhere within the description of process do we find the sphere of labour power's "maintenance" itself, where the transformation of dead labour into living labour capacity takes place. If living labour is expended through the process of production, and this is also the *process of its consumption*, then it must logically *already exist* as a use value prior to the process of production. As Fortunati explains: *Marx...does not realize that the individual male worker's consumption is not a direct consumption of the wage, that the wage does not have an immediate use-value for the male worker and that consumption of the wage's use-value presupposes that some other work has taken place—either housework or prostitution. Only work can transform the wage into the use-values required in the male worker's reproduction; but even then the use-values are not directly or immediately consumable by him. More work is necessary to transform these use-values into use-values that are effectively usable, i.e. ready to be consumed.*[17]

Through what process is the use value of labour power "maintained"? How does a sum of commodities, of objectified labour, turn into the use value of labour power? In sum, where is the "hidden abode" of reproduction? These questions, expertly addressed throughout *The Arcane of Reproduction*, are at the heart of Marxist-feminist interpretations. What Fortunati's text excels in demonstrating is that we must attempt to use Marx's categories not only to solve the problems he gave us but also to understand that *new categories* can and must be proposed where they are missing in *Capital*, and such can be done without undermining the entire system he set up. In short, the aim is to Marxologize nondogmatically.

The categorical placeholders Fortunati indicates can be developed without recourse to a discussion of the "productivity" of reproduction. Her conclusion that the reproduction of labour power is value productive can be understood as a political one, necessary in its historical moment and within the heritage of Italian *operaismo*.

Housework and the Housewife

The Arcane of Reproduction does two important tasks in defining the theoretical foundation of the Wages for Housework movement. It delineates the gendered character of reproductive work, housework, and sex work as well as the structural category or gendered subject who performs this particular kind of socially necessary work specific to the capitalist mode of production. The character of this "labour" is, in Fortunati's terminology, "indirectly waged reproductive work," and the subject assigned to this category of work, "the housewife," names a novel category of *reproductive* labour power. While these aspects of the capitalist totality are insufficiently theorized by Marxists, they are absolutely imperative to understanding the *reproducibility* of a system based upon the accumulation of value and the exploitation of wage labour.

Mariarosa Dalla Costa was actually the first to outline this problem in *Potere femminile e sovversione sociale* (*The Power of Women and the Subversion of the Community*, 1972).[18] Here she makes the initial distinction between housework and production, the latter being *directly* productive and mediated through production relations specific to capitalist society. However, as she writes in the English translation of the essay, co-authored with Selma James, an American member of Wages for Housework: *These are social services inasmuch as they serve the reproduction of labour power. And capital, precisely by instituting its family structure, has "liberated" the man from these functions so that he is completely "free" for* direct *exploitation; so that he is free to "work" enough for a woman to reproduce him as labor power.*[19]

Although Dalla Costa indicates that waged labour is directly mediated by class relations, relying upon a sphere of "nonwork" in which male labour power is reproduced by women, and she indicates this is done through the *capitalist form* of the family, it is not clear if this feminine labour of reproduction is capitalist in nature—that is, a performance of living labour in the creation of a *commodity's* use value—or if it is merely a holdover from traditional family formations found in older modes of production.

In addition, while addressing that which is not directly mediated by the market, Dalla Costa relegates reproductive labour to a sphere outside the capitalist market. She states firmly: "where women are concerned, their labor appears to be a personal service outside of capital."[20] The ambiguity as to the capitalist character of "the outside" leaves open the question of dual modes of production—one capitalist and the other domestic. Though Dalla Costa affirms throughout the text that housework and the family are absolutely capitalist in their social form, the theory required to demonstrate precisely *how* they are capitalist was left to Fortunati.

She takes this initial distinction and develops "the outside" theoretically. She names the form of labour conducted in this liminal space "non-directly waged reproduction work."[21] The housewife's fate is not that of a "feudal serf"; under capitalism, she is "first of all an *indirectly* waged worker."[22] This is not only where a specific category of work is categorized as indirect but also where the site of the historical subject to whom this work is structurally assigned: "within the housework process another, different, labor-power is consumed—that of the female houseworker."[23]

These new concepts of indirectly waged work and the houseworker open up the *sphere* of housework and prostitution as a capitalist sphere within the circuit of reproduction.[24] This sphere contains "the co-existence of the two forms of labor power," productive and reproductive, whose bearers engage primarily in two kinds of work relations—formal and informal (or more often, marriage)—in addition to directly waged exchange. Fortunati writes: "the individual as capacity for production confronts capital," while "in the second case, the individual as capacity for reproduction is confronted not by capital, but by the individual him/herself as [productive] labor-power."[25] The duality of gendered labour powers, corresponding to gendered workers—breadwinner and housewife[26]—are put to work; the use value of their respective labour powers takes place in different times and spaces: the former at the proper capitalist workplace, and the latter in the workplace of the home. While the waged breadwinner spends the "working day" in productive consumption for capital, where their living labour is consumed—a process that depletes labour power while reproducing *the value* of the wage—the indirectly waged housewife spends "her" hours engaged in a different form of reproduction, that is, "her" responsibility for replenishing living labour as the reproduction of "his" labour power. Fortunati explains: "in production, the exchange-value of labor-power as capacity for production is produced and its use-value consumed; in reproduction, the use-value of labor-power is produced and its exchange-value is consumed."[27]

Nevertheless, for Fortunati, this sphere is not simply the opposite of the productive sphere but rather it conceptually "presents itself as a photograph printed back to front, as mirror image of the process of commodity production."[28] Nevertheless, reproduction is not a reflection of production back upon itself (the self-maintaining tautology in Marx's account); in other words, "where the reproduction of labor-power takes place is not simply a producing workshop."[29] Rather, the site where reproduction takes place completes the entire circuit of simple commodity exchange in the sphere of housework and sex work.

This is not foreign to Marxism; it is instead a portion of the circuit of reproduction left open-ended. Marx himself distinguished between two circuits inherent to the wage relation but left one of the most important aspects of the circuit incomplete. He identifies the quintessential and historically specific circuit with the accumulation of money: $M-C-M'$.[30] Within this circuit, production—or capitalist exploitation—takes place (this we might call the viewpoint of capital). However, another circuit also exists, one that waged labourers necessarily engage in for access to means of life: $C-M-C$. This circuit begins with labour power as a commodity (C), which is exchanged for money (M), in order to *buy* means of subsistence.[31] Then the cycle repeats. Or so it seems.

To receive money wages to complete this circuit of reproduction (through capitalist production), the proletarian must enter relations with the capitalist, who buys their labour power (the first C in $C-M-C$) in order to put it to work in the creation of value and surplus value (the M' in M–C–M'). There are many stops along the way in the production and circulation of commodity capital and labour power. What is perhaps most important to say here is that the circuit C–M–C assumes that the wage earner's commodity of "labour power" is purchased on the market ready made, with money wages. The problem identified by the members of Lotta Femminista is the fact that "at no point does labor-power roll off an assembly line."[32]

This feminist critique has located an aporia within traditional Marxist thought, a fetishization—or, in other words, a *structural transhistoricization*. Fortunati has defetishized the seemingly natural process assumed to produce labour power but that is in actuality the "hidden abode" tucked within the C–M–C circuit. Much like Marx, who discovered the origin of profit as a particular *historical* form of class exploitation, Fortunati discovers the *historical* form of gendered exploitation under capitalism. Yet, this does not require that it therefore be value productive. Quite the contrary: according to Fortunati's schema, gendered exploitation must remain external to accumulation, which she characterizes as *indirectly* mediated by the form of value, as socially necessary but not "socially determined."[33]

In other words, whether the non-directly waged work of reproduction is in fact productive is neither here nor there. Between each moment of "the buying and selling of labour power"—which is to say, the *reproduction* of the circuit of labour power itself (C–M–C)—there is a sphere of use-value creation, of the making (and maintaining) of labour power. In the same way that M–C–M' unfolds into its own moments—M–C…P(roduction)…C'–M'— there is an analogous unfolding in the non-directly productive sphere of the reproduction of labour power. As Fortunati expresses in other terms: *The male worker does not transform the money with which he pays for the food into capital, he only transforms it into food. He uses the money as simple means of circulation, converting it into a determinate use-value. This money does not function as capital for him, although in the first two cases it also buys the work done as a commodity, it only functions as money, as a means of circulation. On the other hand, none of these people—houseworker, domestic servant or care worker—is a productive worker in relation to the male worker, despite the fact that the work of each one of them provides him with a product—cooked food.*[34] We might qualify this, though Fortunati does not explicitly, as C – M…R(eproduction)…C and so on, throughout the course of days and years.[35] This moment of R, or reproduction as the mirror of production, is the process through which "food" becomes "cooked food" and "the bearer of the commodity of labor power" becomes revitalized living labour, "the use-value commodity 'he' brings to market."[36]

We might also note that in the above quotation Fortunati explicitly assures us that this reproductive moment within the circuit does not expand capital, that is, it is not productive. The decision to insert a C' at the end of the C – M – C circuit of reproduction is perhaps a political rather than economic surplus. Even if C – M – C as the circuit of reproduction does not expand value, it nevertheless is entirely within the wage relation and therefore a socially necessary moment within capitalist reproduction. On the level of total social activity, both direct *and* non-direct reproduction sustain the capitalist totality. As Fortunati concludes: *Now if, instead of the single capitalist and the single worker, the capitalist class and the working class are examined, and instead of solely the process of commodity production, the entire process of capitalist production—in full flow, and in all its social setting—is considered, it turns out that the consumption of housework and prostitution work is posited as a condition of the constant maintenance and reproduction of the working class.*[37] For every productive moment, there is a corresponding moment in terms of reproduction. These, however, are not one and the same moments occurring in the same time and place but rather an aspect of reproduction occurring in dual spheres, separated in time and space *within the same mode of production*. In fact, it is the duality of these spheres—direct/non-direct, or productive/reproductive—as well as their interconnection that defines this mode of production as one based upon waged labour.[38]

The Work of Love

As I have already mentioned, within this schema we find an analogous form of labour power, which belongs specifically to reproductive workers—typically women. In the context of the Wages for Housework movement, this labour power is entirely relegated to wives, mothers, grandmothers, and daughters, all of whom are assigned both the female gender and this *form* of labour power, by virtue of its structurally enforced necessity within the wage relation. Even if we are to make this category "feminine," as opposed to generally "sexed," we still will find that it is a constitutive category within the wage form. In short, someone must perform this work, regardless of their gender, and *necessarily do so without remuneration*. Therefore, the demand for wages is a demand that strikes at the heart of capitalist exploitation. This is a separate question from whether this form of labour power produces value; in fact, it must remain *non-valued*: "a condition of existence of labor power as capacity for production, and hence of capital, is that labor power can have exchange-value only insofar as the individual reproduces it as non-value."[39]

This identification of housework as the reproduction of "the individual as nonvalue" through the creation of "pure use values" has the effect of representing reproductive labour power as "a natural force of social labour," donated by Mother Nature to both capital and the male working class *for free*. As Fortunati claims, reproduction is "posited as 'natural production,' which has enabled *two* workers to be exploited with *one* wage, and the entire cost of reproduction to be unloaded onto the labor force."[40] Nevertheless, this exploitation is not unloaded equally, because it must be inscribed onto female biology, disguising its origin in the historically specific capitalist mode of reproduction. Fortunati continues: *The woman, under capitalism, reproduces the waged male worker; yet she is not waged herself. She is instead a "natural force of social labor." The "free" male waged worker thus corresponds to the "free" female non-waged houseworker, a profound formal difference which is reflected in the equally profound inequalities of their mutual relationships under capitalism, and their unequal status within the capitalist system, which arises at the point in which capital transforms the male/female relationship from an exchange of living labor into a formal relation of production between them.*[41]

It is here that we strike at the heart of the demand for housework wages. As I have already noted, and as feminists have repeatedly made clear, the point of the demand for wages for housework is to denaturalize this form of labour power, to dismantle its biological justification, so that those who perform this work can be understood as proletarians in the full sense of the term—not just as waged workers but as socialized proletarian subjects with the power to struggle as a sector of the exploited class. This struggle begins from a definite point of capitalist exploitation and work *for capital*: (non-directly waged) reproduction.

The question remains: Why is this work reproductive of

the capitalist system gendered? Or, in other words, why is this the *feminist class* struggle and also the *communist* struggle? Fortunati does the excellent work of outlining this problematic. Not only is it naturalized but it must *remain* naturalized. Marx uncovered the wage fetish. But with regard to gendered exploitation, he seems to be subject to this fetish himself. He does not recognize, as Fortunati does, that not only is *all labour "unpaid" and yet appears to be paid* for the work it actually performs but that this fetish inherent to the wage relation and our very understanding of justice also requires that *all life outside work appear absolutely "free" of work for capital.* However, for those given the duty of reproduction in this sphere of life, as their biologically determined role, there are no illusions as to its "work-*like*" character. It is so much *like work* that it ought to be paid (and in fact often is). Federici recalls a "welfare mother" who remarked that "if the government is willing to pay women only when they take care of the children of others then women should 'swap their children.'"[42] Why, when it is one's own child, is it not work but *love?*

Once we understand the "work of love" in the context of total social reproduction, we can see why debates over the value productivity of feminized labour obscures the analysis. If we can draw anything from Marx's analysis of the wage fetish, it is that, under capitalism, whether on the commute to work or at the office and factory, none of what we do is paid labour, or even payment for the "value" that labour produces. It is the payment of *money for the purchase of the "raw materials" that go into the process of the reproduction of labour power (and that of the indirectly waged labourers who perform its reproduction).*

This defetishization has always underlain the communist understanding of wage struggles—that is, that demands for wages are only the beginning of class struggle to end the wage form. The theorists of the Wages for Housework movement, as a revolutionary feminist struggle, were more aware of this than anyone. As Mariarosa Dalla Costa bluntly put it: "there has never been a general strike."[43] To strike at the point of production, or in the sphere of waged labour, is to address only half the unpaid work that capital exploits. Perhaps we now can see why it was necessary to make this work *appear as work* by theorizing it as *productive.*

In this regard, we can understand Wages for Housework and its complementary theoretical strategy as a political move to mobilize communists of all genders around the reproductive sector. What, however, does this movement and its theory mean to us today? In the context of wage stagnation and high unemployment, in which women and mothers attempt to scrape by within the waged sphere, we must recognize that value productivity cannot be understood as the condition for revolutionary subjectivity. What we today can draw from the Wages for Housework movement is the call to resist the augmentation of unpaid reproductive "maintenance," which rightfully should be called housework, as a result of the crisis of capitalism and austerity measures—especially since that maintenance may not even "maintain" the price of labour power but only do the work of mere survival, in order to keep not only us but also the system of exploitation alive.

This work will inevitably fall upon women because, as Fortunati has demonstrated, work outside direct market mediation is biologically assigned to women. The outcome of austerity measures and restructuring will continue to be the *capitalist attack on women*—unless we resist it and place the viewpoint of reproductive labour at the centre of our struggles.

This text was originally published as "The Gendered Circuit: Reading *The Arcana of Reproduction*" in *Viewpoint Magazine*, September 28, 2013.

1. See the introduction to Harry Cleaver, *Reading Capital Politically* (Edinburgh: AK; Leeds: AntiThesese, 2000), 1–82.
2. Leopoldina Fortunati, *L'arcano della riproduzione: Casalinghe, prostitute, operai e capitale* (Venice: Marsilio, 1981), published in English as Leopoldina Fortunati, *The Arcane of Reproduction: Housework, Prostitution, Labor and Capital*, trans. Hillary Creek (Brooklyn: Autonomedia, 1995). For Aufheben's critique of Fortunati's text, see Aufheben, "The Secret Life of Housewives (The Arcane of Reproductive Production)," in *Aufheben*, no. 13, 2005.
3. Aufheben, "The Secret Life of Housewives," 24–25.
4. Aufheben, "The Secret Life of Housewives," 25.
5. See Mariarosa Dalla Costa, Silvia Federici, Leopoldina Fortunati, et al., "Mille fiori sbocciano appassiti," *Le operaie della casa*, numero speciale/document, April 1977.
6. Silvia Federici, *Counter Planning from the Kitchen* (Bristol: Falling Wall, 1975), 6.
7. Aufheben summarizes this criticism in their review of *The Arcane of Reproduction*. Fortunati, according to Aufheben, abuses Marxist "categories of productive, unproductive, value, abstract labour" in order to render reproduction "essential in the political (or moral?) evaluation of the role and antagonism offered by sections of the proletariat." Aufheben, "The Arcane of Reproductive Production,"

Libcom.org, submitted February 6, 2007, https://fillip.ca/lb70.
8. Silvia Federici, "Wages against Housework" (1975), in *Revolution at Point Zero: Housework, Reproduction and Feminist Struggle*, Common Notions (Binghamton, NY: PM Press, 2012), 15.
9. Federici, "Wages against Housework," 18.
10. Federici, "Wages against Housework," 15.
11. "Nothing can be more effective than to show that our female virtues have already a calculable money value: until today only for capital, increased in the measure that we were defeated, from now on, against capital, for us, in the measure that we organize our power." Federici, "Wages against Housework," 20.
12. Silvia Federici, "The Reproduction of Labor Power in the Global Economy and the Unfinished Feminist Revolution" (2008), in *Revolution at Point Zero*, 93. Federici cites two passages from Karl Marx, *Capital, Volume 1*, trans. Ben Fowkes (London: Penguin, 1976), 276–77.
13. Silvia Federici, "The Reproduction of Labor Power in the Global Economy" (2008), in *Revolution at Point Zero*, 93–94.
14. Marx, *Capital, Volume 1*, trans. Fowkes, 275.
15. Marx, *Capital, Volume 1*, trans. Fowkes, 279.
16. Marx, *Capital, Volume 1*, trans. Fowkes, 274.
17. Leopoldina Fortunati, *The Arcane of Reproduction*, 49.
18. The original publication of Dalla Costa's essay was released as Mariarosa Dalla Costa, *Potere femminile e sovversione sociale. Con*

"Il posto della donna" di Selma James (Padua: Marsilio Editori, 1972). Later that same year, the text was released in English translation as Selma James and Mariarosa Dalla Costa, *The Power of Women and the Subversion of the Community* (Bristol, UK: Falling Wall, 1972).

19. James and Dalla Costa, *The Power of Women*, 33–34. Emphasis in the original.

20. James and Dalla Costa, *The Power of Women*, 28.

21. Fortunati, *The Arcane of Reproduction*, 15.

22. Fortunati, *The Arcane of Reproduction*, 14. Emphasis in the original.

23. Fortunati, *The Arcane of Reproduction*, 69.

24. Italian studies scholar Andrea Righi calls to our attention this discovery in his book on the biopolitical character of Fortunati's work, though he does not draw out the further implications of indirect labour. See Andrea Righi, *Biopolitics and Social Change in Italy: From Gramsci to Pasolini to Negri* (New York: Palgrave Macmillan, 2011), 58.

25. Fortunati, *The Arcane of Reproduction*, 16.

26. This is not to say that housewives do not also work for wages or that breadwinners win all the bread. The point is that they are two different categories of gendered labour power. Fortunati explains: "The female worker, in order to reproduce herself, can exchange her labor power as capacity to reproduce either for the male wage or, if she works in the production of commodities, for her own wage.... the female proletarian must, in order to reproduce herself, exchange her capacity to reproduce both for her own wage and for the male wage at a mass level. 'His' wage has rarely been able to allow 'her' not to do a second job." Fortunati, *The Arcane of Reproduction*, 13–14.

27. Fortunati, *The Arcane of Reproduction*, 69.

28. Fortunati, *The Arcane of Reproduction*, 8.

29. Fortunati, *The Arcane of Reproduction*, 69.

30. Karl Marx, "The Circuit of Money Capital," in *Capital, Volume 1*, trans. David Fernbach (London: Penguin, 1978).

31. Marx, "The General Formula for Capital," in *Capital, Volume 1*, trans. Fernbach, 250.

32. Maya Gonzalez and Jeanne Neton, "The Logic of Gender: On the Separation of Spheres and the Process of Abjection," *Endnotes*, no. 3 (2013): https://fillip.ca/ft45.

33. Fortunati, *The Arcane of Reproduction*, 106–07.

34. Fortunati, *The Arcane of Reproduction*, 53.

35. Let us not forget generational reproduction, which is the process through which another generation of the proletariat is reproduced for years until it can enter the market and the circuit of waged labour.

36. This process of "cooking," for instance, can and historically has always been paid for (at least potentially) within the sphere of direct production, in the service and waged sector; however, as Fortunati notes (*The Arcane of Reproduction*, 53), this is not *structurally* in the economic interests of *any* member of society, and, furthermore, this wage is, under conditions of competition, reduced to its bare minimum. Many studies have

been done—in particular the work of economist Michael Perelman—to show that the formation of waged relations, through enclosures of the commons and so on, has relied on a purposeful augmentation of the wage and household, such that a large portion of "reproduction" is done structurally outside the productive sector in order to create the very conditions of surplus-value extraction. Today, it may be the case that even women can relegate this labour to paid domestic workers within their homes and remunerate them through their own (middle-class) wages; however, these workers, often poor women of colour, are themselves unpaid domestic workers in their own homes, and this unpaid portion of labour power's reproduction not only is done by the *same women* rather than their male counterparts but is in aggregate passed off inevitably to those least able to "purchase" reproduction; rather, it is done "for free" through capitalist relations of gendered exploitation. This is part and parcel of the post-Fordist turn toward feminized production and uneven development globally—a discussion far beyond the scope of this review. For more recent theorizations related to Fortunati's thought from two of her former in Lotta Femminista colleagues, see Federici's *Revolution at Point Zero* and Dalla Costa's *Women and the Subversion of the Community: A Mariarosa Dalla Costa Reader* (Oakland CA: PM Press, 2019).

37. Fortunati, *The Arcane of Reproduction*, 51.
38. For a complete analysis of the logic of gendered spheres, see Gonzalez and Neton, "The Logic of Gender."
39. Fortunati, *The Arcane of Reproduction*, 11.
40. Fortunati, *The Arcane of Reproduction*, 9.
41. Fortunati, *The Arcane of Reproduction*, 31.
42. Federici, "The Restructuring of Social Reproduction in the United States in the 1970s" in *Revolution at Point Zero*, 45.
43. Mariarosa Dalla Costa, "The General Strike," in *All Work and No Pay* (Bristol, UK: Falling Wall, 1975), 127.

Claire Fontaine, Jaleh Mansoor,
Giovanna Zapperi, and Matilde Guidelli-Guidi

A Conversation on Carla Lonzi's
Autoritratto (*Self-portrait*)

The following conversation took place online on February 23, 2023, as part of Dia Talks by Dia Art Foundation in Beacon, New York. Fulvia Carnevale of the artist duo Claire Fontaine was joined by art historians Jaleh Mansoor and Giovanna Zapperi in a conversation moderated by Matilde Guidelli-Guidi, associate curator at Dia, on the work of Italian art critic and feminist theorist Carla Lonzi (1931–1982). The discussion took place in conjunction with the publication of the first English-language edition of Lonzi's 1969 book of experimental art criticism, *Autoritratto* (*Self-portrait*), translated by Allison Grimaldi Donahue and published by Divided in collaboration with Dia.

Matilde Guidelli-Guidi: Little known in English scholarship, Carla Lonzi was an important art critic and feminist theorist operating in a period of political and social transformation in Italy and elsewhere spanning the 1960s and '70s. In Lonzi's trajectory, *Self-portrait* constitutes a liminal book that at once unsettled and reimagined the form and value of art criticism and also marked a shift in emphasis in her life from art writing to feminist theory and practice. Claire Fontaine, Jaleh, and Giovanna: You have done so much to think through the legacy of Lonzi in your writing and art, and we are very lucky to have you here. And thanks to our colleagues at Dia and Divided. Congratulations again to Alyson Katz and Allison Grimaldi Donahue, who designed and translated this wonderful English edition of *Self-portrait*. Now, I will pass things off to Giovanna, who will begin our discussion.

Giovanna Zapperi: Thank you, Matilde. Thank you, Dia Art Foundation for inviting me to participate in this conversation. I would like to start my brief presentation by stressing the significance of *Self-portrait* for our understanding of the art of the period. In her reading of the 1960s Italian art scene, Lonzi leaves aside the linear model based on the art historical fiction of the artistic renewal and replacement of one movement after the other, which was dominant at the time. Rather, she proposes a radically different epistemic structure. Instead of promoting a group or a movement, Lonzi cultivated nonhierarchical relations involving artists associated with different groups or generations. While contesting the verticality of male genealogies, Lonzi fostered a horizontal model that left behind the admiration for the "great artist" and focused instead on the relations, experiences, and forms of life that emerged in the art of her time. In spite of the formal heterogeneity of the practices she was interested in, she proposed a form of intergenerational dialogue that challenged the avant-gardist logic of formal innovation and rupture.

During the 1960s, Lonzi tried to develop her own practice as an art critic, which culminated in *Self-portrait*. The book is based on her self-positioning as a subject and on a sharp critique of the social and epistemic structures defining the critic's activity. *Self-portrait* is based on conversations that Lonzi recorded, transcribed, and assembled between 1965 and 1969. Each dialogue is fragmented and edited in a way that preserves the colloquial quality of spoken language. By constructing the fiction of an uninterrupted conversation, Lonzi ceases to ask questions or discuss the artist's work. She rather speaks for herself in her own voice. In other words, with this book she wanted to challenge art criticism as an activity based on an authoritarian posture—the aesthetic judgment—while at the same time she tried to rethink art itself outside the ideological framework that defined it. Lonzi's undoing of the conventions of art criticism was an attempt to experiment with a different relation to artists, one that was based on mutual recognition and avoided established hierarchies.

So, with *Self-portrait*, which she published in 1969, she was looking for a way to escape what she saw as the inauthentic profession of art criticism in favour of a participatory process that could be personally transformative. Accordingly, the conversations unsystematically address each artist's work and career, but also aspects of their lives and relationships, their shared frustration with Italian art institutions, as well as a number of reflections on the current political situation. These range from discussions of the 1968 protests, the Civil Rights Movement in the United States, the Vietnam War, and the emergence of a feminist consciousness—especially in the dialogues with the abstract painter Carla Accardi.

Lonzi requested that the artists send her pictures, so the ongoing conversation is punctuated with a number of illustrations, thus simulating the traditional text-image format of art history books. However, the majority of these images are personal or travel snapshots, and consequently their presence throughout the book provides a biographical element within the conversations that comprise the text. These interspersed photographs convey the entwinement of art and life that was crucial to Lonzi's critical project while at the same time echoing the nonlinear temporality that structures the book.

Lonzi thus quite literally undoes both the practices and the poetics of dominant forms of art writing, abandoning the authority of interpretation in order to participate in the creative process. Her focus on the artist's subjectivity and nonhierarchical exchange undermines the primacy of the visual of the artwork as a formally expressed epistemic foundation—and of course formalism was the main language available to art criticism in the 1960s. Lonzi's undoing of art history's epistemic structures emerges from a cluster of issues addressed throughout the book: the dispersed heterogeneous and collective subjectivity that challenges established notions of the author; the adoption of a nonlinear temporality created through editing and montage; and the rejection of formalism, with its privileging of vision. What is perhaps even more striking is the way these counter-discourses emerge from the actual construction of the book, which performs a deconstruction of canonical narratives, thereby encouraging alternative forms of knowledge production. For Lonzi, who was interested in connecting her activity to the facts of life, the need to rethink arts institutions went hand in hand with the reconsideration of her own role. As she writes in the book's preface, her intention in assembling the book was not so much to collect information but rather "to spend time with someone in a fully communicative and humanly satisfying way,"[1] introducing herself into "an activity and a humanity to which I was drawn…[but which] were not my own."[2] Consequently, the book's assemblage-like construction enacts a complex process of becoming a subject in the male-dominated art world of 1960s Italy, whereby the roles and identifications that sustain it collapse altogether. What remains is a sort of relational space that is the precondition for a possible liberation from the myths that constitute what we call art. "What remains," she writes, "now that I've lost this role [as critic] within the art world? Maybe I've become an artist myself? I can respond: I am

no longer alienated."[3]

Lonzi's assemblage of the book embodies the search for an outlet that rejects the critic's coherence and unity by dispersing her own voice within a nonlinear dialogic and collective narrative. In these terms, the book resonates with her later feminist writings, where issues of subjectivity, participation, and self-representation are crucial. *Self-portrait* is not a feminist publication, even though it was assembled shortly before Lonzi's decision to abandon art criticism—and actually all the artists in the books are male, except for Carla Accardi. The book's topicality for feminist thinking resides, in my opinion, in its method and epistemic structure. It breaks away from the notion of the creative act as a solitary gesture, allowing for a rethinking of the artist's subjectivity in opposition to the notion of the autonomous and coherent individual. *Self-portrait* strongly resonates with the transformative potential of 1968, which required new strategies in the field of art and culture.[4] Lonzi's critical project foregrounds the possibility to experiment with new forms of being together that were incompatible with the kind of discourse advocated by other critics of the time, such as, for example, Germano Celant. In conclusion, with *Self-portrait*, Lonzi proposed a radical alternative to the hegemonic linear and historical construction that we still suffer the consequences of and that we have not yet left behind. Her unsystematic attempt to develop a different epistemic framework can perhaps contribute to an alternative genealogy of knowledge production in Italy and beyond, one that we need today to redefine our own practices as art historians, critics, and curators.

Guidelli-Guidi: Thank you, Giovanna. We'll hear now from Fulvia Carnevale of Claire Fontaine.

Claire Fontaine: Thank you, Matilde, for this beautiful invitation. I'm very, very happy to be here with Giovanna and Jaleh, because they are dear friends and important interlocutors and we had wonderful conversations talking about this day—so thank you for creating this space for us. I have decided to tackle the refusal to work in Lonzi, her refusal of professional life, which played an important role in the disagreements she had with her close friend and comrade Carla Accardi and their long-term companion Pietro Consagra. Disagreements that led to the end of the relationships, in both cases. I would like to approach *Self-portrait* as a pivotal book, a book of irreversible refusal. In our afterword, we compare it to *Vai pure* (*Go Then*), which is Lonzi's book recounting the end of a long love relationship, because *Self-portrait* also marks the end of a romance: the one with the idea of an art criticism based on the intuition that Lonzi had early on in her life that "extraordinary things were possible between beings."[5] It was a promise that art criticism didn't keep, because, for Lonzi, the discipline turned out to be a judgmental and pedantic activity that ultimately ended up replacing rather than eviscerating the expressions of the artists.

To retrace her journey toward feminism, she wrote in *Self-portrait*: *I began to look, being certain that it was expressed somewhere, that it would be manifested somewhere, a potentiality that I felt humanity possessed. I knew I had it and that I felt that it belonged to everyone.*[6] Although she became afraid of getting stranded on the border of this promised land, Lonzi pursued this "existential feeling," as she called it, but she realized she wouldn't find it in a professional context, and for this she had to make feminism, as she put it. Because, as Giovanna has already noted, her consciousness-raising practice with women's circles was transformative; it wasn't a form of liberation, but it was already a practice of freedom. There were immediate existential and political possibilities of forming relationships in which women could express themselves, not only in the few spaces allocated to them by men for this purpose—the making of art or the creation of cultural products—but with their entire lives. Lonzi is very critical of women who seek professional recognition within society and give up the need to completely transform it, that is, who just bring feminist content into the world of culture. In one of her diary entries, Lonzi wrote: *The person she was before couldn't have helped me, but in the group that I formed she'd found a way of becoming herself and of pushing me to do the same. So I've come to understand why I had to make feminism: in order to make Sara exist, so that she could make me exist.*[7]

Feminism was a space where people could transform themselves and others by concentrating on how they saw each other outside the influence of any other value system, outside the complementarity with or the imitation of men. Lonzi radically refused the segmentation and compartmentalization of different parts of life because she saw how insidious this was for women, how unsustainable in the face of the double militancy of professional work and the work of care. She resolutely stood against the blackmail of multitasking: "For me, doing one thing has a value because it prevents me from doing two."[8] She was entirely absorbed by the pursuit of freedom but this was far from being a selfish and socially privileged goal; rather, it was a way of creating emancipatory relationships that couldn't be borne outside of feminist contexts—a way of inflicting subjectivization, and definitely more powerful than art or art criticism. This plan of political radicality is still a horizon of hope nowadays, as politics have become a space of scandal and regret. They become the context of inevitable corruption or repression. The importance of Lonzi's position lies precisely in its resolute indifference to what is commonly considered as privilege, in fact. If, in order to be included in something, her research of freedom and the making of feminism were threatened, then it was better to remain illegible, unrecognized, and misunderstood by the vast majority of people. Any social or professional recognition appear as derisory in light of the possibility of resonating with other women's subjectivities on a deeper level.

In a text from 1972 entitled "The Meaning of Consciousness Raising within Feminist Groups," Lonzi states that through consciousness raising women will gain the historical, psychological, and mental space where they no longer need men's approval. Maria Luisa Boccia, a very important critic of Lonzi, wrote that what was truly revolutionary about this conception of consciousness raising was that it was a real gesture of attributing value to the feminist and feminine experience as such. To quote Boccia: "Without having to define what needs to be preserved and what should be discarded in the feminine or masculine universe, the practice of consciousness raising showed to every woman the possibility of looking at herself and at her own life as to a resource of knowledge and autonomy."[9] The unexpected subject is the one who, ignoring what is said to be good for her, finds what is in fact good for her by trusting only her own pleasure, her own feelings, her own judgment, without calculating the consequences that this will have in her personal and professional life. In another diary entry, Lonzi wrote: *Women's gestures are bound not to become a product precisely because their value comes from relationships and people. There are gestures made in the air like the ones of acrobats, gestures made of air, on these gestures without an outcome we build our lives. These are the gestures that men appropriate as the meaning providers so that they can say that the material of our lives belongs to them.*[10] I just think that in order to understand why Carla Lonzi left the art world and dedicated all her energy to the adventure of feminism, we also need to understand the scope of this revolution of values, which wasn't only imagined but that actually happened. Those feminist gestures made of air have now transformed the world irreversibly.

Guidelli-Guidi: Thank you so much, Claire Fontaine. Now we will hear from Jaleh.

Jaleh Mansoor: Firstly, I need to acknowledge that I'm currently speaking on the unceded ancestral lands of the Musqueam, Tsleil-Waututh, and Squamish peoples in what is known as Vancouver, Canada, and this is the condition for the possibility of everything that I could be thinking and saying right now. I'd also very much like to thank Matilde for this generous invitation and Giovanna and Claire Fontaine for their sustaining friendship and their unbelievable scholarship on the figure of Carla Lonzi, who, as we look back on the twentieth century, I think should and will be a very important and notable figure.

Lonzi asks herself: "Have I become an artist?" I want to answer that in a way that informs the specificity of her feminism and her elaboration of a creative collective feminist subject. To answer her question simply, I would say yes. I'm also interested in *Self-portrait* as a kind of artwork in and of itself that hybridizes documentary and fiction in a way that I think was very important for Lonzi's later feminism.

Lonzi spent four years conversing with fourteen artists. These discussions were recorded on audio tape and then transcribed. She then took this content, scrambled it, and reassembled it into this extraordinary, long montage in book form, which she then presented under the cover of a self-portrait. I find it utterly fascinating how she's dismantling and reassembling a model of subjectivity. I'm interested in how she unworks this genre of self-portraiture by replacing self-reflection, expression, and interiority with the understanding that a self is constituted through an external field of social and material relations. And this turning of things inside out is where I think the crux of the project is, which then enabled her elaboration of a very special kind of feminist praxis. But to get there I want to point out the way in which she turns things inside out across her work. I'm interested in her privileged term "authenticity," which Giovanna also

brought up. Giovanna's work has in fact meticulously traced this term to Lonzi's early readings of French existentialism and of Theodor Adorno's *Minima Moralia*—a really interesting influence. I think Adorno's influence stayed with Lonzi, or rather she shared a great deal with his position, at least up to the point that she exited the art world. She insisted on the opacity of the artwork: that it should never be a form of propaganda and that it is political when it is least political. So, she didn't like activism—she's pretty harshly critical of the protesters at the Milan Triennial of 1968 and then the famous protests at the Venice Biennale of 1968. But the next year, she exits the art world to become a full-time feminist activist with the inauguration of Rivolta Femminile (Women's Revolt), and with this a plastering of the streets with visual material to attract other women into the group. This alternative way of turning things inside out and the way she gets there is fascinating.

So, in answer to her question, "Have I become an artist?," she's doing something that seems to me very much in parallel with the artists she liked best: Luciano Fabro, Giulio Paolini, and even, to some extent, Lucio Fontana, whom she collected. These artists each summoned the outside—and I'm sort of floating this idea of the "outside" from Maurice Blanchot and others, where these artists took up the material constraints of the outside. For Paolini, for example, we see this in his use of the frame and showing the back of the canvas and the materials that constitute the condition for the possibility of the work. I think that familiarity with artists' practices such as these is how Lonzi arrived at both authenticity and a collective feminist subject, by turning all of these social relations inside out and recognizing that it's the *material and social constraints* of a really unbearable social field—the outside world—that one has to fully acknowledge, internalize, and then carve out from within. It was through this method that Lonzi was able to try to map this other path for a collective feminist subject, one born of creative exploration and experimentation, without entering into this kind of mimetic inscription of heavily ideological forms of protest and activism, which were the types of protests and activist gestures she disliked so much in the 1960s. So, yes—I'm interested in answering her own question of herself and thinking about how her exiting the world of criticism and entering the space of art making enables this peculiarly energetic and dynamic form of feminism. It was here that she seemed to have finally found a satisfying model of authenticity.

Guidelli-Guidi: Thank you all very much for these thoughts and preliminary topics for our conversation. I think something common in all your presentations, and so perhaps a first point to start our conversation, is Lonzi as writer and *Self portrait* as object. Giovanna, in your writing you describe Lonzi's work as experiments in ways of writing differently, where writing literally wears out or undoes the disciplinary languages of art criticism and philosophy. As you all—especially Giovanna and Jaleh—eloquently described, Lonzi literally does that via montage. So, the interview replaces the specialized language with dialogical utterances, and the indexical record of the artist's voice on the magnetic tape generates this kind of expectation

of authenticity, where the authoriality of the artist supposedly remains unaltered—but, in fact, *Self-portrait* is a highly mediated book. As you explained, authoriality is dispersed and transformed by Lonzi's textual and visual montage. I would like to see, then, whether we could comment on and think about Lonzi's writing differently as an experimental strategy in relation to power, one that simultaneously dismantles and builds anew in the present tense of writing, resulting in internal transformation. Most interesting perhaps to our conversation today is: What implications does a work like *Self-portrait* have on traditional systems of meaning and value creation in what we today call the art industry?

Zapperi: Thank you, Matilde, for these remarks. Maybe I should start us off, because you are mentioning this idea of "writing differently." I don't know if I mentioned that specific notion today, but I must have in one of my texts on Lonzi. I think that this idea of writing differently has to do precisely with what you just said: the fact that she was experimenting with something different from the canonical ways of producing knowledge on art and the canonical ways of looking at artworks and of thinking about art, and especially the primacy of her vision, because there's no commentary in *Self-portrait*. Actually, maybe I should underline this point further: *Self-portrait* is not a book where an art critic discusses artworks or even looks at artworks; she rather talks with artists about why they are doing things and how they are doing things, but she leaves space for their own narratives. So, this is for me a very important point: Lonzi is withdrawing from a position of exteriority that is mediated by vision as the dominant way of accessing art, but also the dominant way of producing knowledge, to perform this distance from the subject to the object of knowledge. When I was thinking about and suggesting this idea of writing differently, I was really thinking about the fact that she's *experimenting*, as you said, which also means that she does not necessarily know where this is leading her. She's experimenting, she's trying to, on the one side, think about art from this other, biological, relational perspective; but this writing differently also has to do with her—how can I say—with something that has to do with the process, with something that is unfinished and that will remain unfinished throughout Lonzi's trajectory. This last aspect has to do with what I call her "process of disidentification": she withdraws not only from the fractures of knowledge production but also from her identification with the role of art critic and the kinds of activities and acts that an art critic is supposed to perform and her position as an art critic with respect to the artist, and so on. And this first step in the process of withdrawing from established roles really would become crucial in the years when she was thinking of the subject position of woman—of woman as an already available construct or product or subject position. This notion of authenticity that you brought into the discussion, Jaleh, has to do with this unfinished process of undoing oneself as attributed to the role of woman, to the place of woman. I don't know if that's clear, but maybe Fulvia or Jaleh would like to develop this idea further.

Mansoor: Yes, I want to build on your pointing out that she's working from the outside in. In your work, Giovanna, you point out that Lonzi refers to women as "readymades," which is quite a radical thing to say in 1969 or 1970. This way that she works from the outside in, by reworking the medium that she's working in—writing itself—I think is really extraordinary, and it might be useful to compare her position to the kind of experimental creative writing that happened a little around the bend in the context of French feminism. Take, for example, Hélène Cixous, whose *Laugh of the Medusa*, published in 1975, calls on women to write themselves. But Cixous is mobilizing the kind the kind of format that we're all pretty used to: this avant-garde manifesto format. So, it's really Lonzi's retooling of media itself, which I think is part of her project in a really interesting way, that ends up being political. I think one thing she does is cross the boundary between formalism and social consciousness and that's…I love that. I defer to Fulvia.

Claire Fontaine: I don't know how much I have to offer in terms of a critical perspective applied to Lonzi's use of language and her use of knowledge, philosophy, and politics in general. For her, everything needed to have a use value. There is a real passion for immanence, there is a constant production of intensity and a constant production of the present in her writings that I think is still relevant today. Of course, Allison [Grimaldi Donahue]—who's here with us today—I guess must have suffered while translating Lonzi, because she really does bend the Italian language, and the Italian language is very bendable, but there is also a form of disobedience, a form of freedom, that she takes in using this language. And I wouldn't compare her with Cixous—and I wouldn't compare her actually with anyone else. I mean, other people were using recorded language at the same time in Italy. But it was a laborious process, because the technology was not portable and it was a real commitment to record, transcribe, and all of that, but I think there is a real materiality of language that she says, in *Self-portrait*, she's passionate about. It's explosive because it's unaffiliated. It's really straight to the point, it's not timid.

So, it's not that I do not want to historicize Lonzi, and I certainly think the political context that she was part of and that she created is absolutely essential for her interpretation. But I do think that there is actually a very interesting attitude in her relationship to history, to the official narratives, and to the use of the official language of criticism; it is, as I was saying, very irreverent. So, Lonzi actually does invite everyone to historicize her ideas many, many times in her writings, but she doesn't trust the existing narratives. I think she harbours the same skepticism toward art historical narratives, because she does not express, as Giovanna said, any specifically feminist choice when she puts together these artists, who were her friends, but most definitely she had doubts about the way art history was constructed and how authority was distributed and attributed to artists. And she's not mysterious when she talks about the culture of men at that point, and I think she is not exaggerating.

Guidelli-Guidi: I have another question, which addresses some of the threads that you brought up today: both the question of the horizon

of freedom that you spoke about, Fulvia, as well as the question of Lonzi's legacy that we were just discussing. There's a beautiful turn of phrase you use in a Claire Fontaine essay describing Lonzi's legacy as being "as precious as it is problematic," and you go on to describe a vivid image that brings us to questions about legacy, but also tools and process. In your essay, you use as an analogue to Lonzi's process an image of the Baron of Münchhausen escaping quicksand by pulling himself out by his own hair,[11] which is such an incredible image. I would like to see if you have comments around this almost couple-like set of terms: "precious" and "problematic." Alongside the acrobatics of Münchhausen, another image that comes to mind is Claire Fontaine's work in which you actually engage with Lonzi with floor-bound sculptures that are essentially bricks covered with book covers of Lonzi's Scritti di Rivolta Femminile publications.[12] So yes: a question around the legacy of Lonzi being precious and problematic, as well as around tools, and also how in your writings Lonzi comes to be an example of what you theorize as "human strike."

Claire Fontaine: Yes, most definitely, human strike owes a lot to feminism, and particularly to the revolutionary part of Italian feminism, which itself draws from other feminist thinkers. I mean, the legacies are connected and there is a specific flavour to Italian feminism that we love and that we always bring up in our texts and often in our work. But to begin with the end of your question: human strike is a strike that takes place on an existential level, that is, the inflection of all subjectivity in a direction that can increase one's power. So that avoids the dynamic of domination, which extracts one from the dynamics of subjection, and it also creates a situation of nondefinition, of relative illegibility, which is this category of Lonzi that I have also tried to work on.

I must say, it's painful to work on Lonzi—we were talking about this with Giovanna—because her work always moves deeply, not only emotional but…how would I say it. It questions the theoretical approach that we have to the object of our work, because it invites us to reflect on the ways we are giving value, giving authority to things, to references, which processes we are going for materially and symbolically, how we are evaluating the decisions that we are making on the basis of a set of values that is always there. So, I would say that Lonzi has, yes, made feminism out of nothing—not because there weren't other feminist thinkers around (although she has a specific singularity, of course) but because these kind of revolts that were taking place after '68 were generic revolts, they were human strikes, as Lonzi contextualizes, of course, in *Sputiamo su Hegel* (*Let's Spit on Hegel*) in particular. These weren't corporate revolts—they were moving away from the blind spots of Marxism to get to the places that weren't related only to production and to the professional identification with one's life. So, definitely, there was this refusal to work that existed not only with the feminists.

I will briefly mention the conflict by subtraction that also existed in Italy, where women were leaving their jobs because they were finding that they weren't emancipating them. They called this gesture "conflict by subtraction," because they didn't want to have a conversation about it; they just left. So, these are definitely all movements that have a lot to do with the idea of human strike, because they are movements of subjectivities looking to acquire more freedom and more potentiality and to transform themselves, and they are not related as much to the process of production as they are related to the process of reproduction—including reproduction of the self in the broad sense, not only biological reproduction. But I don't want to take too much space, I want to hear from my friends too. While I haven't spoken so much about the work, I think these questions are maybe useful for the audience to put everything into context, because Lonzi hasn't been so widely available and the '70s in Italy are mythologized, and so I don't know what set of references we all have in common.

Zapperi: Maybe I can jump in from what Fulvia was discussing—this question of the strike—which for me has to do both with the question of authenticity that we discussed earlier but also with Lonzi's practice of withdrawal from the roles that constitute one's own social relations. I was thinking, Jaleh—you mentioned the possible connections with the French feminists, and I was thinking, more than Cixous, of someone like Monique Wittig in her famous text "The Straight Mind," where she claims that "lesbians are not women."[13] So she performs this idea of radical disidentification from women as "What's the meaning of women?" I think Lonzi does something similar in her own practice, of course, through the Rivolta Femminile group and with the practice of *autocoscienza* (consciousness raising). But also when she theorizes, when she imagines, this figure that she calls the "clitoridean woman"—you know, there's this idea of the "vaginal woman" and the "clitoridean woman"—who is another political fiction in a way: it is not a real person or a real subject, but it's a way to imagine a possible subject position that is based precisely on what Fulvia called the human strike or the radical refusal of the gestures, acts, behaviours, and relations that situate us in social and gender relations. Jaleh, you mentioned this idea of woman as a readymade, and Lonzi considers the term "woman" as something already available that we need to deconstruct and to undo in our own practices. Of course, it's a process that is by definition unfinished, because "woman" is what constitutes us as subjects. Maybe I'll leave it there.

Guidelli-Guidi: Jaleh, do you want to jump in?

Mansoor: No, I'm curious to hear what the audience might be thinking.

Guidelli-Guidi: Yes, I have a question from [art historian] Raffaele Bedarida. Raffaele asks: "Starting in the 1960s in the social sciences, oral historians have emphasized nonlinearity, shared authority, intersubjectivity, self-reflection of oral sources as critical tools in a way that has little parallels in art history and art criticism. I wonder if Lonzi was aware of or interested in the emergence of oral history?"

Zapperi: Maybe I can try and answer this. Carla Lonzi, in the 1960s, was a regular contributor to a journal called *Marcatré*, which was published in Geneva and directed by Eugenio Battisti, a very important and very interesting art historian at that time. *Marcatré* was a transdisciplinary journal, and this is where she published her first conversations with artists. Lonzi had a series called "Discorsi" (Discourses) in *Marcatré*, where she published her conversations with Luciano Fabro up until, I believe, the conversation with Pino Pascali. With Pascali, she erased her questions, so you have practically the page with dots and then Pascali speculating on a question that we are not able to read. I mention *Marcatré* because this was a journal where you had texts not only from art but also from architects, cultural producers, as it was transdisciplinary. Many important or famous people, like Umberto Eco, wrote for it, alongside a number of researchers working in the fields of anthropology and folklore, which were also experimenting with oral history, with research conversations and oral inquiries based on conversations that were taped. So, of course her interest in tape recording her conversations with artists has to do with this general framing in Italy. I hope that answers the question.

Guidelli-Guidi: Maybe we have time for one last question. [Art historian] Tenley Bick asks: "Giovanna, I was struck by your comments regarding Lonzi's experimentation with new forms of being together in such a way that was incompatible with what other critics proposed at the time. I was wondering if you could say a bit more on that point. Is there a theoretical model or framework outside of art criticism that might help elucidate the resonance of these forms? Was perhaps the revived legacy of Piero Gobetti and Carlo Rosselli in the new Italian left important to Lonzi, for example?"

Zapperi: Um, I don't know. I don't think so. I've never encountered those names in Lonzi's texts, but who knows? However, I'm a bit skeptical about this idea that she's inspired by some male predecessors, for example, and also of constructing such a precise genealogy. I think she was operating in a context in which those practices were being experimented with by a number of subjects—by activists, by scholars, by writers possibly—and she was part of it. I don't think that there is a vertical relation. I think it was more like a general atmosphere and milieu in which she was enmeshed. So, yes, the precise names, I don't know. The names she refers to most are, of course, the art historian and critic Roberto Longhi, of whom she was a student, and also Carlo Giulio Argan, another important figure in the field of art criticism and art history. And she contests both in different ways, more frontally in the case of Argan, partly because Argan was so connected with the Italian Communist Party, which had a hegemonic role in the field of culture. Lonzi herself had been part of the Italian Communist Party in the early 1950s, like every intellectual in Italy at that time. But she had withdrawn from the party by, I believe, 1956, after the Hungarian Revolution, and so she was very suspicious toward the left or, in any case, toward leftist groups and leftist intellectuals or self-identified leftist intellectuals.[14]

Guidelli-Guidi: We're coming to an end and don't have time for any further questions, but I thank you all so much—both the panellists and the audience—for your participation.

This transcript has been lightly edited for publication.

1. Carla Lonzi, *Self-portrait*, trans. Allison Grimaldi Donahue (Brussels: Divided; New York: Dia Art Foundation, 2021), 13.
2. Lonzi, *Self-portrait*, 16.
3. Lonzi, *Self-portrait*, 16.
4. The global upheavals of 1968 saw a remarkable coalition of leftist social movements and organizations, most famously in the seven weeks of turmoil that temporarily destabilized the Charles de Gaulle government in France. The period takes a distinctively durational form in Italy, often referred to in terms of extended revolutionary upheaval as "the long '68" (*sessantotto lungo*) or "the Creeping May" (*il maggio strisciante*), and sometimes rather more reductively as "the years of lead" (*anni di pombo*), which characterizes the period primarily through its political violence. The events claimed by historians to bookend the period are also diverse, although the massive wildcat strike actions in the industrial centres in Northern Italy initiated in '68 loom large in the historiography and gained in intensity through the Hot Autumn (*autunno caldo*) of 1969–70. The end of the period is often dated to the remarkable proliferation of political and cultural experimentation among the Autonomia groups and the subsequent political repression of 1977–78. For a thoughtful consideration of the long '68 period in the Italian context, see Evan Calder Williams and Alberto Toscano, "Wrong Place, Right Time: '68 and the Impasses of Periodization," *Cultural Politics* 15, no. 3 (2019): 273–88.
5. Lonzi, *Self-portrait*, 43–44.
6. Lonzi, *Self-portrait*, 44.

Colophon

Fillip Folio Series: G
Gendered Labour and Clitoridean Revolt:
Leopoldina Fortunati and Carla Lonzi
Published by Fillip
ISBN: 978-1-927354-41-4

Editors: Arlen Austin, Sara Colantuono,
   and Jaleh Mansoor
Translation: Arlen Austin and Sara Colantuono
Copyediting: Jaclyn Arndt
Proofreading: Kate Woolf
Transcription: Robert Dayton
Printed in Belgium by die Keure

Cover: Carla Accardi, *#639*, 1974. Transparent Sicofoil
on wooden frame, 148 × 150 cm.

Fillip
305 Cambie Street
Vancouver, BC
Canada V6B 2N4
www.fillip.ca